D0169668

BISON
BOOKS

EUGENIA ZIEBER
Courtesy of Oregon State Library,
Salem, Oregon

HARRIET BUCKINGHAM
Courtesy of Oregon Historical
Society, Portland, Oregon

JEAN RIO BAKER
Courtesy of Jeffery O. Johnson
Salt Lake City, Utah

LUCIA WILLIAMS
Courtesy of Helen S. Felker
Tacoma, Washington

Covered Wagon Women

Diaries and Letters from the Western Trails
1851

Volume 3

Edited and compiled by
KENNETH L. HOLMES

Introduction to the Bison Books Edition
by Susan Armitage

University of Nebraska Press
Lincoln and London

♾ The paper in this book meets the minimum requirements of American
National Standard for Information Sciences—Permanence of Paper for
Printed Library Materials, ANSI Z39.48-1984.

First Bison Books printing: 1996
Most recent printing indicated by the last digit below:
10   9   8   7   6   5   4   3   2

Library of Congress Cataloging-in-Publication Data
The Library of Congress has cataloged Vol. 1 as:
Covered wagon women: diaries & letters from the western trails, 1840–1849
/ edited and compiled by Kenneth L. Holmes; introduction to the Bison
Books edition by Anne M. Butler.
p.   cm.
Originally published: Glendale, Calif.: A. H. Clark Co., 1983.
"Reprinted from volume one . . . of the original eleven-volume edition"—
T.p. verso.
"Volume I."
Includes index.
ISBN 0-8032-7277-4 (pa: alk. paper)
1. Women pioneers—West (U.S.)—Biography.   2. West (U.S.)—History.
3. West (U.S.)—Biography.   4. Overland journeys to the Pacific.
5. Frontier and pioneer life—West (U.S.)   I. Holmes, Kenneth L.
F591.C79   1996
978—dc20   95-21200   CIP

Volume 2 introduction by Lillian Schlissel.
ISBN 0-8032-7274-X (pa: alk. paper)
Volume 3 introduction by Susan Armitage.
ISBN 0-8032-7287-1 (pa: alk. paper)

Reprinted from volume three (1984) of the original eleven-volume edition
titled *Covered Wagon Women: Diaries and Letters from the Western Trails,
1840–1890*, published by The Arthur H. Clark Company, Glendale, California.

Introduction to the Bison Books Edition

Susan Armitage

One of the earliest and most evocative portraits of the overland pioneers was penned by Francis Parkman in *The Overland Trail* (serialized in 1847, published in book form in 1849). Observing a group of overlanders as they reached Fort Laramie, Parkman wrote:

> A crowd of broad-brimmed hats, thin visages, and staring eyes, appeared suddenly at the gate. Tall awkward men, in brown homespun; women with cadaverous faces and long lank figures, came thronging in together, and, as if inspired by the very demon of curiosity, ransacked every nook and corner of the fort.

This remarkable vignette, which captures the moment when the pioneers made their last contact with organized American society before moving farther west into the unknown, provokes our curiosity to know more about them. Parkman, whose real interest lay with Indians and mountain men, tells us little more. To get closer, we must turn to the diaries the overlanders wrote about their westward journeys.

Until about twenty years ago, the Overland Trail story was generally understood as a male adventure epic. The vast majority of known diaries were by men "rushing" to California after gold was discovered in 1848. Because of the preponderance of these Gold Rush accounts, the smaller Oregon migration was neglected, and so was the family nature of it. In contrast to the temporary intent of California-bound travelers, families went to Oregon to settle, to farm, and to stay. Family migration, as opposed to the individual urge to get to California quickly, was a minor theme in most accounts of the Overland Trail.

As women's history developed as an academic specialty in the 1970s, women's trail diaries were rediscovered, and two historians, John Mack Faragher in *Women and Men on the Overland Trail* (1979) and Lillian Schlissel in *Women's Diaries of the Westward Journey* (1982), made important contributions to their interpretation. Their most important finding was simply that the trail experience, like every other kind of life experience, was gendered. Women's feelings about the westward journey differed from men's in small but vital ways. For men, the trail experience was a break from customary farm routines. Planning and safely executing the trip posed a significant challenge and there was adventure in meeting the challenge. For women occupied with the customary female activities of feeding their families and caring for young children, a significant part of the trail experience was the struggle to maintain customary family household patterns under difficult circumstances. In the female experience of the westward journey, endurance rather than adventure predominated.

At first, this gendered analysis of the trail diaries was resisted by many western historians, who tended to defend older, well-documented interpretations. Today, however, postmodern scholarship and women's history alike direct our attention not to unifying myths but to the complexity and variety of individual accounts, in which gender is one important (but not exclusive) variable. Furthermore, the decidedly antiheroic tenor of contemporary thought has affected the interpretation of the Overland Trail as much as it has other national icons. John Unruh's monumental *The Plains Across* (1979) emphasized not the adventure but the overwhelming tedium of the four- to six-month westward trip to California, Oregon, or Salt Lake City, an emphasis fully corroborated in women's diaries. The *Covered Wagon Women* series contributes to this antimythic spirit by publishing hitherto unknown women's accounts in all their variety. The diaries in this particular volume, of women travelers in 1851, add new information to the historical record. As Kenneth Holmes's story of their acquisition makes clear, new diaries are still being discovered today, almost 150 years after their recording. Taken together and separately, the seven diaries in this volume tell us some things about general trail conditions in 1851, about the particular circumstances of individual trains, and about the experience of the women diarists themselves.

The approximately seven thousand people who ventured west in 1851 found it was a good year to travel the Oregon Trail. The dramatic decrease in numbers from 1850 eased the competition for good camping spots (those with adequate grass, water, and fuel) and decreased the chance of a recurrence of the deadly scourge of 1850, cholera, which was caused by contaminated drinking water. Because of the vast numbers of gold rushers in 1849 and 1850, the trail was now clearly marked in wagon ruts that remain in some places today. Guidebooks were more reliable, and an ever-increasing number of trading posts and ferries—in addition to the major Mormon settlement in Salt Lake City—had sprung up along the route.

For all of its improvements, the overland journey tested each of the seven very different diarists, as it doubtless did the other approximately three thousand westering women of 1851 who did not leave accounts of their journey. What can we learn about the 1851 journey from these seven women? Who were they, and what do their diaries tell us about the female trail experience?

First, the matter of identification. Women's historians have found that identifying women by age and social class (the criteria by which we generally distinguish men) is inadequate for women. Family status is a crucial additional variable, and this is abundantly clear in this volume's diaries. Three accounts are by young, unmarried women: Harriet Buckingham (age nineteen), Elizabeth Wood (twenty-three) and Eugenia Zeiber (eighteen). Buckingham and Zeiber traveled with family parties and had at least partial responsibility for younger kin and probably assisted with cooking. Elizabeth Wood apparently traveled with others who were not kin and seemed to have no childcare responsibilities. All three of these young women offer cheerful accounts of their largely enjoyable trips. Two other young women, Amelia Hadley and Susan Cranston, married but childless, write rather more somber diaries. Cranston's diary in particular, with its obsessive grave-counting, can only be described as depressed. The two oldest women, Lucia Williams (age thirty-five) and Jean Rio Baker (forty-one) each suffered the death of a child during the journey and their accounts reflect this loss. Thus even within this small sample, the range of experience and attitude is enormous.

All of the diaries map the general contours of the journey: the gradual ascent to South Pass along the Platte River, the long dry stretch across present-day Idaho and eastern Oregon populated by "our old friends Sage and Sand" (as Harriet Buckingham called them), and the final difficult and exhausting transit of the Cascade Mountains. In this common western journey, the wagon trains represented by these diarists shared some difficulties, such as the ferocious rains and "tornados" that struck in the earliest stages of their journeys, upsetting carriages and soaking everyone. Similarly, the end of the journey was a desperate struggle for all of them. Few diarists of any year can match Lucia Williams's account of the hellishly miserable struggle over the Cascades summed up in her simple phrase, "I cannot describe these mountains."

Another common experience involved encounters with American Indians. The frequency and variety of these encounters deserves our attention, as does the range of responses from the first meetings with the

Omahas (described as "beggarly" by Lucia Williams and "filthy" by Amelia Hadley) to friendly visits with the "Soo" (Hadley's spelling) and the highly regarded Nez Perce in Oregon. Universally loathed and feared were the Shoshone Bannock and Paiute of eastern Oregon who stole horses and cattle from weakened trains late in their journeys. As Elizabeth Wood remarked, "The Indians we have met with here are more savage, cunning and treacherous than any we have yet seen," but she went on to comment, "It is not always the Indians that are the aggressors."

There were important differences between trains. The critical difference lay in train organization and management. Harriet Buckingham traveled west in relative ease and comfort because her uncle, Hiram Smith, was an experienced and skilled leader. But other trains were not so lucky. Elizabeth Woods describes a miserable train riven by dissension. When its unnamed leader ordered all the dogs to be shot in an effort to end recurrent stock stampedes, he faced open rebellion and eventual replacement as leader. Jean Rio Baker, the Mormon widow from England whose diary is included here, describes an entirely different experience. Although the beginning of the American part of her journey began badly with dreary daily struggles against rain and spring floods, the minute she became part of an organized Mormon train in early July most of her troubles were ended. The journey to Salt Lake City had physical rough spots, but the organization and communication that linked trains together on the Mormon Trail made the trip easier for everyone. Baker must have received a psychological boost from knowing that the closer she got to her goal the more help she would receive from organized parties sent out from Salt Lake City.

Another common controversy that few trains escaped concerned rates of travel. One train took too long in the early stages of the journey and was pressed for time toward the end, while others who moved more swiftly found themselves with exhausted stock at the same late point in the journey. The question of pacing could also raise religious issues. Many devout Christians (including Susan Cranston and Eugenia Zeiber) wished to lay over on Sunday to observe the Sabbath, but others within the same train disagreed. Clearly, this issue provided endless opportunities for contentious discussion, as in Eugenia Zeiber's train, where the rival parties split, rejoined, and squabbled over the loyalty of uncommitted members of the party.

For all of the things the diaries tell us, there are many silences in them. Some of the omissions are puzzling. Why, for example, does Harriet

Buckingham refer to her niece (with whom she nightly shared a tent) only as "the young girl"? Why don't married women mention their husbands? And why do mothers so infrequently write about their children? A more general lack is emotional reticence: few deeply personal thoughts are recorded here.

Some of the silences can be explained by physical factors. Most diaries were very small, the size of a 3 x 5 card, so there simply was not room for extensive entries. Writing time was limited as well, for pen(wo)manship was impossible in a moving wagon, and the daily tasks of cooking, cleaning, and child-tending occupied the vast majority of the remaining time. But these seven diarists rarely mention their routine daily tasks. Only the occasional allusion to the use of buffalo chips for cooking, to a stop long enough for washing clothes, and to the discovery of saleratus (carbonate of potash, the forerunner of modern baking powder) suggests women's daily routines. And only the horrifying death of young John Williams, "lively as a lark" (his mother wrote) moments before he was thrown from a wagon and crushed, remind us of the constant anxiety mothers must have felt for the safety of their children. Nor do these diaries provide full descriptions of the social life that developed on many wagon trains. We can infer the sociability from occasional details like Amelia Hadley's accordian playing, appreciated by a "merry crowd," and Lucia Williams's vivid glimpse of the five horsemen who serenade her with "Araby's Daughter." But the complex relationships between strangers in the same train and even the stresses and strains that developed between kin and spouses are rarely mentioned. Again, we have to infer from sparse clues. Susan Cranston's grave-counting becomes significant when we realize that only a few graves were new. They were almost all several years old, dating from earlier cholera epidemics. Her obsessive count was not therefore an expression of current fear of epidemic and death, but perhaps an expression of lost hopes and of a deeper unvoiced resistance to her husband's westward urgings. But perhaps not. There are permanent mysteries in these simple-seeming diaries.

If they are not accounts of daily or collective life or repositories of true confidences, what *are* these accounts? They are, it seems to me, goal-directed accounts in which each day's miles and each night's camping place serve as markers of the remaining distance to the desired goal. Along the way, unusual sights and occurrences are noted, just as in any travelogue, but the real topic is distance and how much of it remains. The daily mileage notation is a count, very much like crossing

off the days on a calendar. And perhaps the campsite descriptions func-
tioned in the same way that we sometimes take travel photographs not
to show others but to remind ourselves afterwards of the complex inter-
personal reality, which cannot be fully captured on film or in a diary.

Nevertheless, each diary, in its own way, traces a trajectory from east
to west, from early ignorance and optimism to understanding and endurance. Few diarists, in any year, trace the trajectory as clearly as just-
married Amelia Hadley. She begins in exuberance: "It is amuseing and
delightful to travel over these plains, and is not such a task as many
imagine." Early in June she confidently remarks, "It is true that a great
deal suffer during this long journey, but It is one half owing to carelessness and Mismanagement, little or no sickness as yet. . . . I for one
never enjoyed myself better and never had better health." But just a few
days later she complains of "this abominable mountain sage, which I
have got so tired of that I cant bear to smell it." By mid-July, she says,
"It seems the nearer we approach Oregon the worse roads we have, and
a worse more rough looking country." Three days later her brother-in-
law is shot by an Indian during an attempted horse theft. She fears for
his life and the safety of the party: "This is a wretched place to camp. . . .
I can hardly lay down to sleep without It seems as though The Indians
stood all around me ready to masacree me." Then she herself comes
down with dysentery and is unable to write in her diary for two weeks.
As she revives, the party comes to the Columbia River, and after a final
struggle through the Cascade Mountains reaches Portland on August
23. Hadley's final entry brings her travel trajectory to rest: "This is the
end of a long and tedious journey."

And so, indeed, it was for everyone—long and tedious, but a journey
to look back on with pride of accomplishment, intermixed with other
feelings, some of them captured in these seven diaries, some kept only
in the personal memories of the women who made the covered-wagon
journey west.

Contents

Illustrations

Introduction to Volume III

From best information . . . but few persons will emigrate to California or Oregon this year. This time last year our town literally was crowded, but now very few are in the place. – St. Joseph, Missouri, *Gazette,* March 26, 1851.[1]

The first volume of *Covered Wagon Women: Diaries and Letters from the Western Trails, 1840-1890,* dealt with the records of women traveling overland during the 1840s. The second volume contained the diaries and letters of those who went west in 1850.

The real news of wagon travel to the far west in 1851 is found in the quote from the St. Joseph *Gazette* above. On June 6 the report of emigrant trains passing Ft. Kearny indicated that up to that date only 837 wagons had passed with 1,156 men, 928 women, 799 children, 5,975 oxen, cows, horses and mules.[2]

The most reliable modern study of numbers on the trails, that of John D. Unruh, Jr., in *The Plains Across,* indicates that the number of emigrants to California dropped from 44,000 in 1850 to 1,100 in 1851, a staggering decrease. Those to Oregon fell not so radically from some 6,000 in 1850 to 3,600 in 1851. The number of Mormons going to Utah dropped from 2,500 in 1850 to 1,500 in 1851.[3]

When one considers that the male-female relationship of those going to California was generally nine men to one woman, it is easy to see why there is a

---

[1] Quoted in Louise Barry, *The Beginning of the West* (Topeka, Kansas, 1972), p. 986.

[2] *Ibid.,* p. 1008.

[3] (Urbana, Illinois), pp. 119-120.

dearth of women's records for the California Trail.[4]
In fact, so far we have found none for publication.
The six to four female ratio in the Oregon emigration
means that there would have been about 2160 men
to 1440 women — a family migration, as was the case
with Utah.

Why was there such a drop-off in California emigration in the 1851 overland season? George R. Stew-
art in his study of *The California Trail*[5] suggested
that there were three reasons:

1. The reports of hardships of '50 discouraged migration. This would include disease, especially cholera,[6] with one count of 963 graves, as well as the
incredible loss of cattle and wagons on the desert
crossings.

2. The hysteria of the gold rush could not be main-
tained. Everybody did not get rich overnight. There
were returned stony-broke '49ers in many eastern
towns, and they were reported in the newspapers.

3. The new federal donation land law for Oregon
by which for the year 1851, each man and wife could
settle on a full section of land diverted no fewer than
2,000 overlanders from California to the Willamette
Valley of Oregon. Those who came after 1851 and
through 1853 were to obtain a donation half as large.[7]

The next year, 1852, there would be another amazing reverse in overland numbers again as the trails
were once more inundated with people, mainly going

---

[4] *Historical Statistics of the United States to 1970* (Washington, D.C., 1976),
pp. 24-36.

[5] (New York, 1962), pp. 299-302.

[6] All of our women diarists of 1850 had mentioned the disease.

[7] Lester B. Shippee, "The Federal Relations of Oregon," *Oregon Hist. Qtly.*,
xx, No. 4 (December, 1919), pp. 345-70.

to California, but many also to the Pacific Northwest
and to Utah. That year, 1852, would be a golden one
for women's diaries and letters, so many that our
volume IV will deal only with the travelers to California, and volume V with those going to the Pacific
Northwest. More overlanders reached the western
destinations in the 1852 migration than in any of the
preceding years.

So we publish the diaries and/or letters of six
Oregon-bound women in 1851 and one delightful
journal of an English Mormon woman, who kept
a diary all the way from the Old Country to Salt
Lake City. We do finish with one dynamic paragraph
from a published letter written by a California woman,
probably in 1851, which appeared in an eastern publication in June of 1852.

The 1851 diaries and letters are arranged here in
chronological order, from the date they crossed the
Missouri river. This was the mental beginning of the
journey for most of them. The dates for the Missouri
crossing for our 1851 women are as follows: Harriet
Buckingham, May 4; Amelia Hadley, May 6; Susan
Cranston, May 8; Lucia Williams, May 13; Elizabeth
Wood and Eugenia Zieber, late May; Jane Rio Baker,
July 5.

For those readers who have not read our introduction
to the series in volume one, a reiteration of a few sali-
ent points which guide our editorial hand are in order.
It is our purpose to let the diarists and correspondents
tell their own story in their own words, with as little
scholarly trimming as possible. The intent is to transcribe each word or phrase as accurately as possible,
leaving as written whatever mis-spellings or gram-

matical errors are found. The only gestures we have
made for the sake of the reader have been as follows:

1. We have added space where phrases or sentences
ended and no punctuation was to be found in the
original.

2. We have put the daily journals into diary format
even though the original may have been written con-
tinuously line by line because of the original writer's
shortage of paper.

Many geographic references are mentioned over
and over again in the various accounts. The final
volume in the series will include a gazetteer, in addition to the index and bibliography to aid the reader.

We have sought out the scarce and unusual in overland documents. Readily available accounts are not
included, but will be referenced in the final volume
in the bibliography. If you know of a special account
written at the time of the journey, please let us know.
Our goal is to add to the knowledge of all regarding
this portion of our history – the story of ordinary
people embarked on an extraordinary experience.

KENNETH L. HOLMES

Monmouth, Oregon, 1983

The Diaries, Letters and Commentaries

Crossing the Plains in 1851

∮ Harriet Talcott Buckingham

INTRODUCTION

A major problem with the diary of Harriet Talcott Buckingham is that there are two diaries that cover essentially the same journey over the Oregon Trail.

One of the diaries is written in pencil in a small journal typical of the time. It is artless. There was no attempt to make what we would call a "production" of it. It covers the dates May 12 through August 15, 1851. We call it Document A.

The second diary is written neatly in ink in a larger book, and it covers the dates May 4 through September 26, 1851. We have labelled this one Document B. Both journals are in Harriet Buckingham's hand.

It is our theory that the small pencilled book is the original, done day by day on the wagon or in camp. There may have been three of these little books done in pencil, or else there were loose pages before and after the core of the diary, which we have here.

Later on — just when, we don't know — Harriet sought to produce a more polished copy of her overland journal, possibly for publication. She revised her original into a more finished piece, adding a long segment about their stay in Salt Lake City, a segment that is not found in the first journal.

The question naturally arises for the editor: What shall we do with these diaries? Our solution has been to use the original diary, Document A, as the central record of our copy. Where the original prelude and postlude of Document A are missing, we have used Document B.

The manuscripts of both of these versions of Harriet Buckingham's hand-written diaries are in the collection of the Oregon Historical Society in Portland, and we are grateful for permission to publish what follows.

Harriet Talcott Buckingham was born on March 31, 1832, in Norwalk, Ohio. She celebrated her nineteenth birthday early in the journey with her uncle and aunt, Hiram and Hannah, as they pursued the long trail to Oregon. Henry, her brother, two years younger, was also along. The teenagers were particularly fortunate in having their uncle as a guide, since Hiram Smith had already made one trip over the plains to Oregon in 1846 and then had returned east to recruit a party of settlers.

Upon arrival in Oregon, Harriet was wooed for a few months by a vigorous Portland businessman, Samuel A. Clarke. On February 23, 1852, they were married. Her life was one of excitement with this partner who was a sometime poet, prolific writer, successful editor, as well as an entrepreneur in railroading, mining, and farming. He was editor for one year of the Portland *Oregonian,* and for three years of the Salem *Statesman.* He is most re-nowned today for his two-volume history of Oregon, *Pioneer Days of Oregon History,* published in the year of the Lewis and Clark Centennial, 1905, by J. K. Gill Company, which is even now a major bookselling concern in the region.

This book was published after the passing of Harriet, who died on January 27, 1890. Samuel's tribute to her in the "Preface" of *Pioneer Days* is a classic in emotional expression, and we publish it here in full:

> My work as a writer had the encouragement and assistance that association and inspiration with another soul can afford, and for forty years had depended on. She, who had aided and inspired whatever success had been attained, planned that we should work together to mould the historical labors of the past

into connected form. It was a beautiful suggestion, that our labors should close with such effort, and the result remains a joint tribute for posterity. Death sundered that alliance and left me for years discouraged as well as suffering from nervous prostration. But there comes to me, after all these years of waiting, the ambition to complete the work as she had planned it; to leave the product as an humble monument to the past of which it will treat, also as a remembrance of the lovely character and beautiful soul of the woman whose life was blended with mine, and was a blessing to all who knew her. (p. vii).

Samuel and Harriet Clarke had four children, three daughters and a son. They are listed in the 1870 Federal Census of Oregon as Minnie, Hattie, William J., and Sarah A. It was Sarah (Mrs. Sarah A. Dyer of Salem) who presented a vast collection of family materials to the Oregon Historical Society in Portland, and among these, Harriet's manuscript diaries are found.

The editor would like to acknowledge three sources that have been invaluable in understanding the Buckingham/Clarke manuscripts: The most helpful biography of Samuel Clarke, with particular emphasis upon his life with Harriet, is to be found in Alfred Powers' massive book, *History of Oregon Literature* (Portland, 1935). There is a second source, a manuscript book on the shelves of the Oregon Historical Society that was particularly helpful: It is a multi-person production of a thesis, "Diary of Harriette T. Buckingham," done by eleven students in a history class of Professor Allan H. Kittell at Lewis and Clark College in Portland. The diary they chose to edit as a "final examination and as a reward for its young authors" was what we have called Document B, the more polished of the two journals. The editor commends creative teachers of this kind who would give such an intriguing "final exam." The last source, in the Bancroft Library (Berkeley, California), was an interview done by Mrs. Hubert Howe Bancroft and Amos Bowman, for the historian Hubert Howe Bancroft. The interview was with Mrs. H. T. Clarke in "Salem, Oregon, Sunday, June 16th, 1878." This is an early example of what we call "oral history." The editor used this valuable record called "Young Woman's Sights on the Oregon Trail" as a resource.

THE DIARY OF
HARRIET TALCOTT BUCKINGHAM

[DOCUMENT B]

May 4   Crossed the Missouri at Council Bluffs, where we had been a couple of weeks making the final preparations on this outskirt of civilization

The weather has been mild, and we have walked evry day over the rolling hills around – one day found a young physician and his wife who were interested in examining the numerous skulls and human bones that were found near the surface of the ground. After much speculation the fact was elucidated that, large tribes of Indians from the middle states had been pushed off by our government to this frontier region to make room for white settlers, and had here perished in large numbers by starvation consequent upon removal from familiar hunting grounds: they had been buried in large trenches with heads to the east. Skulls were thick: of peculiar shape differeing from the Anglo Saxon type.

We number seven wagons – one carriage, a large band of oxen & cows, horses & mules – the latter are for the carriage – oxen for the wagons. Mrs Smith myself and a little girl occupy the carriage – we have a driver – Mr Smith rides a little black mule that is very intelligent & a pet with him.

There are drivers for the wagons and loose stock. Mr E. N. Cooke & family[1] have a nice carriage & about the same equipment. Mr Hiram Smith[2] has crossed the plains twice before & so knows how to do it Mr Smith & Cooke travel together intending to go by the way of Salt Lake City for the purpose of selling to the Mormons Goods & Groceries with which most of the wagons are loaded so we make quite a cavalcade as we slowly move along. We have tents & small cook stoves.

Mr & Mrs Smith have had the carriage so arranged that a bed can be made of the seats, & when the curtains are all buttoned down there is a comfitable sleeping apartment The little girl & I sleep in one of the big covered ox wagons in which is a nice bed – really makes a cosy little low roffed room, it has a double cover – Mr Smith has a coop fastened on behind the carriage which contains some fine white chickens – three hens and a rooster. We let them out evry time we camp, and already they seem to know when preperations are made for moving & will fly up to their place in the coop. Mr & Mrs Cooke have a niece Miss Brewster,[3] & a little daughter, an uncle & a young gentlman Mr T. McF Patton,[4] with them, so we have a nice little society of our own.

---

[1] Edwin N. and Eliza Cooke from Ohio settled in Salem in mercantile and hotel business. He was Oregon State Treasurer from 1862 to 1870. Howard M. Corning, *Dictionary of Oregon History* (Portland, Ore., 1956), p. 61.

[2] Hiram and Mary Smith were from Missouri. He was one of the main promoters of overland travel to Oregon. *Ibid.,* p. 227.

[3] Sue Brewster, niece of the Cookes, later became the wife of Charles P. Cooke. H. K. Hines, *An Illustrated History of the State of Oregon* (Chicago, 1893), p. 553. See also footnote 19, below.

[4] Thomas McFadden Patton, a member of the bar in Ohio, became a

May 5 We are now travelling through the country
of the Omaha Indians. They demand toll for passing
so Mr Smith promises them a feast, & they have sent
sumners [summoners?] out to bring in all the tribe
who are not already out Buffalo hunting

[May] 6" Hosts of the Indians have arrived on
Indians Ponies. Squaws & little Pappooses – young
men in the glory of fine feathrs paint & skins – their
war costume, for they are just now about to go to fight
the Pawnees. The girls who are in the market are most
grotesqely painted in vermillion & Green – they have
not yet assumed the cast off garments of white people –

The Calf which Mr Smith & Cooke gave them was
killed and eaten even to the very entrails, some hard
Bread was given to them too.

In the evening they gave us a war dance by an
immense fire, that lit up the wiered [wierd] hob goblin
scene – their fiendish yells, as they tossed their arms
about and swung the gory scalps just taken from their
enemis, the Soux: helped to give the whole affair an
informal aspect.

Old women sat squatted on the ground chattering &
screaming their delight at the sight of evry freshly
shown scalp

Not till morning did quiet come, then when we were
ready to move we missed the mother of the calf – which
was soon found tied in the brush some distance off. it
required some nerve to take the animal away from
them, who outnumbered us

---

practicing attorney in Salem. He served in the Oregon Legislature and in
1884 became the United States Consul to Japan. He and Frances Cooke
were married on August 3, 1854. H. O. Lang, *History of the Willamette
Valley* (Portland, Ore., 1885), p. 743.

11 May   The Platte river is beutiful here – many
islands dot the stream & are covered with cotton wood
trees –

We ladies went to visit some Indian Graves near
here & were piloted by Mr Patton. Some of the graves
were larger than others, all were mounds from five to
six feet in highth. Earth & stones heaped up in a conical
shape

The Indians were so hungry & persistent – They
levy tribute on all who pass – do not always get anything – but it is wise to do so as they will stampede the
cattle some dark night if not well treated

[DOCUMENT A]

Monday, May 12   This is a beautiful day pleasant
sunshine after rain makes us feel cheerful. We cannot
cross as the water is so high. Our boys are now making
a bridge   Six Indians stopped with us last night. We
gave them supper & breakfast.

Tuesday May [13]   We were quickly wakened this
morning by the singing of the Indians. Our men all
went to work with the three other companies building
a bridge. It was completed by afternoon when we
crossed. It is a matter of surprise that over 500 head
of cattle, & fifty wagons should cross without accident
The Waggons were all drawn over by hand & the
cattle & horses swam. This day was pleasant   we
encamped a mile from the creek   The Evening was
delightful   the moon shone so Clearly but before
morning, it clouded up & one of the most terrifine
storms I ever witnessed. The heavens seemed to be
opened   The rain fell in torrents   The lightning was
most vivid. We were obliged to move as soon as pos-

sible for fear of being overflown Our cattle was
skatered miles around us. they were not together till
nine Oclock when we traveled on some 3 miles in
water up to the axeltrees. The 13 & 14 of May will
long be remembered by this bunch of Oregonians
We still continued on for we wished to be in advance
of so large a company We did not leave our former
camping ground as soon as the other company & consequently ran far behind We pushed on amid most
terrifine thunder & lightning & passed the other companies in five miles, when we camped on the open
Pararie. I had often read and heard of the Platt river
storms & we realized it beyond the most vivid description

June 1 This is the first day of summer. beautiful
day went 27 miles. Mr S & Mr Patton crossed to
the south side, to call upon other emigrants from Mr
Cranston's Cy [5] & Mr. Knight [6] They had had a
severe hail storm at the same time that we were upon
the island it fell there 10 inches. Camped upon a
fine creek The clearest water we have yet had since
we left: Crossed the Missouri. The Pararie is covered
with beautiful little flowers. Whose fragrance sur-
passed any garden flowers. There is a modest little
white flower which peeps up among the green grass.
Which particularly strikes my fancy. I call it the
Pararie Flower Autumn sun will bring the more
gorgeous flowers

Jun 2 Came 23 miles camping near the Platt –
opposite – McFarlans Castle. From here it has the

---

[5] See "Letters from Oregon," by Susan Amelia Cranston, in this volume.
[6] So far unidentified.

appearance of a splendid castle a huge mass of stone It takes its name from a man who was murdered here by the Soux. At about noon we passed Ancient Bluff ruins Mr & Mrs Cook, Sue, Tom, Joe & I climbed the highest ruin which commanded a fine view of the country.

This is of Solid Rock with five scraggy gnarled cedars, Throwing their twisted arms over the overhanging precapice Many a name was carved with knife upon the bark We left our names upon a Buffalo bone which lay bleaching upon the top from the river it presents the appearance of a fortified city falling to decay, but the nearer you draw nigh the illusion valishes. Thornton [7] speaks of this, though he went upon the south side he crossed to see it his description is vivid from our camp we see Chimny Rock which is 10 miles from the Castle. It is 600 feet high. Whoever has read the Pararie Flower & Leni Leoti [8] will see that it is spoken of as a spot of eventful meaning very poor grass

June 3 Cattle wandered. We consequently did not leave camp till late, fine day & good roads John spilled over his wagon, soon after we started but soon picked up again passed several small sheets of water which looked tempting but Death was lurking there in its limpid waters Today an antelope stood close by the road side so that I could see it quite distinctly it was a beautiful little creature. It gazed at us for a moment & then bounded away to the Bluffs Came 17 miles & encamped upon the Platt three miles from

---

[7] Jessy Quinn Thornton, *Oregon and California in 1848* (New York, 1849).

[8] Emerson Bennett, *The Prairie Flower* and *Leni-Leoti: Or, Adventures in the Far West* (Cincinnati, Oh., 1849).

the main road. Which we left for better grass & to avoid the alkeli water which stands in pools on the road. The ground is encrusted with this substance saw two indian Lodges near us of the Ceyeon tribe [Cheyenne]

Chimney Rock is opposite our camp & Scotts Bluff in view ahead so named from an Indian trader by that name whose party had been robbed of their provisions & this one fell sick & desparing of ever reaching his home & family pursuaded his companions to leave him. He was left some miles from this place but some years afterwards human bones were found at this spot & it was supposed that he had crawled here to die

June 4   Made 16 miles & camped upon Spring Creek.

June 5   Started at six   made 10 miles & nooned upon the banks of the Platt. The Prickly Pear, & a species of the Cactus grow in quantities by the road side Modest sweet little flowers are springing up among the grass   an hour and a half after noon a violent hailstorm arose & we were obliged to lay by some time   Came 18 miles. Camped upon the Platt   our vision was delighted with the view of a few small trees that grew upon the banks for they tell strongly of good cheer after having to cook so long with Buffalo Chips   For 200 miles we have no wood. Bluffs are not so high on the south – more sandy, rainy & unpleasant.

June 6   Started early road by the first of the day over level plains   Nooned upon Raw Hide Creek In the afternoon passed three companies travel rocky passed the fort in front of which was a Soux village of some hundred Lodges & great numbers of ponies. The squaws were just herding them in as we passed They are a smarter race than either the Omahas or pawnees Could not find grass & came 27 miles camped at nine near Mr Kinneys camp [9] five miles from the fort.[10] Bluffs still continue ever higher and more rocky with a few stunted pines & cedars. Small wood upon the banks of the river

[June] 7 Our road to day lies over high river bluffs steep precipitous patches most beautiful rugged scenery. Mountains covered with a growth of cedar & pine. Nooned between two high hills or almost mountains where was a beautiful spring of water. Giles [11] & I led the horses down to the spring & then washed our faces in the cool stream It was refreshing on that warm day. Road still was very bad steep & rocky. Camped near a beautiful grotto where Sue and I discovered under the rocks a little spring whose water dripped so slowly upon the stone basin under several gigantic cedar trees Their thin branches over The grape vine too was twining above, forming a complete arch. It was a delightful little spot.

Sunday [June] 8 A warm beautiful day Scenery more tame can still see Laramie Peak which has been in sight five days Nooned near a small brook where Sue & I as usual ventured upon a voyage of discovery found our garden Larkspr flowering currant choke cherry in great abundance Wild sage in great abundance camped near a small creek. do not know how far we came

---

[9] There were a number of Kinneys who traveled to Oregon, but their big year was 1847. This one is not identified.

[10] In her June 6 entry in Document B she says this was Fort Laramie.

[11] Giles is so far a mystery.

[June] 9   Another beautiful day of warm sunshine.
The pure air of the mountain breeze is so invigor-
ating. Rode to day upon horse back   We have again
struck the Platt, but were not in sight of it in the afternoon. Road is now level   We were nearly three days
crossing these Black Hills. They are a spur of the
Rocky mountains   We could not find grass & water
& as night drew on were upon the point of camping
with out water & poor grass for our teams had had a
hard drive & were weary, but after a short consulta-
tion it was thought best to travel on & find water too
The moon now shown brightly – Our road lay through
the belt of a mountan forest   Camped upon the Platt
at 10 oclock.   (All cross)

[June] 10   started early. Most tremendous horrid
barren hills "The heathey hills of Scotland will not
bear comparison" so sais "Uncle Ed" [12]   broke our
buggy but not so bad as to be fixed. Camped early
upon the Platt a pretty spot   good grass wild sage
in abundance

11 June   our road to day lay more upon the level
high banks of the river. made 17 miles & camped 2
miles from where the south road crosses & comes upon
the north. we are in sight of the ferry where a company is now crossing   camped again upon the muddy
Platt, in a thick grove of cottonwood on one side &
the Black Hills sloping to the right. Prickly Pear in
great abundance. Very dusty. Upon these hills is
manufactured the storms which are driven down upon
the river & forms the Platt river storms so much
noted by trevelers. One of our boys found a coal bed

---

12 Edwin N. Cooke.

yest[erda]y I think this part of the country can never be settled for the scarcity of timber There are but few trees upon the Platt & those in patches & entirely of cotton wood. (sick at heart) Mr Cook lost a cow, The first loss yet. Other companies that we have passed complain of lame cattle, sore feet &c. we have passed the horse company that ferried the Loup Fork just before we did & made their boasts that they would see Oregon two months before any other company we passed them four days ago.

12 of June Made 23 miles road was fine reminded me of the macadamised road from Bellevue to Perrysburg [Ohio] our camp last night was a delightful spot It was a luxurient grove of cotton wood & as we sat under their grateful shade we thought that we could now appreciate our own lofty forest trees. The Eglantine & mountain currant formed a dense undergrowth we now begin to see bestricken, broken waggons, stoves, lanterns, & indeed almost everything that could be well dispensed with high rolling bluffs coverd with the wild sage. nooned in a cotton wood grove. Many of the trees were peeled of their bark & names of many emigrants upon their white trunks told of the effects of the California mines.

Friday 13 June Started early for we were to make a long drive so as to pass through the alkeli regions to do which we were to travel 32 miles. To day we bid farewell to the Platt which from here presents a strikingly picturesque appearance. We have followed its windings more than 500 [700? – not clear] miles, & are loth to part with it. We could always see its waters glistning in the sun as it flowed so quietly by our side. From the higher bluffs it looks like a silver thread binding the base of the hills. But good bye, Shall we ever meet again? Here at this point, the morman trail crosses the river. I suppose that their object in thus ferrying twice is to avoid those formidable Black Hills passed at 4 through what must have been the crater of an old volcano, huge rocks lay in upturned masses by the road & in such unnatural positions that some voilen convulsion of nature must have produced these results. Soon after passing this we came to the first alkili spring the cattle were rushed through & some tasted it, but the bones that lay bleaching upon its banks testified to its poisonous qualities scattered along for many miles we saw these bones. We passed the other also without the cattle drinking. at nine we came to good water, & camped upon Willow Creek. Cattle very tired, no grass

[June] 14   Early we left & went six miles & camped some ways from the road, upon waggon creek, so called from the quantity of waggons which must have been left, left by last years Californians here we stop to rest the rest of the day

[June] 15   At noon found us underneath Independence Rock. from the distance it has the appearance of an oblong sand hill of no great dimensions, but as you approach nearer we find it a stupendous mass of granite standing isolated between two ranges of mountains (for I suppose they might be so called.) The Sweet Water runs at its left, I think it is some 120 feet high. I looked in vain amid that medly of names engraven & written upon its sides for one familiar *one*. It ought to be called the Sweet Water register – I walked I suppose a mile upon the north side, and seeing the names still as numerous as when I first started gave up the search. But I had hoped to see Patricks or b - r sturges Fremonts name still there We that is Sue [and] myself for Cook & Gibs [13] left our cards upon the highest peak for Mr Williams of Ill. & Mr. Black. We spent a pleasant afternoon in rambling over the rocks & in the cool fissures which we found, for it was an exceedingly warm day. Towards night we bid adieu to it. I was riding "Tamir." Went five miles further – & passed the Devils Gate & Gap. The first is a wild opening through the mountin about ¼ of a mile long of rugged appearance. Much I saw was of 2 parts. Many names engraved here also. The gap is a narrow opening of but few feet through which the Sweet Water runs. it is but a short distance from the first. The water is good in this stream, – In the forenoon we visited the dried bed of an alkeli lake. from the road it seemed like a patch of snow it was of such brilliant whiteness we found it quite thick & is good for use. We went two miles from the gate & camped under a massive rock, solid granite & some 500 feet high. Mountin sheep here. I have seen a many of horned toads, they are very poisonous. They are of the size of our common toad, but more resembling a lizzard of a greenish colour. Roads good & hard. The gravel hurts oxen feet. Larkspur abundant –

Monday 16 June Came 8 miles today and camped again upon the Sweet Water. Its water is slightly impregnated with alkeli. High rocks of granite upon our right – within firs scrubby pines & cedars, grow in crevices where a little soil had accumulated. F

---

[13] Gibs is so far unidentified.

Cook discovered something which risembled gold dust
but I think it is some other mineral substance   gravely
roads, rather warm   cattle. feet rather sore   Called
at Johnsons camp whose name might be seen upon
evry bleaching skull board & stone   good grass. Wild
sage here grows luxuriously almost small trees which
makes good fires. There is another little shrub intermixed with the sage called grease wood   it looks like
cedar, but its leaves are very tender & has a disagreeable *smell* of grease & turpentine –

17 of June   fine day, roads hard & gravly wending
between granite hill to our right, sand upon our left.
since we struck the Black Hills there has been no
good grass unless upon the bank of some stream. Grease
wood, sage & wild mustard predominate   In the morning the ground is pearley white with a blossom resembling the portulacca   camped upon the Sweet water which we forded.   our camp ground lay between
high granite Rocks.

Wednesday 18   Twas soon after we left camp we
again forded the stream & soon reforded it – this was
quite deep above the waggon beds. This might be
avoided by crossing in another place. The rocks here
as well as in every other prominant place bear the
names of many who have crossed before   This afternoon we saw the Wind River Mountains 70 miles
distant covered with perpetual snow.

It looked novel upon this warm day to see snow
apparently but few miles distant. The atmosphere here
is so clear, that distances & objects are very deceiving
came 9 miles & camped upon the Sweet water which

we again forded some distance from the main road. Last eve Mr Smith Cook & Marvin [14] had gone hunting & were to meet us they did not get to camp till afternoon tired & sick killed one deer & antelope *little* grass boys went hunting

Thursday [June] 19 Sruck our tents early for we had 16 miles sandy desert to pass without water, though there is an Ice spring ¼ of a mile from the road. it lies under the sod & can be dug in large pieces & very clear too. It is singular that it did not melt, it was so warm – Mr Smith was taken sick Mrs S. got off the horse & I had to ride alone. We camp upon the Sweet water. Made 14 miles.

Friday [June 20] Day was very windy & dusty. I rode all day 20 miles. passed at noon Rocky Ridge. I had just begun to realize that we were upon the rocky mts for it was very rough for a few miles. I *do not* realize my anticipations in that respect for I had expected to see it rugged mountainous & difficult passes but on the contrary, I should think myself upon a high rolling pararie. The soil is sandy & much gravel mixed with it, roads hard & good Met two returning Cal trains. Crossed many streams but found grass all eaten off. Went further than we expected to Camped upon Willow Creek where were already two other companies. passed several snow banks. The ground upon which we camped was a carpet of flowers

---

[14] She spells this name both Mervin and Marvin. On July 8 she tells of a Kate Mervin. There is an interesting reference to one Albert M. Marvin in H. O. Lang, *History of the Willamette Valley, op. cit.,* p. 739. Lang tells of an 1851 emigrant by that name who at age 11 traveled over the trail to settle first in Portland, and then in 1853 to move to Salem, "and has lived there ever since." He was serving as a steward in the Chemekata Hotel; had been married in 1873 to Lucinda Coffin.

mountan moss just in bloom, & small purple flowers
sent up a rich perfume. Pleasant but cold nights.

Saturday [June 21] Pleasant, cool mountain breeze
road lay over rolling sandy bluffs, covered with wild
sage   at noon we passed the dividing ridge which
separates the water which flows into the atlantic from
the pacific. In a short time we came to the Pacific
springs where we had expected to camp but it was
already full.

passed the Twin mounds which are the opening to
the great mountan pass   Came five miles beyond pass
& camped upon Pacific Creek, rode 19 miles   road
good,   we every day see many bones of horses & oxen
who have been left.

Sunday [June 22] This morning after herding in
the cattle found one which was much crippled in the
hind quarters.   boys drove it some ways & were obliged
to shoot it   The flesh was yellow & green, had been
bitten by a snake. Keeler [15] was taken sick last night &
is now very unwell   was doubtful whether to proceed.
He was put into the carriage. I rode horse all day.
No water but one alkeli stream, passed many dry beds
of this   about noon we came to the junction of the
Salt Lake & Oregon roads   here Mr S took in a
Mr. Brown [16] an old gentleman. Came 23 miles &
camped upon a fine spot excellent grass wood & water.
Willows grow upon the banks. T. sold sugar to some
Cal — for 50 cts cup ful, Ten ds. Box. The scenry
is not as I had anticipated so level.

---

15 So far unidentified.

16 The only "old gentleman" named Brown in the 1860 census was one
G. Brown, 76 years old, from Tennessee, a farmer in Marion County.
What would now be called "senior citizens" were very rare in Oregon
in the 1850's.

Monday [June 23] To day we laid over for cattle, as well as men needed rest. S is better. Condit [17] is a convelescent. Keeler better but Mrs S. was taken very sick indeed. Mountan fever, Several alkeli springs here. there are frogs in the ponds, talk a different language from our common ones. The creek is very crooked. It is called, little Sandy The night that we were upon the mountans water froze an inch thick we have cold nights & the mornings but warm dys. Snow capped mountains upon our right, Wind river range Two Indians passed our tents the first we have seen for many hundred miles.

Tuesday [June 24] Came 7 miles & camped upon the big Sandy good grass Company of returning Cal. camped with us. Mrs S better. Her & I wrote home by them. to day we passed a small grove of trees where hung an Indian wrapped in his robes & blankets. This is the method of burial among this tribe (crows) his arrows & bows were placed around his head.

[June] 25 Came 17 miles across a desert no grass or water. Roads quite stony several ascents nothing grows but grease wood & wild sage & something resembling Camomile. [Two unreadable words] upon the banks of the stream.

We have left the first range of wind river mounts & see upon the north & west we catch a glimpse of the snow capped mountains. It is very warm about two hours in the day This day at last we came in sight of the formidable Green River which we have so much dreaded. There is a good ferry boat – kept by

<hr>

[17] Sylvanus Condit, who in 1854 married Sarah A. Brown. They became farmers in the Turner area of Marion County, Oregon.

Mormons & worked by French & Indian half breeds
Mrs S. & I visited the wigwams after we crossed.
disgusting looking beings. by each tent was made a
shade of brush in which they cook, using the former
for sleeping. In one shady bower was an old squaw
one dog & four puppies & a calf, above hung cups
& other dishes used for culnary purposes   Came 14
miles & camped upon Green river   gravly roads, wild
sage & grease wood, poor grass uncomfortable times.
Ferry men dishonest. Uncle Israel's [18] Brown & Tom
cross. This now is a fine stream some what impregnated with alkeli   cotton wood. Yesterday Mr Marvins
"much [unreadable word] took Grand leave & also
a horse bag of bacon & hard bread & took his departure.

[June] 27   came 19 miles   camped upon the Black
fork of the Green river. poor grasss,   one of Charles [19]
oxen died   very cold   Sue & I were horse back &
I was obliged to seek shelter of the carriage had a
touch of the ague   When we came to camp we found
our way to the river bank and in the shelter of a thicket
of rose bushes,   soon were warm. some fish here
snow mountains on our left, good roads.

[June] 28   Came 5 miles & camped on Black fork near
where there were some traders & Mr S. & C. succeeded
in trading off poor cattle to good advantage, & just
as our cattle were giving out too. it was quite providen-
tial   Uncle Gid [20] laid it to that & alcohol of which

18 Israel Cooke.

19 Charles P. Cooke later married Susan Brewster on October 30, 1851.
They became Polk County settlers on Claim #4218. They later moved to
the Klickitat Valley in Washington. *Genealogical Material in Oregon
Donation Land Claims,* ii (Portland, Ore., 1959), p. 85.

20 The "uncle" for whom this nickname was used is so far not known.

they drank freely. One of the traders was a fine looking man he was of French extraction he spoke of his family I innocently asked if his wife were not lonesome in this desert place. he said Oh no for she was a native of these wilds [i.e. squaw] he then said he was going to Oregon & wished to know if he could go & his boy too. Thus alluding to the manner in which they treat their wives keeping them only to cook & tan hides for them & leaving them as caprice dictates but they seem to expect this & seldom grieve.

[June] 29 came 18 miles & camped upon Muddy Creek a stream was never more rightly named for we could not step upon its margin without sinking into the mire we are in sight of Bear River Mountains. I am better no more ague poor grass.

[June] 30 came 18 miles camped in sight of Fort Bridger an independent trading company Built of hewn logs we visited it Mrs B. [21] a dark eyed lady & children accompanied us home This is a beautiful valley the only habitable looking place that I have seen since the Elkhorn. Bear river mountains in sight. Smith & C. are trading goods & cattle so we will not proceed today. Mailed a letter to Cornelia. A coquettish little stream darts along among the green grass dividing & uniting & then parting again Its clear cold sparkling water as it comes rushing from the mountains over the rocky bed is grateful to the taste

---

[21] "Little Fawn," the Shoshone Indian wife of the famous trapper, Jim Bridger. She charmed all who met her. Mrs. B. G. Ferris described her thus: "His wife was simplicity itself. She exhibited some curious pieces of Indian embroidery, the work of her own hands, with as much pleased hilarity as a child; and gave me a quantity of raisins and sauce berries — altogether it was a very pleasant interview." J. Cecil Alter, *James Bridger* (Columbus, Ohio, 1951), pp. 242-43.

& after drinking of the Big Muddy we can better appreciate it. This leaves no whitened margin   I do not wonder that squaws are so indolent for since we have been dwellers in tents I feel that to throw myself upon the ground is luxuriant ease – free from restraints of etiquette is pleasant.

[July] 2   came 12 miles & camped on muddy Fork. It ill deserves this name for it is a clear cool stream winding its way through willows & rose bushes. Caught trout here. They are speckled & destitute of scales. An hour before camping we came down a bad hill worse than any we have yet descended.

[July] 3   This day was one of interest to me   The road lay through the Bear river mountans   scenery fine but tame   passed two soda springs running out of the mountain close by the road side. One hill that we descended was a mile in length   some 18 miles from our last camp are the tar springs   It is very much like that in ordinary use. it oozes out of the ground into holes dug for this purpose – first a coat of tar then a scum of oil & clear water underneath   several cold springs come from the mountan   20 miles brought us to Bear River.

[July] 4   This morning of the glorious fourth, we breakfasted at six upon Trout Strawberries & cream. We were roused by Mr Patton's firing two guns in honor of the day & crossed Bear river which is difficult fording for it is a swift stream & uneven rocky bed at noon we entered the Kanyon or canon which had been told us was extremely bad to pass through. came 18 miles & camped upon a little spring. The grass is excellent as indeed it has been since we left green river

[July] 5 This pass is called Echo Cannon & this Evil little stream whose crooked windings cursed us to bad roads is Echo Creek. Here we saw wild oats wheat hops & cherries much resembling those growing in our own country, snow drops & willows & single rose bushes grow thickly over it completely hiding the water. 13 times we crossed this & the banks being so steep as scarcely to afford footing for the cattle but it was passed safely without one broken axeltree, though Charley was so unfortunate as to turn over. All have had his luck but Condit with his "Rocky mountain schooner" & the boys declare that it shall go over befor we see Salt Lake. Came 19 miles & camped upon Weber river, a right smart charmer of a stream. Caught many speckled trout which are deliceous The scenery through this Cannon is magnificant Sometimes the mountan seems to hang over our heads as the road passes close under it. on the left is smooth high mountans covered with green grass, and in the ravines fir & cedar but upon the right these mountans rise almost perpendicular 1000 feet They are of gravel & stone cemented together by some earthy substance tops covered with cedars & scrubby oak sides perforated with many holes in which birds have built their nests & whose chirping we could distinctly hear & there is a substance oozing from the crevices which when burning emits a naceous effhusin resembling assofirdita Masses of rock had fallen in many places by the road side & becoming subjected to the influence of the weather, & had crumbled leaving only a heap of gravel. Cotton wood & willows the only timber Here we leave this cannon Kenyon is a spanish word signifying a armed or large gun, & the water rushing

over rocks through these ravines – making a noise like
firearms & out all openings in these mountains are
called by this term   In some of the ravines between
the Bluffs the rocks assume such fantastic shapes caused
by the waters washing down each side & leaving this
mass in the center   near our camp was a fine specimen

[July] 6   came 4 miles & camped for after 3 long
drives cattle needed rest   here were a company of
returning Cal.   one gentle[man] showed us coins &
fine specimens of gold in a crude state   Boys went
fishing   Caught fine trout.

[July] 7   Came 19 miles   bad roads   we crossed
this creek 10 times as it winds from side to side ne[c]es-
sarily makes many crossings. One redeeming thing it
was shady   flies gnats musketoes very annoying to cattle as well as us   John turned over again. camped upon
Canyon Creek under the brow of the mountan   Uncle
Israel & Mr Patton stopped at last camp with sick
cattle   camped at the mouth of Mountain Kenyon.

[July] 8   This days travel was hard. commenced the
ascent of the mountan   5 miles   a garden of flowers
roads extremely bad. tall pines & balsum   many
springs running by the road side. Sue & I walked
the decent of the mountain 2 miles very steep. Chained
the wheels   I was almost afraid to walk down myself
for the first decent was nearly perpendicular. Many
rocks and holes & sudden turns   Sue & I also walked
down this carrying Kate Mervin   when at last we
found the bottom we threw ourselves upon the grass
under a large cotton wood & waited for the carriages
washed our faces in the cool creek. came 9 miles
camped on Browns creek a small stream lined with

willows. I think that "Uncle Sam" could find employment for convicts in breaking stones between Fort Bridger & the City.

[July] 9 Mr S, C & Mervin went to the city. we washed & baked. Keeler & I tried our luck in fishing but could get none Trout are very timid fish Men returned disappointed in the City – The floor of our tent was exremely dirty – dusty so we made a carpet of willow boughs. very warm

[July] 10 Came 4 miles bad roads [line crossed out]

[July] 11 This day at noon we came in sight of the City of Salt Lake from the distance of 5 miles it, the valley, presents the appearance of an immense ploughed clay field but as we approach nearer it is a garden of Luxuriant growth The most pleasing feature of the city is the brooks & water which flow on each side of evry street & rows of young cotton wood by the side. It is conducted from the mountin streams. It looks so cool on these sultry days to see & hear the water rippling over its gravely bed the city is five miles square & is divided into lots of 1¼ acres Houses of adobe [22]

August 2/1851 Valley of Salt Lake Saturday yesterday was a busy day The new cattle were brought together & branded at two oclock we were on our way & most truly rejoicing for we were but [unreadable word] happy to be once more upon our journey & also to be beyond the precents of Mormanism. We have been in the valley three weeks. the cattle were

[22] A long section telling of life in Salt Lake City in the following days is found in her second, revised Version B, as we have labelled it. This is not in her primary record of the journey, Document A.

25 miles from the City & most of the boys either herding the cattle or working in the harvest & fields   With
the valley I am much pleased, indeed its fertility
far exceeds my expectations & I think that no more
river is Lost in irrigating the land than is by rainy
days in the states. Corn & potatoes are about medium
but this the wheat fiels of the world for no so near
does it thrive with such luxuriance   It often yields
100 to the acre. 70 & 80 are average crops   There are
about 40,000 Mormons in this & other valleys for there
are many other equally populated settlements here
Little Salt Lake San Pedro &c   It is reported that
extensive beds of coal & gold have been found there,
for instance that a man had been digging post holes
& throwing the dirt in heaps in which the chicks
scratched & having later decapitated one for his supper his wife displayed to his wondering eyes pieces
of gold to the amount of 150 $!

One would hardly think that in four years such
improvements could be made. As you enter the valley
each way as far as the eye can reach we see fine
farms & herds of cattle grazing upon the range &
lands so regularly laid out too. And we see the cheq-
uered patches of every mans farm, Square fields of
green corn one equally as large of ripening wheat
oats & grass each with its varied hues of yellow. This
day we went 10 miles & camped apparently near the
margin of Salt Lake, but found to our disappointment
that it was no less than ten miles! so deceiving are
the distance here.

August 3   We came 13 miles & camped upon the
Weber with the boys who were herding cattle. Our
eyes were once more greeted with our old friends

Sage & Sand, whose acquaintance we had formed
in the black hills Our road lay through a pass in
the mountains to a by place some distance from the
main road. scenery wild & grand. O for a lodge in
some vast wilderness, a home in some deep lone "kenyon" We were under the brow of the mountan by
the side of a cool spring. There were two of these,
one they had used to wash dishes in & dress fish –
the other for drinking for they had dammed it up
to form a basin allowing the water to run from one
side – we went further up the kenyon in search of
Raspberries not finding any. Sue & I took off our
shoes, & walked upon the shallow pebly bottom of
the noisy Weber while Mrs S & C sat upon the bank
trying to frighten us with stories of snakes & toads.
To day again we thought to try our fortune in berry-
ing some of the young gentlemen of the camp went
with us & taking each a pail & basket of hard bread
& venison we started invoking the gods to be more
propiteous for it was a long toilsome walk to climb
the Rocky Mountan & then not to get one raspberry
it was too bad though we did find wild currants &
service berries but we were a merrie party. O it was
so hard to climb – to jump from rock to rock sometimes swinging ourselves by holding a shrub & cling-
ing to the roots after ascending about a mile, we
heard the tricling of water & pushing the bushes by
my side found a small spring where the water was
dropping from between the stones we held a cup
under & were quite refreshed with a drink of ice
water Two miles brought us to the long sought berries – O my poor hands – mess – but never will our
dinner [be] finished & pails filled in a short time. I

never saw larger ones cultivated in our gardens at home
both white & black but now came the tug of war for
we were to come down again. found another spring
& sitting around it we thought we would improve it
This by combining art with nature   The next ram-
bler will wonder who did this! We cleaned out the
sand leaves & sticks laid a wall of stones around it
piling them so as to form a pretty little fall – as we
came down upon the bottom we met two of our men
panting & out of breath, with their guns   They had
seen two Indians on the opposite side & they had shot
at them, and hurrying to camp got their guns & came
in search of us. We hastened home but I will confess
that I cast a suspicious glance behind every big rock
or thicket. These are the Utah, & quite ugly. This is
one of the pleasant days which linger long in the
memory and are often spoken of – for all we [of]
that little party will not soon forget it. There came a
young man who was anxious to go to O[regon]   He
is engaged to a young widow in the City, & not being
himself a Mormon, Mr Young would not marry them
& says he will kill him if he attempts to take her
from the valley   I think Mr. Mervin will take him
& the widow too & should we meet a Minister before
we enter the territory we shall probably have a wedding : –

[August] 5   We came 18 miles & camped in another
kenyon near a settlement where Mr S and C were
trading for cattle. You would be surprised in the
growth of this industrous people   soon will evry ravine & in these mountans be teaming with life   now
in evry kenyon you will see the smoke of their hearth
stones

[August] 6 Today two Utah indians visited our camp with skins & service berries to "swap" weather delightful though rather windy at sunset lasting until the rising of the sun. our cattle number 203 horses & mules d[itt]o.

[August] 7 Today we camped upon a small creek beyond Fort Ogden This is a settlement which is rapidly improving, situated upon the west side of Ogden river a beautiful stream of clean cold mountain water. There has been two Indian burials not far from our camp The last was the Chiefs brother. He was wrapped in skins tied around him with Lariets & laid upon a horse. He was carried up into the mountans followed by the whole tribe who were howling & screaming most hideously

His horse & colt were sacrificed upon his grave. His bow gun & other implements were placed in the grave too. After this ceremony was over they returned in great glee through the Fort. We passed many untenented wigwams built of brush walls quite good. O you who live in Ohio do not know the good or bad roads I used to think that hill between M[?] & M[?] with fear for it was so steep. But one who has crossed these R[ocky] M[ountains] would say that that was only a little pitch. We have waded miles at a time in Sloughs up to the hubs of the wheels down hills that seemed perpendicular half a mile threatening to throw the carriage over the horse upon the sides of mountains where the waggons had to be held for fear of tipping upon one side evening warm discussion but it is always so people have nothing to gossip about but their neighbours & murder will out sometimes & so it was this time, but thanks to the good fairy who

has always attended me I was quietly day dreaming
in my own *little room* A Mr Brown came to camp
said he wanted to speak to the Ladies too for he so
seldom saw them — He has but 7 & is contemplating
two more. He can not get the daughter without the
widowed mother — he bought 140 yards of calico
he said it [will] not more than go around.

August Friday 8 Early this morning we were on
our way at noon we passed the hot spring very
salt — some were boiling. one of the cows ran in &
Mr S after to save her for she would soon be par
boiled He went in over his head & as he came up
caught hold of a piece of rock & came out dripping
with red & yellow slime which collects there forms
a marshy piece of ground encrusted at the edges with
salt I picked out a fine specimen came fifteen miles
& camped a mile beyond Box Elder creek upon which
was the bad [?] settlement found plenty of fine choke
cherries

[August] 9 This morning found that one cow & mule
was missing John & Simon went back we passed
Hollidays Train for Cal Came to salt springs, some
were warm and some boiling Here were feathers
as though some one had been dressing fowls Near
this a clear cold stream bubbled from under a pro-
jecting rock passed a company camping upon the
banks of the Bear river who had started for O[regon]
& taken the cutoff from [Lookout?] springs & intending to settle in the valley Forded Bear river and
over upon the opposite bank we were beyond the
precincts of mormonism This is a wide but shallow stream water rather brackish came 19 miles &
forded Noland Creek which is another small creek

very deep & narrow Camped just before sun down
There had been a camp here before & things looked
quite suspicious remnants of trunks clothing waggons & boots partly burned &c on the first watch
the guard said he saw indian prowling. They were
upon the opposite side in the brush imitating the mo-
tions & breathing of cattle to ensnare him across.
fired two guns & they were quiet. thanks to the vigi-
lence of our guard none of the stock were stolen but
I did feel timid for they are very troublesome now.

[August] 10 Came 18 miles & camped upon Bear
springs brackish water again O how I long for
a good drink of pure water. no fuel but sage & little
grass. We saw an Indian galoping through the ravine
Extremely warm roads good. They lay over a barren wash which can never be cultivated springs
strongly impregnated with salt and copperous &
warm at that.

[August] 11 After a tedious ride of 28 miles we
came to a small spring where we camped some time
after dark. we had passed but one small brook &
consequently the poor cattle had not drunk since
morning & were crazy when they smelled the water
– We took a cut off which lay through a vast field
of wild sage we gained nothing by it hereafter I
eschew all cutoffs as being longer than the right road.
However we had a beautiful moon light we met
a large band of packers. One smilingly gave us papers
He was from Cal He liked it better than Oregon –
which latter was a fine country but he had not lived
there long enough to fall in love with it. They had
seen the bodies of 7 men exposed to sight – they were
murdered by Indians who would not allow them to

be buried The rest of the 14 escaped Horses &
mules were packed some with baggage & some with
provisions fine moonlight

[August] 12 To day we passed stony creek & camped
upon Casia in a valley. fine grass good water &c all
prepared for Indians but as it proved this morning
we needed not fear though I presume that we are
watched & when we cease to be very vigilent then
we may expect an attact.

[August] 14 We found after starting this morning
that six cattle were missing so we went but few miles
& camped Trout for breakfast

[August] 15 Last night about midnight were awakened by the sudden tramping of the cattle who were
herded in the correll. Indians! Stampede! before two
moments elapsed all hands stood ready to fire imagine to yourself forty men rising like specters from
under waggons tents & carriages with guns & bowie
knives – cattle, scattering with speed & the bright
moon rising over our heads & then form a faint idea
of the consternation & chagrin that momentarily de-
picted itself upon their countenances – when the guard
said it was he who accidentally frightened them caus-
ing this small stampede soon all were gathered in
the correll Then the laughter & merry jests –Then
all was quiet again Passed the body of an Indian
who had been wilfully shot by some daring fellow
& farther on lay the bodies of eight white men who
innocently fell to revenge the blood of the redmen
one week after Finis

[DOCUMENT B]

[August] 18 Travelled over sage plains, roads rocky

and dusty Rocks sharp and hard. Bear River vally
is the most inhabitable looking since we left the Platt
The Crickets are large often an inch and a half or
two inches in length – Black & shiney, the Indians
make soup of them – They catch them by driving
them into pits dug for this purpose – they are dried
for winter use, its laughable to see our White Chickens try to swallow them, it often takes two or three
efforts to get one disposed of, they are so numerous
that one cannot avoid stepping on them.

Snake river here is narrow & the banks very steep,
from 8oo to a thousand feet to the water, only now
& then a fissure by which access can be had to the
water. Camped where the cattle were driven a mile
before a pass could be found down. Many dead cattle
all the way.

[August] 21 Hot & dusty, worn out, scenery grand
Salmon Falls near by. The water falls over the black
Basalt in numerous cascades

Numbers of *Shoshone* Indians are camped here,
We bought enough Salmon of them for a fish hook
to make us wish never to see any more. The Fish is
poor by the time it gets this far from the ocean.
The falls prevent them going farther, so the water at
certain seasons are alive with them, some of enormous
lengths – as long as a wagon bd [bed]

Our road is often through light sand ten inches in
depth – which is hard on cattle – whose feet are now
very tender.

[August] 22 We crossed snake river to an Island
& then to a second Island, where was nice grass, with
plenty of wood & water. Here we missed some Horses
& the tracks showed that they had been run off by

Indians at Ft Hall. Volunteers went back under the control of Mr Cooke so as to get to the Indian camp before sunrise that they might be taken by surprise, & so be able to capture the Horses. The camp sorrowfully watched the departure of our warriors, & a sleepless night followed – After twenty-four hours of anxiety the absnt ones were seen returning with all the missing stock.

They reported the consternation of the Indians at the apprence of hostile whites. The squaws & Papposes took to the hills for refuge & were seen issuing from evry Lodge. The men half dressed with bow in hand stood at bay ready to repel intruders. But viewing the rifles pointed at them folded their arms and awaited events. Mr Cook gave them by signs to understand that he wanted Horses   they signified that they had none,   after some more strategy one seized a Lariet & soon returned with the missing stock Mr Cooke recovred his old favorite "Barnabas" with delight, so ended the battle of "Wagon Hill"

We recruited [23] a few days & as the ford was dangerous it was thought best to recross & travel on the same south side of snake river, to Boise   Had a beautiful camp good grass water & wood   soon after the corell was formed we had supper and all gathered around the camp fire & a song was sung composed by Mr Cooke. Roads rocky, of volcanic aspect, often doubling teams on the hills

4 sep   Crossed Burnt river many times   scenery most beautiful

[September] 8   we are in the Powder river country

----

[23] The meaning of "recruited" here is that they rested to regain strength.

and begin to see forests of Pine & Fir. Came down the mountain into Grand Ronde vally – a perfect gem – an oasis in a desert The descent was made with difficulty – the wagons being chained & let down with ropes much of the way.

Grand Ronde river flows & winds through this basin surrounded by high hills

Thousands of horses – many of them curiously spotted feed upon the mountain side.[24] Hundreds of Indians of the Nez Percies tribe, are camped here, & lazily greet us with invitations to swap, saw one child almost if not quite white among them. The women are all dressed in native costumes of dressed antelope skins – fringed & ornamented with moccasins on their dainty little feet. They came to see us mounted astride of great sleek horses, & laugh & chatter among themselves like just so many gay school girls. Their long black hair is braided into two long plaits that hang down & on top of the head is a gay little hat shaped like a flower pot – made of woven grass – it serves to pick berries in or to drink out of, as it holds water it being so closely woven. Brass rings are to be seen on waist & ankle they have an air of maidenly reserve that wins respect. The men are all fine specimens of physical development, & have not yet become contaminated with the vices of white men and the whole tribe are very superior to any we have yet seen. One pretty squaw took my knitting & very proudly took a few stitchs – the remains of some of the teach-

[24] This is a primary reference to the Nez Perce "curiously spotted" or Appaloosa horses, named for the Palouse branch of that tribe. Francis Haines, *Appaloosa: The Spotted Horse in Art and History* (Fort Worth, Tex., 1963).

ings of Mrs Whitman that had been remembered
Grass was tall & luxuriant in this Indian Paradise.

[September] 15   Crossed the Dechutes river – very
rocky & difficult. We were told the story of an emigrant woman who was afraid to cross with her train,
but was persuaded to get on a horse behind an Indian
that had just crossed. When in the middle of the stream
with dizzy brain she cried out in fear. The Indian
turned his face to her & said, "Wicked woman put
your trust in God" These words in good English
frightened her worse than ever – He was one of Whit-
mans good Indians & he had been taught this by that
missinary martyr

[September] 23   found us at the Dalles of the Columbia. Most of the train went on crossing the Cascades
mountins & the rest of us came by boat & raft to the
Portage of the Cascade, where we camped. The little
steam boat James G Flint [25] brought us part of the way

Indians were salmon fishing at the Portage & were
drying their fish there. They had a great dance dressed
in costume – none but the young men danced. The occasion that called for it reminded me of some of the
customs of the ancient Iseralites and I wondered if
indeed, they were of the lost Tribes of Iseral.

Many fine canoes were to be seen, made of great
length out of trunks of great cedar trees – some might
be fifty feet in length hollowed out & carved with high
sculptured prows, glistning with brass headed nails
& it was wonderful to see the skill with which they

---

[25] Her reference should be to the *James P. Flint,* an amazing river
steamship that was built above the cascades of the Columbia by hauling
an engine overland and literally building a ship around it upstream. Randall
V. Mills, *Stern-Wheelers up the Columbia* (Stanford, Calif., 1947), pp. 27-28.

would handle them. The squaws all seemed to be rich in ornaments of beads & brass strings of beads of all colors weighing pounds hang from the neck, – all looked happy and contented sevral Indian burial places we passed as we walked from one end of the portage to the other. Mr Chenewuth [26] was living there These burial places seemed to be pens built of huge slabs of wood ornamented with grotesque carvings & paintings, where the bodis were deposited

26 of sept we landed at Portland a little town of a couple hundred inhabitants, just as the guns were booming in honor of the completion of the Plank Road to Tualatin plains.[27] The Town was completely deserted evry body having gone to the Road

There is a small Catholic Church, a good Methodist building The Episcopalians have service in a school house & sometimes in the Methodist church. The pastor is Rev Dr Richmond [28] who called immediately to see me, and I heartily enjoyed the service of the

---

26 Francis A. Chenoweth was an attorney who emigrated from Wisconsin to Oregon in 1849. Later he became an active politician, serving in both the Oregon and Washington legislatures. *Dictionary of Oregon History, op. cit.*, p. 52.

27 There was a colorful story about the laying of such a road in the Porland *Oregonian* for September 20, 1851, just six days before Harriet Buckingham made this entry: "PORTLAND AND VALLEY PLANK ROAD. – We are requested to give notice that the first plank will be laid on this road on Saturday, Sept. 27th, a which time, all persons who feel interested in this work are invited to attend and lend a helping hand. Mr. Coffin who has taken the contract to put down the planks, assures us that one mile or more, at the commencement near Mr. Carter's, will be ready for the plank by that day. It is proposed to have a pic nic dinner on the occasion. Should the weather be favorable. Let us all turn out upon this important occasion and give the road a volunteer impetus towards its completion."

28 Another *Oregonian* story in the September 27, 1851, issue of the paper, says the following: "Notice. – The services of the Episcopal Church will be held at the School House in Portland, every Sunday but the last in the month. W. Richmond, Rector."

church once more in the little school house. The Pastor is zealous but rather executive

The steam ship Columbia [29] comes in once a month & all the town sit up two nights before its arrival lest they should be sleeping, when the gun fires the population go to the little wharf – a crowned head would not be received with greater Eclat than the Captain & Purser of the staunch little Columbia Gentlemen go about with big boots suitable for mud, as there are no side walks, & the Main street is full of huge fir stumps & deep mud holes. We were invited the second day of arrival to the house of the Editor of the principal paper the "Oregonian" Mr Thomas J. Dryer,[30] who with his family welcomed us travel stained & weary from our seven months journey – a welcome that made us feel at home was offered by his excellent wife and charming daughter.

One other paper was in circulation – the Times a democratic organ.[31]

29 The first river steamboat constructed in Oregon at Astoria in early summer 1850. Mills, *Stern-Wheelers, op. cit.,* pp. 16-17.

30 Thomas Jefferson Dryer, a New Yorker who crossed to San Francisco among the forty niners. He published the first issue of the *Oregonian* on December 4, 1850. George S. Turnbull, *History of Oregon Newspapers* (Portland, Ore., 1939), 55ff.

31 The *Oregon Weekly Times* began publication as a Portland newspaper on June 5, 1851. It was published by John O. Waterman and William Davis Carter. Turnbull, *op. cit.,* pp. 52-53.

Journal of Travails to Oregon

§ Amelia Hadley

INTRODUCTION

Sigmund Freud would not be born until 1856, but that did not stop Amelia Hadley from using a Freudian slip in the title of her overland diary in 1851. She really intended it to be "Journal of Travels," but somehow it came out "Travails." She has special talent for variety in misspelling the word "travel" all through her diary, and many other words as well.

She was born Amelia Hammond near Cleveland, Ohio, on September 21, 1825. It was on April 10, 1851, in Galesburg, Illinois, that she married Samuel B. Hadley, a man from Maine. That was Sam's 30th birthday, having been born on April 10, 1821. Four days later, on Monday, April 14, they left by wagon train for Oregon and Amelia made the first entry in her daily diary. So Samuel and Amelia Hadley's overland journey was a honeymoon trip lasting some 130 days. There was another Hadley who accompanied them on the wagon trek — Sam's younger brother, Melville.

The early part of the diary reveals a very cheerful young lady. On May 29 she wrote, "It is amuseing (*sic*) and delightful to travel over these plains, and is not such a task as many imagine   perhaps I may sing another song before I get through. . ." On June 2 she gazed upon the beauty of Courthouse Rock and emoted, "I for one never enjoyed myself better and never had better health." She blamed the bad luck of others on "carelessness and Missmanagement." Then the "travails" begin to make their appearance: On July 15, while chasing an Indian who had

stolen a horse from the camp, Melville Hadley, her husband's younger brother, received a gun shot wound in his
right side, "the ball passing in between his ribs and out
within an inch of his back bone." If it had not been for the
presence of a medical man in the party, Dr. James C. Cole,
who went out with a group of men and brought him in,
Melville might well have died. As it was, he lay in the
wagon for a number of days suffering repeated bumps
and jolts.

Then, on July 20 she wrote, "Do not feel verry well
my self," and for the next three days she did not improve,
and on July 23 she added, "I am no better will have to
give up journal for few days." She did not add more until
August 10 when she wrote, "After striking the Columbia
I again resume my journal. I have been verry sick for the
past 2 weeks and not able to wait on my self and of course
my book neglected." By the time she wrote her last entry
on August 23 in Oregon City, the final words were, "This
is the end of a long and tedious journey."

One noteworthy feature of the Hadley's overland journey was its speed. The very idea of reaching the Willamette
Valley as early as August 23 is unusual. More often, it
took other travelers another month or two. The main
reason for this was that the Hadleys used horses. Amelia
constantly refers to passing the ox teams of others all
along the way.

For the first few months in Oregon, they lived in the
little town at the confluence of the Willamette and Columbia
rivers: Portland. Then they moved south to the valley of
the Umpqua River and settled a claim near what was to
become Roseburg, which, at that time, was being founded
by their cohorts on the cross country trek, Aaron and Sarah
Rose.[1] The claim record indicates that the Hadleys took
up their claim on December 1, 1851. That richly timbered

---

[1] Howard M. Corning, ed., *Dictionary of Oregon History*. (Portland, Ore.,
1956), p. 212.

part of Oregon was to be the main center of their activities for the rest of their lives. There were two short periods away, one near Yreka in northern California's Siskiyou County, the other in eastern Oregon on the banks of Summer Lake. Dr. James Cole, who had attended Melville's wound on the westward journey, settled with his family a short distance away in what became known as Coles Valley.[2]

Over the years following, the Hadleys had eight children, generally speaking every two years: Albert in 1852, Margaret in 1854, Samuel in 1856. Then in Siskiyou County, California, on April 22, 1858, there came twins: Melvina and Melville. Later children were Kitty in 1862 and Henry in 1866.

But there was a ninth child, one whom the others remembered vividly. Melvina F. (Hadley) Hayes, one of the twins, told Fred Lockley of the *Oregon Journal* about this child in the issue of July 1, 1938:

> When I was a little tot my parents adopted a Siskiyou Indian boy, 5 years old. His mother was blind and couldn't take care of him. Father named him Joe Bowers. He grew up with the rest of us and was like one of the family. He idolized Mother. He was one of the finest Indians I have ever known. He was perfectly dependable and everyone liked him. Father was a stockman and usually had 300 to 400 horses. Joe Bowers and my brothers, Albert, Melville and Hank, rode the range and were expert horse wranglers. They would break horses to ride, before Father sold them.

The Hadleys were Methodists. Although she did not deplore traveling on Sunday, as some other covered wagon women did, Amelia did mention it several times. In Oregon, their home became a center of Methodist activities. A friend of theirs, William Grandison Hill, remembered in later years that "Sam Hadley kept a meeting house and

---

[2] O. Larsell, *The Doctor in Oregon* (Portland, Ore., 1947), pp. 267-68.

some of the worst blue rum a man ever got outside of." [3]

In its issue of October 8, 1886, the Roseburg *Plaindealer* newspaper reported the death of Amelia Hadley, and with a segment of the obituary we close our summary of her life. Her first name is spelled wrong, but the rest of the story is authentic:

> Mrs. Emelia A. Hadley was born near Cleveland, Ohio, September 21, 1825, and departed this life at Myrtle Creek, Or., Oct. 3, 1886. She was married to Mr. S. B. Hadley at Galesburg, April 10, 1851. Together they crossed the plains the same year and remained a while in Portland. They settled in the Umpqua Valley in the fall of 1851 where, with the exception of a few years spent East of the mountains, they have remained ever since. For many years her life has been that of an earnest and consistant Christian and she died in full fellowship with the M. E. Church South. Her hands were ready to every good work and the hearty sympathy and help of the community during her last painful sickness and the large number of friends who followed her to her last resting place fully attest the high esteem in which she was held by the entire community.

We have been unable to locate the original copy of Amelia Hadley's diary. We have used, with permission, a mimeographed copy in possession of the Corvallis Public Library in Oregon. There are identical copies in other Oregon libraries as well. The time we have spent with the manuscript convinces us that it is a fairly accurate copy made by someone who was careful to transcribe Amelia's style and spelling as accurately as possible. Amelia Hadley's "Journal of Travails" has to be one of the finest records of frontier life extant and an item of rare significance as a document of American history.

---

[3] "A Pioneer in Oregon" — The Story of William Grandison Hill as told to his daughter, Ella Hill. (Douglas County Museum-Roseburg, Ore.), p. 8.

THE JOURNAL OF AMELIA HADLEY

Monday May 5   Left Mr. Hustons, and traveled about eight miles which brought us to Kanesville, or Council Bluffs. This is quite a town some larger than Henderson in Ill.   the houses are mostly hewed log, 2 story and on main street they have sided them up and they present quite a fine appearance   Here we lay in our provisions to cross the plains, flour 2½ hundred which is reasonable for this place, here you can get everything you want, crossed the Missouri which is a wide mudy looking river   ferried over in a small flat boat, which they rowed, saw several Indians up and down the river which are the first I ever saw, The bluffs are surely romantic and beautiful presenting them in huge collums and if I may so speak in various kinds of architecture. Some of them are verry high while others are still lower reminding us of the work of nature and of the creation when every thing was formed as the creator best saw fit. We are now in the Indian Territory and a more wild barren place I never saw. The sand on the west side up the Mo, is almost insurmountable while each side of the road rushes, are abundant, and you may [see] a vast sea of them, traveled about eight miles from the river and camped on a small stream. There are the tribe of Omahaws the first tribe we pass through, they are the most filthy thevish set and are mostly naked, Their cheif can talk verry good American, also his daughter   she has lived 2 years in St. Louis and had been to school, tried to buy a dress   said she wanted to dress like white woman.

Tuesday May 6th   Lay by to day for the purpose
of organizing a company. There are a good many
camped with us, some with ox, and some with horse
teams, The wind blows verry hard and the sand and
dust is flying in clouds and put me in mind of a mon-
soon, they say that on this river there are always
clouds of sand flying. It is indeed disagreeable. No
timber this side of the river of any account   plenty
of willows.

Wednesday May 7th   Traveled 12 miles and found
a good camping place, grass about 2 hands high, good
water no timber, & great many Indians. Of the Poto-
watamie tribe which is the 2 tribe we pass through.
They are a filthy tribe and barbaroic similar to the
former tribe. They follow us up from one camping
place to another, and were it not for our number they
would, be down upon us. Our company consists of 23
waggons horse teams and some 50 men and 11 women
besides a number of children   passsd the old Morman
burrying ground, and town as the ruins where they
were, there burrying ground covers an acre and were
just as thick as they could dig the graves, It beat anything I ever saw, This place was called Winter Quarters, It lies on both sides of the Mo. and the buildings
are log. I should think there were about 2 hundred of
them. They have all left the west side of the river and
gone to Salt Lake, and it looks from appearance, like
the riuins of Sodom. The old burrying yards stands
open and look[s] lonely and solemn. One cannot but
help drop a tear to see how providence will order
everry thing. True, how short & fleeting is life, we
cannot but reflect what frail creatures we are. We
will muse no longer on the past but call our thoughts
to the present.

Thursday May 8   Here we cross the Elk horn, have
to ferry it, plenty of Indians   travelled 21 miles which
brings us to the platte river, camp on the platte, this
is a mudy sandy stream like Mo. It covers considerable surface, and is cut up with sand bars. It is the
whitest sand I ever saw, and finest and is disagreeable
when the wind blows, which is almost constant, find
verry little timber and that is a mixture of oak, elm,
and a verry little walnut   have seen 2 or 3 cotton
woods, passed by an old Indian grave which had the
appearance of a wigwam and supposed it was untill
reaching it,   It is constructed of sodds and built pyra-
mid stile, and has a hole at the side about a foot acros

Fryday, May 9   Travelled, 22 miles to day   crossed
Shell creek. 12 ft wide, 2 ft deep. We are now traveling on what is termed plains, they are beautiful, but
the land differs verry little from what we have been
traveling over   find little or no timber principaly
Willow and this serves for fuel, that is the dead ones,
good camping places so far, our teams look fine haveing
plenty of good grass. The water of the platte is verry
good when settled which we do by throwing in a little
alumn, and let it stand for a while. The water is as
soft as rain water. camp to night on the banks of the
platte. We form a currelle with our waggons, and at
bed time put our horses in side and tents and then have
a guard stationed. We are a merry crowd, while I am
journalizeing one of the company is playing the violin
which sounds delightful way out here. My accordian
is also good, as I carry it in the carrige and play as
we travel, had a verry hard rain this evening, and
everry thing seems affloat.

Saturday May 10.   Travelled 19 miles   come to Loup

Fork of Platte, it is verry high on account, of the rain and we cannot either ferry or ford it.

Sunday May 11. Camped on the Loup Fork on account of crossing verry rainy and cloudy, and considerable cold, find plenty of grass, and little timber have had no trouble with the indians as yet, they are affraid to tackel us an ox train back of us they atacked and took 2 oxen and 2 sacks of meal. Have seen some antelope and plenty of wolves.

Monday May 12. Still camped, high water and high washes

Tuesday May 13 Still camped, prospects no better.

Wednesday May 14 Try to ferry this morning. The boat is an awful constructed thing and is not fit to ferry with. It sank yesterday with 12, or 15 men on it, no lives lost, some of our company has crossed, and we still remain here, an awful thunder storm accompanied with hail, and heavy wind, is on hand. The waves run high, have to camp again with nothing to eat or sleep uppon our waggons being on the other side, and nothing with us except the carrige, some of our company on the same side and better of[f] than us brought us something to eat and sleep uppon, so we fared verry well.

Thursday May 15 Crossed this morning looking rather rough, but came accross safe a beautiful sun and rainbow presents itself to our view this morning and we feel fresh and invigorated after the storm, a great deal of thunder and lightning we have and terrible storm every one says that has travelled here on the Platte river, we have some 2 hundred miles to travel on it, camp to night about 2 miles from the fork, grass not very good, rather short, plenty of timber for camping purposes. Another thunder shower has come and heavy wind.

Fryday May 16 The light of another day has dawned and with it an awful storm. It seems it never rained harder, But at this we will not complain for we shall soon reach where it seldom or ever rains. Pass a good many Indians, camp grounds and their little wigwams no timber but popple [poplar], and willow which makes when dry verry good fuel I beleive willow grows everry where, and where nothing else will grow, see a good many antelope. Traveled 25 miles, found a good camping place water soft and good, rolling land, good grass and fine scenery.

Saturday May 17 Had another hard rain last night accompanied with hail. The soil is so verry sandy that these heavy rains does not make it mudy. Find in most places excellent grass. Mushrooms in abundance, and also a great variety of flowers, here also are a number of old Buffalo trails, looking a good deal like furrows. We are now in the Pawnees country have not seen any of them yet, traveled 24 miles and camped on the bare plain no timbers, nor no water, seem, as though we should perish for the want of it, tolerable grass, and some dew, which made it better for our horses.

Sunday May 18th Started very early, and traveled to where there was water and breakfasted good grass, no timber. This place is called prarie creek, and is excellent water. here are two graves, on the bank of the creek, one was in memory of A. Kellog, died June 12, 49 aged 23 years, the other the name Edgebert, cut out on a peice of board, serving as tomb stones. They look verry lonesome, away here To day is the sabbath but does not seem much like it, has to travel to where we could get timber, traveled 16 miles and struck wood river about 1 o'clock and camped for the night, found plenty of timber but it is cottonwood some dry willow excellent grass, to day has been verry fogy, and a good deal of thunder and lightining. The wind is cold have not had but one or two days that might be called warm. I hardly can see how the grass can grow, when it is so cold. It is nothing for it to storm on the Platte, they are frequent and verry hard. saw 2 antelope was near enough to see them. They resemble a deer verry much but are lighter collered, and some larger. Their meat is called better than deer.

Monday May 19th Traveled 15 miles good water tolerable grass, and tolerable camp, saw a grave but had no inscription on it.

Tuesday May 20th Traveled 20 miles and camped camp not verry good, saw several antelope, and an animal called prarie dogs, which resemble a puppy. There are acres of them so by speaking I mean that they are like the meadow mole they plough the ground up and form little knolls all over the ground, and also eat the grass of[f] so that the ground looks almost bare. They dig a hole in the ground, and throw it up around like an ant heap, grass in abundance, timber cotton wood and but very little of that.

Wednesday May 21 Traveled 16 miles found a good camping place camped on elm creek, had one of the worst storms that I ever experienced hail as large as quils eggs. face of the country level, plenty of grass, and game.

Thursday May 22   Traveled 21 miles camped on the
banks of the Platte. The river is about a mile wide
where we now are. In it are a great many sand bars
which makes the river very shallow and verry much
cut up but verry wide, timber popple   we are now
at the head of grand Island, and in the Buffalo country, on the south side of the river, is fort Kearny
about a half a mile from the river land flat and wet.
The air is cold almost enough to freeze. It seems as
though summer would never make its appeared. Water poor white with clay of which the Platte and
Mo. are alike   But by taking a pail full, and putting
in a little alum, and it will settle in a short time. This
water is verry soft. One of our company killed an
antelope and gave us some. It is verry sweet and
tender, a good dead like veal. much better than venson.

Fryday May 23 51   traveled 25 miles   grass the most
of the day verry short, and poor I think from the
appearance that it has been tread out by the bufalo
for it looks just like an old barn yard more than
anything else, crossed Buffalo creek, and passed Willow and Tetah Lake. They are south side of the road
long and verry crooked   soil sandy, passed 2 graves
camped again on the banks of the Platte,   our road
some times cuts of a bend in the river and we do not
camp on it for 2 or 3 nights, find good grass on an
Island in the river, have no corn for our horses and
they have to subsist entirely upon grass which seems
hard and work them hard all day and then turn them
out on grass and that sometimes not very good. We
left Kanesville with 12 bush shelled corn, and fed
each horse 2 quarts a piece as long as it lasted.

May 24 Saturday Traveled 20 miles crossed the
Platte, and travelled on an Island, which was about
6 miles and crossed back which shortened our distance about 8 miles. saw a good many buffalo. One
of the company shot eight balls into 3 of them and
killed none they are tremendours hard thing to kill
you can't kill them to shoot them in the head. passed
2 graves to day, one was a fresh one, buryed 5 days
ago. This name Ezekiel Clifton from Michigan. grass
not verry good timber willows and Popple. plenty
deer & antelope There are any quantity of scorpions
and resemble Lissards on these sand bluffs which look
disagreeable, though perfectly harmless. There are
three kinds of them one is a kind of pink one nearly
black and one brown, the brown one is rather different
from the others being nearly round while the others
are long. This round one looks some like a toad head
like a toad and has a sharp tail about 4 inches long,
the querest looking thing you ever saw, Prickely
pears grow spontaneous and 3 kinds of cactus, they
look beautiful. The Platte is a delightful stream although back from the stream on each [bank?] in most
places they are huge sand bluffs which look like snow
drifts being so white and not an atom of vegetation
on them but on the banks of the river plenty of grass,
and some little skirts of timber. It is in most places,
some 5 or 6 miles to these bluffs but does not look
more than half a mile, It is deceiving like any prarie
country. The road leads along the north side of the
river some times near the river and then we near the
bluffs. there is also a road on the south side There
is a kind of grass called Buffalo grass which grows
thick like our blue grass and looks like it at first sight,

but I think that It never grows over 4 inches high, you will see patches of this where you will see grass of no other kind   excellent feed, camped on the Platte while we were driving in camp one of our companys horses ran away with their waggon   tiped it over cleared themselves from it and ran themselves down.

Sunday May 25   Waggon repaired and everry thing to rights   traveled 25 miles   camped on the platte the river here is about a mile wide, here is the last timber we find for the next 2 hundred miles   pass a large company   they are driving about two hundred head of cattle, look well, passed one grave to day   the name Gordon from Dubuque Iowa, died last May 1850, aged 27 yrs   Henry, and wife are acquainted with him. Our company to day have killed 2 deer and 4 buffalo, plenty of fresh meat. It is good and quite a luxury after liveing on salt meat so long.

Monday May 26   Camp to day to prepare for the 2 hundred miles where we have no wood   shall be about 10 days crossing.

Tuesday May 27   Traveled 13 miles, find the best of grass verry heavy sandy, road. These sandy bluffs are tremenduous hard traveling for we sometimes cross them in small ravines, which are sultry hot, beating directly upon the sand. There is however now and then a good cold spring isueing from the hillside which gladdens us poor weary travelers, the water is verry clear the bottom being pure white sand, in some of the ravines where there is water there is verry good grass. It looked almost impossible for grass to grow in such verry deep sand. Saw 3 or 4 head of Buffalo, fording the river had a good view of them   Our curiosity is pretty much satisfied as to Buffalo, haveing had some to eat, you could not tell it from beef. If you were not told and had It set before you, come to examine closely you will perceive that it is a little coarser grain and a little darker. Crossed bluff creek, reproduce as 10 rods and 2 ft, deep water clear sand bottom, some quick sand as also in the Platte, which causes these streams to change greatly and make them dificult to cross   camped on the river   had to cook with buffalo chips for the first time   It makes verry good fuel when dry, and is more prefforable than wood for the verry good reason, (can't get it.)

Wednesday May 28   Traveled 21 miles   some verry sandy and some swamp road, about 2 miles was so mirey that we could hardly get through it   The heat is almost intense in these blufs, crossed Duck weed creek   10 feet wide   here is an abundance of good cold spring water, which was verry palitable, crossed shoal stream, 3 ft wide, On the oposite side of the river from us there is plenty of cedar, which looks rather inviting as we have no wood, camp on rattle snake creek 20 ft wide 1½ ft deep   swift current, sandy bottom, not verry hard to cross, now at what is called cedar bluffs, grass about ½ foot high and good water. We have had no misfortunes as yet   our company are all well and teams look fine. See a good many buffalo, they are not as fleet as I had supposed. you can easily ride up to them, the same as cattle. They do not mind you at all and will not run at the sight of you but as soon as they get the scent they are off, you can get up to them on the windward side.

Thursday May 29   Traveled 17 miles   had some heavy sandy road   4 buffaloes came down to our

camp this morning. It so happened that our horses
did not see them and had no trouble. Some of the company crossed the river and got some cedar for wood,
red cedar, verry nice. It is amuseing and delightful
to travel over these plains, and is not such a task as
many imagine perhaps I may sing another song before I get through, a person wants to take a great deal
of care of their teams, and take a moderate walk and
averagc about 18 or 20 miles a day and they will
stand it verry well.

Fryday May 30 Traveled 19 miles over some of the
heaviest sandy road that I ever saw as much as our
teams can do to drag over it, traveled along side of
the river today, passed one Lone tree, which was cedar,
about 100 yds from the river looks verry singular
there being no tree nor shrub for a hundred miles,
remind me of the Charter oak, scenery delightful, find
some of the most beautiful flowers none that we see
in the states except wild roses, I love to walk along
and gather them, came to an Indian camp about noon
where they had quite a little village of wigwams &
a great many poneys. They are the tribe of Soos. They
are kind and hospitable and are the most polite and
cleanest tribe on the road. They are whiter, to than
any that we have seen. They are well dressed and
make a fine appearance, went in one of their houses
made of dressed skins sewed to gether and verry large.
They are all busy some of them jerking Buffalo, some
painting skins for boxes which looked very nice. The
old chief came out shook hands with me invited me
in, and seemed almost tickled to death to see a white
woman, quite a curiosity.

Saturday May 31 Traveled 21 miles had good roads

and verry good grass. over took an ox train for Oregon, which had just crossed the Platte, comeing this far on the south side passed two graves to day & one yesterday, one a lady the name Margarett Hawk from Ill, died Aug 6, 1849, aged 46 years, camped on a little lake south side of the road tolerable grass, and an excelent spring, cold and clear road lays along the bank of the river, river here not verry wide but quite deep, weather fine but air quite cold.

Sunday June 1st Traveled 20 miles had the best of roads equal to Mcademised road. This road leads over the bluff called Cobble Hills, and one would certainly think from their rude construction they were rightly named, after leaveing these and traveling some miles farther we discover some more hills, or bluffs, Called Ancient Bluffs ruins which are decidely grand and beautiful for such as love such a scenery. It looks like ruins of old castles and buildings of all sises and descriptions one in particular runs up some 100 ft and almost square, and the top of it covered with grass, the ruins being principaly rocks, makes it look more strange, here is part of a company who are the most delightful of any thing I have seen visitors have to be verry careful on account of the many rattlesnakes lurking among the clefts of the rocks camped again on the river verry poor grass, have to be verry careful with our horses on account of alkali water It is to be seen only in places standing in puddles. The ground seems covered with this salt, as potash, and this lye looks and smells as strong as I ever saw in an ashery.[1] It has the same taste and produces the same effect some of our company went up among

---

[1] An ashery was a shop where soap was made by combining lye and grease.

the ruins and found a quarry of chalk perfectly white and pure as chalk can be   look very white from the road

Monday June 2   road runs along the river   to day passed court house rock, south side the river   It is on the top of the ridge of bluffs, and accends up in a square form 2 thirds of its height and then forms another square on the top   looks as much like a court house as anything can. I will give you a draft in the back of the book. It is about 2 hundred ft high above the main ridge   verry romantic. see a company on the other side of the river, stop to dine in sight of chimney rock. I seated myself this day noon to scetch it as near as I can from so great a distance and from observation you with this also in the back part of the book. It is from the level of the river 2 hundred ft high and runs up to a spire similar to a steple. It looks like an old doby house and great big clay chimney, it is a kind of yellow clay, so that It crumbles and washes   In 3 or 4 years you will hardly notice it at all, hardly looks like the work of nature, traveled 23 miles   good grass considerable of this alkali; stake out our horses with a long rope around in places where they cannot get it   Weather fine to day, air warm verry windy, the sand flyes verry bad, makeing it verry disagreeable, Traveling has become a second nature on these plains, but is not so bad after all. It is true that a great deal suffer during this long journey, but It is one half owing to carelessness and Mismanagement, little or no sickness as yet as I know of, health is a great blessing on this road. I for one never enjoyed myself better and never had better health   saw 7 buffalo before us in the road. This road is better than

any laid out road in the states, looks like an old road
in an old setled country, But not much to be wondered
at for there is a continual trail all the time and onley
the one road, we surely wont loose our way

Tuesday June 3   Traveled 23 miles to day   had verry
good road, passed a number of ox trains   some of
their cattle are dying from drinking alkali water
Some of them think they are making great head way,
but have about killed their teams off   they drive some
days over thirty miles and no team can stand it, on
this route passed 2 indians of the soo tribe   said they
were a going to fight the pawnees   were on horseback
had great long spears, and other weappons. As they
passed us they said to me, Soo, and then point their
spears at us saying   me for, Pawnees   and rode off
as fast as they could. Saw some cactus on the bluffs
and mountains some of them in blossom   they were
the prettyest things I ever saw   plenty of mountain
moss and a beautiful variety of stones or pebles, a
great many curiosityes to attract the traveler   passed
Scotts bluffs on the south side of the river, they are
grand more so than any we have seen   named from
a man by the name of Scott that starved to death on
top of them   should like to have drawn them had
we camped where I could have had a chance   camped
on spring creek which was said to produce trout but
saw none   the creek is clear and cold coming from
the mountain formed from spring I suppose. The road
considerably distance from the river   grass is verry
good but later than at this time of the year in the states.
We are, still rising and on a much higher elevation
than the states   grass here now as in April there & it
is now June.

Wednesday June 4 We are now 46 miles from fort
Larrimi   all well in body and spirits   over took another ox team which were driving considerable stock.
See a number of waggons on the other side   travelled
20 miles   found good road   runs considerable close
to river. We are now on the North Fork of Platte.
It is quite small in some places and then again it covers
considerably surface and form a good many Islands,
camped on the Platte plenty of timber such as it is,
it is mostly cotton wood, but in the states we would
not call it plenty but It seems plenty to us after doing
without any   plenty for camping purposes   found on
the bank of the river a log of pine, which I supposed
had drifted there which was delightful wood. It was
so full of pitch that little of it done our cooking verry
well, we carried some of it a number of days.

Thursday June 5   Travelled 22 miles   had some verry
sandy road, road still near the river, cotton wood plenty,
good grass, within 6 miles of Fort Larimi, camped here
and lay by a day. plenty of timber. There is an Indian
village where we are camped where the Sioux wintered
last winter, cut nearly all the trees off about as high
as their heads   here we had a hard hail storm   hailed
about an hour as hard as I ever saw it so that the
ground was perfectly white   hailled also last night
not so much but considerable larger   see nothing much
worthy of note to day but expect to when we arrive at
the fort . It is over 900 miles from home to fort Larimie
shall soon be half our distance.

Fryday June 6   Lay by to day   plenty of grass and
wood on the bank of the platte   Indians around our
camp all day   bought some moccasins of them which
are made verry nice. Some of our company did not

lay by and have gone on   they are anxious to see the
elephant[2] I suppose.

Saturday June 7   travelled 20 miles   came to the fort
which was beyond all expectation   about as large a
town as henderson and much handsomer   on main
street the building are brick 3 story high stores in the
lower stories   here you can get almost any thing you
want. It seems as though I could hardly contrive how
they could get goods there   the town is a square, block,
and brick side walks   It is on the south side of platte
there are quite a number of frame buildings. here is
a good blacksmith shop   here are any quantity of
wigwams and Indians about 5 or 6 hundred, soil sandy
there are only about 80 soldiers here now   some of
them have their wives with them. This town is at the
foot of the mountains in a bend of the river, here we
now begin to accend the Rocky mountains   these mountains are covered with wild sage pine & cedar. These
pines and cedar are scruby some about 1½ ft through
and 20 ft high which is the largest   you may ask I
wonder where they got their lumber to build those
frame houses, I answer   They have a sawmill, about
10 miles from the fort, which is strange for this place.
They have a good ferry at or oposite the fort, we are
not obliged to cross   we still go up on the north side.
some of our boys went over to put some letters in the
office. This road up on the north side of the river is
a new one and comes into the old one about 80 miles

---

[2] The term "to see the elephant" was used by some overlanders to sum
up in one phrase the whole dangerous enterprise. The entire third chapter
of Merrill J. Mattes' *The Great Platte River Road* (Lincoln, Neb., 1969), is
devoted to "Elephants of the Platte." His short definition is, "It was the
poetic imagery of all the deadly perils that threatened a westering emigrant"
(p. 61).

above the fort. these mountains look verry high and
almost insurmountable the road follows up ravines
and round among them so as not to be verry bad, plenty
of rocks as you may suppose look like Iron ore, camp
15 miles in the mountains to night dismal enough,
and pleasant to, feel some timid, here is a spring of
cold clear water side of the road. 2 waggons joined our
company from the fort. There are over a hundred good
waggons at the fort which the emigrants have left
pretty good grass on the mountains. There are about
3 hundred crow Indians in these mountains they do
not show themselves I wish they would I should
not be affraid of them as long as you can see them
there is not much danger.

Sunday June 8 Traveled 21 miles   camp within 8
miles of the platte, as you must know that It hcads
up in these mountains. We have had a verry hard road
to day steep long hills and enormous rocks and cav-
erns. I never saw such ledges on rocks and so awful
high and steep I think sure they are Rocky mountains This part is called black hills range, of Rocky
mountains quite a romantic scenery after all what
gave them the name of black hills is they look like
burnt ruins black the soil and rocks is preasely
[precisely] the collar of snuff Macabay [3] you can
take up a rock and it will all scale and crumble in
your hands, and the earth is the same   looks as though
it would cullar, good springs of water, from the mountain side.

Monday June 9, Travelled 23 miles   good though
hilly road   good watering places at suitable distances

---

[3] Maccaboy was a special snuff scented with attar of roses.

the farthest 14 miles. Traveled up the platte which is
here not verry wide came to a place in the mountains where the platte runs as cuts a place, not over
20 ft wide through which is worthy a travellers notice
The water is deep and swift being in such a narrow
Kanyon. camp on the river plenty of wood, grass &
water, had some antelop to night see some hens called
sage hens, I have heard say that they were good to eat,
some of our company killed some, and I think a skunk,
prefarable, their meat tastes of this abominable mountain sage, which I have got so tired of that I cant bear
to smell it, they live wholly upon it and it scents their
flesh.

Tuesday June 10 Traveled 22 miles found verry
good road and no water except touching the river occasionaly. camp to night on the Platte in a nice little
cotton wood grove with awful great mountains all
around us, the most romantic place I ever saw, overtook and passed 2 ox trains to day.

Wednesday June 11 Traveled 25 miles had some
very heavy sandy road and some bad hills, Though
our road winds around through the mountains at an
astonishing rate and is more lined than I should suppose it could be. It is the most natural road I ever
saw. We see almost all kinds of plants and roots that
grow in our garden and green houses of which is Cactus 2 kinds, Prickely Pear, Wormwood, Southernwood,
and Chamoile and an abundance of sage of which the
latter is not like our garden sage. Flowers of which
are Larkspur Sundials, China asters and roses in abundance 3 kinds, of them one kind are nearly as large
as a tea saucer I never saw the like and just as red
as blood, most beautiful indeed. plenty of peas which

look like our sweet pea have just such a blossom, here
are a great variety of flowers that you do not have in
the states   plenty of wild sunflowers and I do not
know where that does not grow, Our road has run to
the river at intervals to day which has afforded water
for our teams   at one of these watering places there
stood a large lone cotton wood tree, with an indian
grave in it, which was quite a curiosity, could not
think at first what it was. It was a small child from
appearance, the skull was lying on the ground, the
crows had picked it all to pieces and left the bones.
It was first put in a blanket and then rapt in a buffalo
robe, and I should think there were about a quart
of beads about it which they had ornamented it with.
its scull was painted   corpse was lashed to the limbs
of the tree with a number of little sticks layed across
under it, saw also a buffalo to day, and another ox train
camp to night within half a mile of the river in an
awful sandy place   no wood and have to burn sage for
the first time. Any quantity of locusts on our journey
to day the first we have seen –

Thursday June 12   Traveled 20 miles   have found
a most beautiful camping ground on the river   our
road has been verry hilly and sandy this afternoon.
We are now 130 miles from fort Larimie   We have
cool winds and a constant breeze here in the mountains   have good grass which you will probably think
strange but their are small valleys that afford plenty
of grass. I can tell you that we are in sight of snow,
on the top of these mountains. It looks verry strange
to me having seen It so before. This snow lies principaly in the deep narrow ravines and is some 20 or 30
ft deep and from that to 50 ft which is not so easily

melted, and more than that I should think from the air now that It never would get warm enough up there to melt it much.

Fryday June 13   road runs near the river occasionaly touching the bluffs with awful heavy sand at these points. Our road mostly to day has been delightful runing through a nice grove along the river. You may know that it seemed good to get into timber again enough to make any shade. came to a grave his name Glenette died 1849, was burried in a canoe. The wolves had made a den down in his grave. They dig up everyone that is burried on the plains as soon as they are left. It looks so cruel I should hate to have my friends or myself burried here. which all may be. The weather is verry changeable nights verry cold and verry warm in the middle of the day. some times it will turn cold in an hour so that from shirt sleeves, you will be cold with the heaviest of winter clothing. It beats anything I ever saw. travelled 25 miles had not water except what little we carried in our canteens.

Saturday June 14 Travelled 20 miles passed one grave and a great deal alkali water. About 25 head of cattle which had died from drinking it lay around people are not half careful enough. Passed through a plane called rock avenue which was a curiosity one which I cannot describe any more than for you to look at some quarry here are ledges which look as though some one had cut the stone square and layed them up in a wall. I can tell you how it came here is where the Free Massons done their first work. (now you know) camped at Willow Spring plenty of grass, and good water willows for fuel.

Sunday June 15 Travelled 25 miles, about one mile
from the spring is Prospect hill It is a delightful
view, and here you can see the range of Sweet water
mountains we then had a bad slugh to cross, which
smelled awful nooned at Greese wood creek, 6 ft
wide, 1 deep; this takes its name from a shrub which
grows upon it and resembles the gooseberry bush but
the leaves look like hemlock. It is called Greesewood,
we next came to alkali lakes, which were 3 or 4 rods
wide the water dried up and the ground just as white
as snow and this is 3 or 4 inches deep and you can
get chunks of salaratus as large as a pint cup just as
pure as that you buy here I gathered some, and I
send you some It has got durty. We have now left
the platte entirely we had travelled on it so long
that it seemed like an acquaintance camp to night
on the Sweet water river 200 miles from fort Larimie
passed a grade to day. This river is 8 rods wide 2 ft
deep swift current good water as soft as snow water
which it is coming from melted snow from the mountains. This water tastes like sap which gave it this
name. I always had a curiosity to taste of it have to
cross the river for grass, so many have camped here
that they have eat it all up on this side.

Monday June 16 Lay by to day on this river. There
is independence rock, about 200 yds from the river.
which is about 6 hundred yds long and 120 wide. it
is composed of hard granite and is quite smooth, took
a walk upon it pretty hard to accend. I am now
seated on top journalizing. There are thousands of
names and some are verry nicely chiseled on, but
mostly put on with tar, left ours with the rest Here
I have a full view of devils gate where the sweet waters

pass between or through the mountains. This is an
independent rock standing aloof from the rest of the
mountains. and has a singular appearance look like
a great rock rooled down from the rest of the mountains. It has the apearance of a court house standing
in the centre with a block all around. I never saw
any thing more splendid see a great many names of
whom I knew

Tuesday June 17 After leaving here and traveling
5¼ miles west of this rock you come to devils gate
which is from 20 to 30 ft and 400 ft high and a quarter of a mile through this is a great curiosity here
are also an abundance of names The current is swift
through here like foam here is a grave at the entrance and at the outlet, just by the side of the river,
there is also a grave of a lady at independence rock
her name Elizabeth Campbell, died 1850 aged 23
years and on the bank of the river oposite independence
rock are the graves of 2 girls I think these may well
be termed rocky mountains for they are pure granite
rock with no earth on them with now and then a shrub
cedar springing out of a crevice We are now in a
beautiful valley between the mountains which is delightful, considerably alkali grass good in spots
have verry good road by traveling up the river. passed
3 graves this afternoon died in 51 travelled 23 miles
to day camped on sweet water road hard this afternoon, on account of crossing the river so many times
and so many rocks in the river.

Wednesday June 18 travelled 22 miles heavy sand,
tolerable level, crossed the sweet water in all 5 times
came through at the last crossing a narrow Kanyon,
between the mountains just like a narrow street about

as wide as a narrow road   is thousands of names written in here which looked like a street in town with
their signs up   passed 2 graves to day   saw a name
on the rock W. T. Shinn   thought perhaps that it
was W. S. of Newark, Ohio, camp to night on the
S. W. river where there is as you may say no grass
at all and hardly any roots left   here are 5, or 6 trains,
also but will soon have to share or starve   there has
been good feed here, but a number have stoped here
to recruit, and eat it all out, Some of our Company
killed a mountain sheep or more properly a mountain
goat for they look about the head like a goat, while
the body is covered with hair and short fine wool which
looks some like fur   had some to eat. I merely tasted
it so as to say I had eat some, but do not like it   the
rest said it was good but I know they think better all
the time for they taste of every thing they get even to
black birds and call them good. We have 3 English
men in our train who eat everything have a kettle of
soup every day. One day they had a black bird soup.

Thursday June 19   Travelled 21 miles   passed 2
graves to day one by the name of Stantlif   here we
have a grand view of the wind river mountains which
are always covered with snow   they have a verry
white appearance   passed ice spring to day   about
2 yds to the right up the road is where the spring
breaks out and leads of[f] down the road in a marshy
swale, which is mirey   here you obtain pure ice by
diging down to the depth of 4 to 6 inches   dug down
and got some   there is a solid cake of ice as clear as
any I ever saw and more so   cut a piece as large as
a pail and took and rapt it in a blanket, to take along
camp to night on the river   not verry good grass.

Fryday June 20   Passed to day a company of packers comeing home from California   were with mules which were seal fat   they were well fixed one woman packing with them. Travelled 21 miles   camped on Willow creek   tolerable good grass, and Willows for fuel. crossed Strawberry creek so named from the quantity of vines up and [down] the creek   they are just in bloom   found plenty of snow in some ravines side of the road   some of the boys had quite a snow balling   The air has been verry cold to day. passed 5 graves to day all in a row   the wolves had made holes in all of them

Saturday June 21   Travelled 17½ miles   camp on Pacific Spring which is the first camp after you get through south pass. There we saw the far famed south pass, but did not see it until we had passed it for I was all the time looking for some narrow place that would almost take your breath away to get through but was disappointed. It is a body of table land rooling but not mountainous and is 15 miles wide being the pleasantest place I have yet seen. The altitude here is 7 thousand & 30 ft. We have been on a gradual accend since we left Larimi and now we shall decend the same to the pacific   at Pacific Spring the water begins to run to the pacific   verry cold to day   Water standing the night of the 20 froze a quarter of inch thick on a pail   in sight of snow all the time from 5 to 8 ft deep side the road in some places north side mountain.

Sunday June 22   travelled 20 miles   camped on little sandy,   road tolerable level and I never saw nicer in the states. No grass in the distance and no water except a small spring which is verry brackish and fit for man

or brute. From Sweet Water to south Pass is 10 miles.
To Pacific Springs 3 miles ditto creek crossing 1½
dry sandy and brackish water 9 m To forks of road
Sublet cut off 6 m To Little Sandy 2 ft wide 2 ft
deep 4 m To Big Sandy 4 wide 2 deep 5 m To
Green river 45m. This entire road from Pacific Spring
is a verry level sandy and Ashy desert, no green of any
account on the stream. The sand and ashes drift like
snow, altitude 8080 ft here.

Monday June 23 Camped on little sandy here we
lost one of our carriage horses from a kick in the side
good grass along the bank of the stream though high
banks to get to it.

Tuesday June 24 Traveled 6 miles to big Sandy
here we stop until about 4 o'clock and then travel all
night. We here shall take Sublets cut off which is a
barren desert of 45 miles no water we think our
teams will stand it better to travel it in the night. This
shortens our distance about 75 miles.

Wednesday June 25 arived about noon at green river
after such a jant for our teams they were pretty well
go drayed [4] after traveling all night and till noon the
next day. There are 3 deep ravines near the river
they are 4, 6, 8 miles from the river steep hill at
river this is the place to try men and teams here
are 3 or 4 good ferryes, the best we have seen about
30 or 40 white men live here among the indians 4
white familys white women also a small Grocery, and
plenty of indians for the Snake tribe and some Flat
heads The most of these men have squaw wives and
some 3 or 4 and a great many children as funy

4 Dragged out.

sight as I saw was a little pappoose about 2 years old run along the fery almost naked and Its white dady took it up and carried to the wigwam and gave it to its mama   Had to pay the enormous sum of 10 dollars a waggon and 1 dollar a horse to cross, swam our horses rather than pay so much   river 100 yds wide swift & deep   dangerous too   traveled 9 miles from river and camped on Salmon Trout branch 7 or 8 miles above its union with green river.

Thursday June 26   remain in camp to day to rest our teams   caught some beautiful fish of 3 kinds spotted and mountain trout and a kind of whitefish   there are here 4 graves and some Indian wigwam. There is a road leading from green river to salt lake, a great many go to Cal on this road, the road from Green river here is verry hilly and circuitus   this branch is 2 rods wide 2 ft deep

Fryday June 27   Travelled 20 miles   camped on Nettle creek which is a small run. Our road to day has been verry hilly   nooned at Fire wood grove which is Spruce Pine   here is a fine spring, gathered a quantity of beautiful green and some fine strawberryes.

Saturday June 28   Travelled 18 miles   verry hilly road,   some accents looked almost impasible   plenty of indians Snake tribe scattered all along the road snow all around us and above us and cold enough to freeze. good grass and It seems singular how it can grow when it is so cold   camp to night in a nice little grove of pople and birch between the hills or in a ravine   plenty of currents but not large enough to eat. looks rather singular to see currents here   the bushes the same as our tame ones   plenty of Strawberrys vines in abundance. Nooned to day on Hams Fork of Green River. Here is an Indian Camp

Sunday June 29   Travelled 18 miles   had awful hills and verry steep   camp to night on a fork of bear river. good grass, good water plenty of strawberryes and current but the currents are not large enough to cook went out and gathered 4 or 5 quarts which was a great rarity and served fine with bread butter, & tea, stop here the remainder of the day.

Monday June 30   Lay by to day which gives our horses as well as ourselves rest, here is a small grove of timber where we are camped. weather cold, no rain since we left the Platt not a sprinkle.

Tuesday July 1   Traveled 20 miles   had verry hilly and slik road traveled 10 miles to Thomas Fork of bear river   There is an Indian vilage also a bridge across the river which has been constructed by some white men who stay here to receive toll. They also have a small grocery and horses to trade. bought a coupple of poneys camped on bear river about 10 miles from the fork.

Wednesday July 2   Traveled 25 miles   had verry good road, quite level and few hard pitches. Stoped to noon at a small stream   good water   some small willows and a few strawberrys. camp to night on bear river about 2 miles from the river to the road. this is the main river and quite a large stream   large fish in it salmon and speckled trout but the salmon are small here, good grass   awful high mountains all around us.

Thursday July 3   Travelled 20 miles   had tolerable level road. after travelling some 10 miles we came to soda springs which are along the bank of the river. The

water boils up from the bottom sparkles and tastes just
as a glass of soda will, pure and cold. There is one
called steamboat spring which boils up from an opening in a high rock about a foot across and boils up
about 18 inches high. I never saw anything so splendid
in all my life. This water is merely warm, it is thrown
up by means of gass, or something of the kind in the
earth. There is a tradeing establishment here, a number
of whites spaniards and Mexicans. They have droves
of horses and fine looking ones. At Thomases Fork
was a chance to send letters to Fort Leavenworth on
the Mo. and one of the whites who registered the
names of the emigrants. we had ours put down   bought
some horses of the Mexicans. We have now 18 head
which look well we are pretty well in the mountains and among the shoeshone or Snake indians. They
at present appear friendly

Fryday July 4, Travelled 23 miles had good road
except a few stoney hills. stoped to noon on a small
stream   tasted a verry little of soda The air is verry
warm to day and we can see any amount of snow all
the time. camp to night on a fine stream of water
had to cross some few willows on it and excelent
grass. To day has been the 4, Our company and another
joing fired guns and drank toasts and had a merry time.

Saturday July 5 Traveled 25 miles to day In the
fore part of the day had some verry hilly road. excellent spring of water by the road side ozeing from the
mountains. There is an insect which I shall call a
cricket but some resembles a grass hopper they are
as large as your thumb,and everry hush & shrub is
covered as full as it will hold, the coller of a black
cricket The indians gather them and dry them and

pulverize them to put in soups. They wanted us to buy some. camp to night 11 miles east of fort hall, on a fine stream called Port neuf made up from fine springs, good water, willows for fuel, poor grass, being very dry.

Sunday July 6   Traveled 20 miles   found verry level road. The fore part of the day being very heavy sand. Struck a beautiful plain which is called snake river valley. skirted along the banks of the river with better cotton wood and popple, arived at fort hall, about 2 o'clock, passed old fort Lorim an American post about 5 miles above, fort hall.* This is where the soldiers were stationed,   fort hall is about 50 yds from the river and is built of doby brick, only one large building 2 story high and looks verry pretty. this is the Hudson Bays fort as the brittish Although they never had soldiers stationed there it has been used as a fur traders establishment   about there they can get any quantity of fur, plenty of otter and beaver, bear buffalo, and many other kinds   This old house is now filled up with low dirty French, that have squaw wifes any quantity of Indians and half breeds. There are left 60 old United States waggons, and a great quantity of plunder, belonging to the soldiers, they left Fort Loraim last fall and were deposited at fort hall. There will have to be a station as another It will not be safe for emigrants to travel, camp about 2 miles from the fort, on a fine stream delightful grass and a large feild "or as you may say foild although it is not enclosed) of wild wheat which at a distance looks like a beautiful feild of wheat. There are any quantity of wild currents of which are yellow, red, & black. the red ones

---

*Fort Loring was a U.S. Government Cantonment adjacent to Fort Hall, Idaho, from 1849-64.

are like our currents in the states, are quite a luxury,
could gather a bushel in a short time.

Monday July 7   Lay by to day at camp. Plenty of
Indians about us and some not verry well disposed look
rather suspicious.

Tuesday July 8   Travelled 21 miles   had some verry
rough road, and some sand, nooned on an old camp
ground, where is a nice spring an excelent water, good
grass   Camp to night on Snake river at the great
American Falls Which for the most part of them are
more cascades than falls   They extend to the length
of 300 ft and, in that distance their fall is 60 ft, being
150 yds wide. This is in Snake river or Clarks, &
Lewis river. The bank or basaltic rock all together
presents a beautiful prospect. We now have to travel
about 2 hundred miles on this river.

Wednesday, July 9   Traveled 25 miles, had some verry
hilly road, several small streams to cross any one of
them large enough for a mill stream. Camp to night
on Cassia creek, which is quite a stream here. Stay
to night with a company of packers from Oregon returning to the States   sent some letters back by them.
they gave us a great account of Oregon, and California

Thursday July 10   Travelled 22 miles   had verry
rough road, verry rocky, hard traveling. travelled 16
miles without water Then struck a creek of verry poor
water   any quantity of wild wheat up and down the
creek   stock does not eat it if they can get any thing
else. but in most places there is bunch grass which is
good, and will grow on a mountain in the place of the
low lands, were it not for that stock would suffer, In
many places we have found plenty of red top grass,
looks like the tame with the exception of the top which

is not as red, our road to day has been over a sage barren and ashes which has the appearance of an old ashery. The soil all looks more like ashes than dirt. It puts me in mind of the white bean story. An old Indian came verry near stealing a horse from our company last night when he was in the act of leading him of[f] the guard shot at him and he ran, without the horse. We had 2 stolen out of the train at fort hall, that belonged to Mr. Rose [5] of Michigan worth 100 dollars a piece. We have all the Denies [6] in our company. The old man & the surveyor, that surveyed Ontario, and whom you know. The indians are every day commiting some depredation or other, they steal and rob from every train and those dirty french put them up to it. I think if congress knew how bad they were they would protect the emigration as I have said it is cruel, for them to hold out inducements for people to settle Oregon and leave them unprotected and to fight theyr way as best they can, passed 2 graves to day camp to night on Snake good grass no wood but sage, find plenty of currents so far up the river.

Fryday July 11 Traveled 30 miles which we were obliged to do on account of water & grass. traveled 22 miles before we stoped here we found a little grass baited [7] our horses and then traveled 8 miles farther before we could find grass enough to camp. Had some of the roughest stoney road you ever saw.

[5] Aaron Rose, founder of Roseburg, Oregon. See introduction, pp. 54-55.

[6] John Denny was a War of 1812 veteran. With him on this journey was his wife, Sarah, a daughter, Loretta, and six sons and their families. They became Pacific Northwest settlers all the way from the central Willamette Valley to Puget Sound. Sarah H. Steeves, *Book of Remembrance* (Portland, Ore., 1927), pp. 211-13.

[7] "Bait" was an old word for feeding horses during a pause on a journey.

Camp to night on a fine stream plenty of grass and good dry willows for fuel.

Saturday July 12   Traveled 16 miles over verry rough road. It seems the nearer we approach Oregon the worse roads we have, and a worse more rough looking country   Camp to night on a stream of good water   bank basaltine rocks.

Sunday July 13   Traveled 23 miles   had verry good road with the exception of two or 3 hills   crossed warm spring creek to day which at it head or at the spring it is boiling hot, and would boil a piece of meat as quick as if over the fire, some of them tried it. It is about blood warm at the crossing. Camp to night on Salmon fall creek in which there are any quantity of fish   emptyes into snake river about 300 yds below us. This place is an especial resort for the Indians thousands of their old camp, here they come in summer time to fish and secure them for winter. Which with roots & what they steal is their subsistance.

Monday July 14   remain in camp to day to rest our teams, good grass.

Tuesday July 15   Had last night a good horse stole from camp which belonged to Mr. Strong[8] of Michigan. Mellville Hadley,[9] Mr. Strong and 2 or 3 others went in pursuit of him   overtook it about 12 miles from camp the indian riding him still off. The Indian saw them jumped from his horse, and went to a ledge of rocks, wher they said they could look of[f] some 300 ft and secreted himself (knowing every crevice I suppose) and when they rode up on the point of them

---

[8] Mr. Strong of Michigan is so far unidentified.
[9] Melville Hadley, who was shot in this episode, was Samuel Hadley's younger brother.

to ascertain which way he went The Indian shot Hadly,
through the right side the ball passing in between his
ribs and out within an inch of his back bone he is
brought into camp alive Have a good Doctor [10] in
our train, that went as soon as we got the news, which
we heard from a young man by the name of Godfrey,[11]
that was with him, he went out with 7 or 8 others and
brought him in almost lifeless from loss of blood
was shot 12 o'clock in day time, brought in camp 11
o'clock at night.

Wednesday July 16 Lay by to day on H. account.
He is some revived is verry sore and weak can hardly
be moved They did not get the horse. This is a wretched
place to camp all suffer from fear I am sure I can
hardly lay down to sleep without It seems as though
The Indians stood all around me ready to masacree
me, shall be glad to go.

Thursday July 17 Are still in camp, Mell is better
a little are in hopes we can soon travel for we are
in danger stoping here.

Fryday July 18 Traveled to day 12 miles which we
were all day doing on account of Mel. he stood it
better than we expected, we fixed a bed in our caraige
and bolstered him up and drove slow with him, but
after all every little jar he would hollar, and grown
all the time but we were obliged to travel which
seemed awful hard.

Saturday July 19 Traveled 15 miles tolerable good
road, some of our men went ahead and threw out all
the stone so that Mel got along verry well, but was

---

[10] Presumably Dr. James C. Cole. See introduction, pp. 53-54.
[11] Godfrey is so far unidentified.

verry glad to get in camp. Camp on snake river
tolerable grass, heavy sand, killed several large rattle
snakes in camp. There is some of the largest rattle
snakes in this region I ever saw, being from 8 to 12
ft long, and about as large as a man's leg about the
knee. This is no fiction at all. Traveled 20 miles
verry good road, plenty of Sage which has become a
perfect nuisance no grass of any account & poor
water. Melville is quite smart to day am in hopes
he will get well he has every attention that is necessary, and a good phycian, to ride side of him.

Monday July 20 Traveled 14 miles and camped on
a creek, not verry good water, nor grass, plenty of
wild wheat, which our teams eat the head of. The sick
still recovering. Do not feel verry well my self. am
afraid I am going to be sick from constant fatigue,
am not strong no why

Tuesday July 21 Traveled 25 miles had verry good
road or M. could not have stood it to have rode so far,
gets verry much fatigued before we stop to camp
still getting better have to handle him verry careful.
Am no better myself, feel as though I could not hold
out much longer I have the flux,[12] which is fast running me down am doctoring for it, but does me no
good as yet.

Wednesday July 22 A beautiful fine day and Mell
much better, so that it does not hurt him much to
travel, or ride as he is comfortable in the caraige
I have the mountain fever [13] the Doct. say with the

---

12 The "flux" was a term for bowel disorders.
13 The best discussion of "mountain fever" is in John D. Unruh, Jr., *The
Plains Across* (Urbana, Ill., 1979), p. 409. Unruh designated it either as
Rocky Mountain spotted fever or as Colorado tick fever, saying it was
"less virulent than cholera but deadly enough."

flux, and am not able to set up, and hurts me verry bad
to ride   yesterday camped on snake river, I am not
hardly able to keep journal, to day we travel down the
river, From where the road strikes river 6¼ rds to
small creek   plenty of water   above and below crossing the road is level, but deep, dust, & some sand
no grass except on the margin of the river   do not
know the exact distance we have travelled, to day,
shall be brief in my descriptions.

Thursday July 23   From this creek to warm spring,
3 miles, These spring are to the left of the road 150 yds,
the water to hot to bear your hand in. Heavy dust,
from these spring, to a good camp on the road, distance 11 miles. There road leaves river, and takes up
gradual, accend to left, The first 6 miles of the 11,
from springs, road level then hills to accend & decend
over bluff or river. This is a white clay bluff and you
will find many small hills between this and camp,
which is situated as described. Where road leaves river
& on the oposite side from camp on the bottom some
¾ miles from the river is a round black mound of
rock standing by itself, some distance from bluffs, I
am no better and shall have to give up my journal
for a few days, Mell is still improving, I will just
give you the camps, and distances from here to Columbia river, in short, to sturgeon creek from this
camp 11 miles, good camp, good camp on snake river
3½ miles, to the crossing of owyhe 12 miles, good
camp 4 miles from there to fort Bossissee   good
camps all the way, From Fort Boissee to Malheur
river 15 miles   good camp which is the first water
from fort. To Sulpher springs 12 miles   poor camp,
little water good to drink but verry sulphury   10

miles to birch creek, good camp, 3½ miles roads strikes
snake river, good camp. There is the last you see of
Snake river. 4½ miles to (burnt river) good camp,
Travel up burnt river 34½ miles, good camp, all the
way. From head of burnt river to Powder river slough
17 miles, 15 without water of that, good camp at slough,
9¼ miles to crossing of Powder river, good camp, 9
miles to fork of powder river, good camp, 3 miles
to Sechend [second?] fork of powder river, ½ miles
good spring, 14½ miles to grand round, plenty of
water and grass in that distance. Then you have a
splendid country of fine grass. 7¼ to a branch north
side grand round, here you enter the blue montains
7½ miles verry rough road to crossing of grand round
river, poor camp, no grass, plenty of water, Next water
is a spring to left of road, 13 miles, poor camp
spring hard to find.	not many emigrants find it and
suffer for water before they get any. 7½ miles fa[r]ther
is Lees old encampment	good camp, 19½ miles to
Umatila spring, good camp, 14 miles to crossing of
Umatila where road strikes bottom. From here to
Columbia 13 miles ½

Saturday August 9	After strikeing the Columbia I
again resume my journal. I have been very sick for
the past 2 weeks and not able to wait on my self and
of course my book neglected	I am now able to be
about and Mellville able to ride on Horse back, Travelled 20 miles and verry sandy road, and but verry
little grass and that is dry as hay. Camp to night on
Columbia, bank verry sandy, no timber but plenty of
Indians all along the shore fishing	catch a great many
salmon	Columbia is a pleasant river but is not as
large here as I had supposed. We are in the Walla,

Walla, nation and among that was a horrid murder, but the catholicks were the cause, they put the indians up to perpetrate the deed,[14] they are civil to us, and we have no trouble to watch our horse among them.

Sunday August 10 Traveled 16 miles heavy sand, folowed the banks of the columbia, down not much grass, barely enough to sustain life every thing is so dry that you cannot decern any thing green except a clump of willows, But the dry season is almost over, camp to night again on the river, I am getting considerable smart, no other sickness in the train.

Monday August 11 Traveled 14 miles had very sandy road and enormous stony still traveling down the river Camp on willow creek a little stream which emptyes in Columbia not much grass, but plenty of Grouse which is a kind of prarie chicken and you could not tell them from tame chicken they are blacker than a prarie chicken, but the meat is as white and sweet as tame chicken.

Tuesday August 12 Traveled 17 miles roads verry sandy, and rough plenty of salmon weighing from 20 to 30 lbs, 3 or 4 of our company and an ox train bought a canoe, and went down the river, camp to night on river. Had a fine sprinkle of rain which was something new

Wednesday August 13 Traveled 12 miles over verry hilly road, accended a mountain which we had to

---

[14] The work of Clifford M. Drury has proved that the Roman Catholics did not provoke the killing of the Protestant missionaries at the Whitman Mission. See especially his *Narcissa and Marcus Whitman and the Opening of Old Oregon*, 2 vols. (Glendale, Calif., 1973). He discusses this issue on pages 205-265 in volume II. He even shows that Father J. B. A. Brouillet even risked his own life in order to be helpful and helped to save Henry Spalding's life (II, p. 287).

double teams, and could hardly get up at that, Camp to night on John Days river a pleasant stream, upon the mountain just before we crossed the river we saw Mt Hood towering high above the Cascades, A beautiful snow capt Mt.

Thursday August 14 After leaveing camp and river we accended a mountain which seemed almost insurmountable but by perseverance we accended the top, road to day over a mountainous country have traveled 19 miles to day camp to night on the Columbia. There is a small tradeing establishment here and also a place where people can take boats and go down the river this is 6 miles from what is called the dalles, the price is 10 dollars a person, and 50 dollars pr waggon or one waggon for another, We shall cross the mountains ourselves, cant afford to give all we have to get through.

Fryday August 15 Traveled 14 miles over a very hilly road where the hills are dificult to get up without doubling teams crossed the Deschutes river a little above where it emptyes in Columbia had to ferry paid 5 dollars per waggon here we learned the sad intelligence that those that went down in a canoe were drowned. It is dangerous going down especialy when heavely loaded as they were, there being so many rapids in the river, their canoe was found bottom side up, with a pair of boots tied in the captern [15] nothing has been seen of them. camp to night on an arm of the deshutes or fall river, Bought

---

[15] She evidently means the "capstan" of the boat. The Oxford English Dictionary indicates nine variations of spelling in connection with the use of the word. It could mean something to wrap a rope around to secure the anchor or the boat. Amelia Hadley adds another spelling, "captern."

some potatoes at a little grocery here, for which we paid a bit pr pound   seemed like old times but rather dear eating to what we had been used to.

Saturday August 16   traveled 25 miles   had verry hilly and stony road, have seen several peaks of the cascades peering above the rest with their white mantles on   These mountains are heavy timbered with pine, hemlock cedar and shrub oaks with a little popple alder Hawthorn and birch and the largest elders I ever saw, from the size of the arm to some 10, or 12 inches through and many larger, Camp to night on the arm of the deshutes   good water   plenty of wood and the best kind, several indians here the Canakees,[16] the most filthy set I ever saw.

Sunday August 17   Traveled 12 miles over the most hilly rough road I ever saw   after we left camp we accended a mountain where we had eight horses to a wagon   camp to night at the foot of cascades called barlow gate, have only to travel 4 days before reaching Oregon Citty   what a joyful time will that be.

Monday August 18   Travelled 15   road awful hilly and mountainous, exceding anything yet   one hill was 1 miles ½ long, and verry steep, plenty of water isueing from the mountains, any quantity of plunder and waggons on the road.

Tuesday August 19   Traveled 12 miles over the worst road and mudy, it is indescribable   camp to night on a small opening, good grass to night but last night had none, there is little or no grass in these mountains except in spots, and hard to be found.

Wednesday August 20   Traveled 20 miles over a much

---

16 By "Canakees" she probably means the "Kanakas," or Hawaiians who were found in quite some numbers in those days in old Oregon.

worse road than yesterday, accended a hill called Laurel hill steep & dangerous, enormous rock in the road so that waggons precipitate from 1, to 2 ft, perpendicular cut a small tree and tied it to the back end of our waggons to keep them right side up.

Thursday August 21 Traveled 15 miles over a mudy stony road over dividing ridge all the team can do to strugle along.

Fryday August 22 traveled 18 miles some of the day had verry good road have had verry good luck in finding grass, cross the big and little Sandy, camp to night within 10 miles of settlements.

Saturday August 23 traveled 10 miles camp to night at a farm, the mans name is Foster [17] from state of Maine was kind and entertained us verry fine I could not walk strait after not being in a house for so long when I got up to go across the floor I was like an old sailor that had not been on land for a long time, They had about 2 hundred bushels of peaches which looked delightful And now you have seen me through this great Western thorough fare and you wonder where I have settled I came from thence to O, citty and from there to Portland where I now remain, This is the end of a long and tedious journey.

E. A. Hadley
Oregon

This is all I can tell you by pen and paper my love to you all and should providence again call us together I can tell you more in an hour than I can write in a week.   E. A. Hadley

---

[17] Philip Foster, a native of Maine, traveled to Oregon in 1843 by sea. His farm of Eagle Creek was a first stop for many travelers over the Oregon Trail, those who came the Barlow Road route south of Mount Hood. There is still a Foster Road leading in a southeasterly direction out of Portland.

An Ohio Lady Crosses the Plains
₰ Susan Amelia Cranston

INTRODUCTION

"Matter-of-fact, with an occasional flight of fancy": that is how one might describe the daily journal of Susan Amelia Cranston. She just told it like it was — most of the time. She discussed day after day the finding of those three basic needs for wagon train travel to the West: water, fuel, and feed for the animals. A typical statement is the one written on May 9, 1851: "encamped at night in the prairie with tolerable grass and water but no wood cooked with weeds." Susan saw countless graves along the way, but she simply counted them and recorded the number seen each day: she did not write down the name of even one of those who had died and were buried there.

Susan and Warren Cranston were married in Woodstock, Champaign County in western Ohio on April 18, 1850. She was Susan Amelia Marsh before that date. She had been born in Stowe, Vermont, on August 31, 1829. Warren was two years older.

They really started for Oregon immediately after the April marriage. However, as family members remembered in later years, when they got to St. Joseph, Missouri, "he was offered a position as a school teacher, so he taught school until the spring of 1851, putting in his spare time studying surveying. He brought his compass across the plains, thinking it might be handy to survey land claims." [1] It was true; Warren Cranston did work with surveying teams in the mid-Willamette Valley of Oregon later on.

[1] Fred Lockley, column, "Impressions and Observations," *Oregon Daily Journal,* Portland, Ore., November 9, 1931. Interview with Charles Cranston, Pendleton, Ore.

The young Ohio wife would only live a little less than six years in the Willamette Valley when her death took place due to tuberculosis in Salem, Oregon, on June 2, 1857.[2] She was buried in the Odd Fellows Cemetery.[3] During those short six years she gave birth to three daughters: Amelia, born on Christmas Day, 1852; Ella Rozetta, born on December 5, 1854; and Hulda Orpha, born September 28, 1856.

The Cranstons were part of a fairly large community of Ohio emigrants who traveled overland in 1851. Many were named in her journal. They tended to be of a strong anti-slavery sentiment and would become active in the development of the Republican Party in their new homeland during the pre-Civil War years. The folks from Ohio tended to settle east and northeast of Salem in what is known as the Waldo Hills region and in the Siverton country. There was, in the early 1850's, a small town named Lebanon [4] out in those Marion County hills, and Susan's husband, Warren, became postmaster of the community for a time. In 1858, that Lebanon died (and its post office closed) but gave way to another community of the same name a few miles farther south in Linn County. That town is still viable.

Warren Cranston was devastated by Susan's early death. There is a letter written by him on July 25, 1859, two years after her passing, in which he told relatives in the east that he was teaching school in Albany, Oregon, and still felt the impact of Susan's death:

> It has been over two years since Susan died and a long time it has been for me I assure you. I often times regret having come to Oregon, thinking perhaps had I not done so Susan might

---

[2] Portland *Weekly Oregonian,* June 13, 1857, page 2, column 5.

[3] Daughters of the American Revolution, *"Oddfellows Cemetery," Cemeteries of Marion County,* part IV. (Salem, Ore.), p. 43.

[4] Lewis L. McArthur, ed., *Oregon Geographic Names,* 4th edn. (Portland, Ore., 1974), p. 435.

perhaps still be living. She always told me that she did not regret coming, but perhaps it is all for the best. It would be better for man if he could be reconciled to the mysterious workings of Providence. I cannot do otherwise than to submit. My aim shall be to try and raise these little ones in such a manner that they will be as much respected as was their mother . . . but to do that I must be with them more than I have been since Susan died.

It is the very simplicity of Susan Cranston's journal and its occasional revelation of her inner self that make it of such value in understanding the problems faced by women of her time in the settling of the West.

There are typescrips of Susan Cranston's journal in several libraries, but the original is Manuscript P-A 303 in the collection at the Bancroft Library at the University of California in Berkeley. There is also a collection of Cranston letters, one of which is quoted immediately above, in the Bancroft Collection. We are deeply grateful for permission to publish the material used here.

There is another collection of Cranston family letters in the library of the Genealogical Forum of Portland, Oregon. They were written by Warren Cranston's father, Ephraim, who with Rosanna, his wife, traveled with the same wagon train of 1851. The letters are in typescript form and have been invaluable as reference material.

THE JOURNAL OF
SUSAN AMELIA CRANSTON

May 8th   crossed the Missourie river   drove 2 miles and encamped   our company consisted of 14 wagons with from 4 to 6 yokes of oxen to each and about 30 head of loose cows and young cattle and 14 horses.

May 9   drove 12 or 15 miles   had a hard rain in the

forenoon stopped an hour at noon encamped at night in the prairie with tolerable grass and water but no wood cooked with weeds.

Saturday May 10th. drove to Weeping water, stopped an hour at noon and arrived early at camp not very good grass but wood and water There the company organized chose a camp and guard master numbered the wagons to take turns driving ahead There were 30 men 13 women and a No of children Passed 11 graves

Sunday 11th drove 12 miles crossed Salt Creek and encamped near the bottom where there was good grass wood and watter 3 or 4 wagons camped on the other side of the creek with horse and mule teams Salt creek derived its name from the saltness of its watter which is not for use although our stock drank it without any perceptible injury. The country thus far that is between the Missourie and Weeping water, Weeping Watter and Salt creek presents an extensive prairie which is very rolling. The eye scans the open distance in vain to find an object upon which it may rest at times the eye is employed in scanning the coursing of a stream which may be seen from ten to fifteen miles according to the hight of the hill from which you look except the scattering trees upon the banks of the streams there is scarcely a stick large enough for a riding whip nothing but the rolling prairie one hill has not ended before another is begun at this time the grass is not high or long enough so far to find good grazing on the hills and on the creek bottoms sufficient for our teams but if we had better we should like it the grass will soon be good on the high prairie and we have had plenty of rain lately

Monday 12th started at 7 oclock stopped at . . . . .
There was not much grass but water for the cattle
. . . to cotton wood ditch Passed 16 graves had
good grass and water We have not been in sight of
timber to day only at our camps at morning and night

Tuesday 13th No one knew the camping ground any
further untill fort Carney [Kearney] our camp master Mr McAlexander[1] has been to calafornia but he
started from St. Joseph We took some wood and
water and drove untill noon when we stopped an hour
for the cattle to rest and graze and encamped a night
in the prairie We had tolerable grass but neither
wood or water except what we had brought The
prairie has been more broken to day there has been
shrubs and small trees in sight in the ravines most of
the time 3 indians the first that we had seen met us
just at night and followed us to camp they appeared
very friendly and were begging They had a paper
and on it was written with a pencil (these are friendly
indians you had better treat them well) they seemed
unwilling to leave but we sent them away at dusk
8 graves

Wednesday 14th Had a very hard shower with wind
and hail which scattered the cattle so that we did not
start very early drove about 10 miles and encamped
with neither wood or water except what we brought
with us passed 2 graves the appearance of the country about the same as yesterday

Thursday 15 drove about 15 miles in the afternoon
we struck the plat bottom the grass in the bottom is

---

[1] Andrew McAlexander and his wife Violinder settled in Lane County.
They later became citizens of eastern Oregon. *Illustrated History of Union
and Wallowa Counties* (Portland, 1902), pp. 573-4.

good the best that we have seen we encamped at
night on a little stream of good water we had brought
wood with us from a stinking creek which we had
passed in the afternoon Passed 2 graves The Platte
bottom is about 10 miles wide a low flat plain

Friday 16th drove about 20 miles struck the Platte
river and encamped on the bank The Platte is full
a mile wide the water is not good as the Missourie
fuller of sand The Mail from New fort Carney to
the Missourie staid with us to night We are 90 miles
from N Ft Carney 3 indians passed our camp they
were packing on 3 ponies showed a disposition to
be off

Saturday 17th Followed up the Platte stopped an
hour at noon encamped at night on the bank the
bottom and river are not so wide there in some places
it is not more than half a mile from the river to the
blufs We have a shower every day and sometimes
two or three since we come to the Platte Passed 2
graves stopped early and began washing calculated
to finish the next day Passed an old deserted indian
village the largest wigwam was 30 feet in diameter

Sunday 18th Raining in the morning so that we could
not wash Hitched up and drove on stopped 2 hours
at noon had a hard shower stopped early on the
river The bottom has been narrow to day on this
side of the river in some places the blufs come to
the river consequently we have had some hilly road
Passed 4 graves

Monday 19th The morning was cool and pleasant
In the fore noon we finished our washing and dried
our clothes in the afternoon we drove about 12 miles

Encamped again on the river   grass was not very good
The road has been to day about the same as yesterday

Tuesday 20th   Drove about 20 miles   stopped an
hour at noon and encamped at night opposite Grand
island   we had good grass   Passed 1 grave   the bottom has been wider to day   we have not been on the
blufs

Wednesday 21st   Drove about 12 miles and encampcd
on the river in sight of fort Carney   it has rained
most all day some of the time very hard   it cleared
up at night so that we had a chance to get our suppers
The bottom has been wider to day   Some of the oxens
necks begin to be sore   Passed 4 graves to day   we
expect the reason that we have not seen more since
we struck the river is that we have traveled in the
bottom and the graves are on the high land

Thursday 22nd   Drove about 15 miles   passed fort
Carney at which we stopped a few minuets and encamped on the river   had poor grass and nothing but
green willows for wood   fort Carney is situated at
the head of Grand island which is 50 miles long and
5 wide   There are 2 stores at the fort and a No of
good dwelling houses   3 graves

Friday 23rd   drove about 20 miles   stopped an hour
at noon where there was good grass and water for the
cattle   In the afternoon we found some wood that had
been cut and dried   we supposed by the indians   we
encamped at night in the prairie in sight of Platte
we had poor grass and water   no wood except what
we had brought   Passed 2 graves

Saturday 24th   started at seven   drove till noon when
we stopped an hour   crossed Plum creek which takes

its name from the plum bushes which grow on its
banks   at night we encamped on the bottom which is
wider since we left fort Carney   there were two little
ponds by our camp the water of which we used for
washing   our drinking water we got from a little
running stream between us and the river

Sunday 25th   Drove about 15 miles   stopped an hour
at noon   It was the warmest to day that it has been
since we started untill the middle of the afternoon when
we had the hardest hail storm I ever saw for which
we were unprepared   we saw the cloud but thought
it would be only a slight shower   Some of the stones
were as large as hens eggs   they had to hold the horses
by the head and unhitch the cattle from the wagon
it knocked some of the men down and the stones lay
so thick on the ground that they picked up pails full
after the shower was over   They soon found the cattle
hitched up and drove a little ways and encamped near
the river   Grass was poor

Monday 26   Drove about 12 miles and stopped to dry
our things that got wet in the hail storm   we encamped
on the bank of the Platte   had plenty of wood   grass
short   We washed but did not get our clothes that
we washed dry   Some of the boys went hunting on
the islands in the river and at night brought in 2 deer.

Tuesday 27th   Drove about 15 miles   stopped an hour
at noon near a slough and encamped at night on a little
stream   had tolerable grass wood and water   Some
of the boys stayed back to hunt and soon after noon
overtook us bringing two deer. Passed 3 graves

Wednesday 28th   Drove about 20 miles   stopped an
hour at noon on a slough and encamped at night 2 or

3 miles above the forks of the Platte   had good grass
and water but no wood except what we brought with
us and buffalo chips which burn very well   7 graves

Friday 30th   Drove about 15 miles   stopped an hour
at noon and encamped at night at the ford across south
fork   The appearance of the country since we struck
the Platte bottom has [been] about the same every day
The bluffs on the right and the river on the left

Saurday 31st   started early   crossed south fork at the
upper ford which is very good   the water did not
come over the axel tires of the wagon   here we come
up with 12 wagons which crossed the night before
we started ahead of them but they soon overtook us
and drove with us until night when they passed us
When across the river we left the bottom (which was
narrow) and ascended the bluffs which were not steep
then crossed a high roling prairie 12 or 13 miles across.
The grass was so short that we did not unhitch the
cattle at noon only stopped a few minutes for them to
rest   When we come towards the North fork the bluffs
became very steep and stony with deep ravines between
them but the road kept along on a ridge that appeared
forward for the purpose untill we come to a steep hill
when down we found ourselves in what is called Ash
hollow which leads out to the bottom of North fork
this hollow is two miles long and from 15 to 30 rods
wide winding around he bluffs which tower up on
either side some times to the highth of 60 feet   The
road through the hollow was lined with shrubs and
flowers wild roses cow cherries and scrub ash and up
on the blufs small cedars   We drove out into the
bottom and encamped near the river   grass short   We
took along a quantity of wood from the hollow as we

learned there was no more for 60 miles. we were soon
visited by a number of indians squaws and papooses
there was a large encampment of them across the river
opposite to us   they were Shions [Cheyennes] and
Sioux who marry and live together yet have each their
separate chiefs   The Shions a very intelligent looking
nation are said to be wealthy   a little papoose attracted
the attention of the whole company   it was dressed in
a wild cat skin taken off whole and lined with red
flannel and trimed with beads   There was a frenchman
living with them said he had been there 32 years

Sunday June 1st   did not start very early   drove 5
or 6 miles over   hard road   in some places very sandy
fine loose sand 6 inches deep and in others the ground
was covered with alkaline salts and where water stood
it looked like lye   we have seen some alkali before to
day but not as strong   the first we saw was 1 or 2 days
drives this side of New Fort Carney   about noon we
come to tolerable grass and encamped intending to go
no farther to day but we learned that grass was better
two or 3 miles ahead so we hitched up and drove to
good grass   in the morning when they went to hitch
up one of the oxen was missing   some staid to hunt
and after searching some time found him in the possession of the frenchman and indians   they overtook
us with the ox at noon   Passed 5 graves

Monday 2nd   Started 30 minuets after 6 Oclock
Drove about 15 miles in the forenoon   the sand and
alkaly was about the same as yesterday in the afternoon
we saw no alkali but sand was worse   Encamped at
night and noon on the bank of the North fork   grass
short   Passed 13 graves

Tuesday 3rd   drove about 18 miles   had good road
crossed Little creek before noon and encamped at night
on Big creek (passed 13 graves) in sight of the lonely
towers and Chimney rock   We saw them both a little
after noon   we were 5 miles from the tower and 24
from the rock

Wednesday 4th   Drove 24 miles   stopped an hour at
noon and encamped at night 5 miles beyond Chimney
rock on the river   The tower is 5 miles from the road
from which it appears very much like a ruined deserted tower or strong hold but on approaching nearer
it looks more rough and irregular   it is composed of
a kind of cement, or very soft sand stone which can
be cut or crumbled of[f] easily   it stands alone over-
looking the surrounding country   those that visited
it judged it to be 300 feet high 200 long 50 wide
when we first come in sight of Chimney rock it has the
appearance of a chimney or stove pipe as you approach
it looks like a hay stack with a pipe on it   it was of
about the same composition as the towers between two
and three hundred feet high   the chimney or pipe is
perhaps 50 or 60 feet high   it can easily be ascended
to the base of the pipe   Had very good roads in some
places the ground was covered with alkaline salts so
thick that we could pick up hands full of it   good
grass   Passed 8 graves

Thursday 5th   drove 21 miles   had good road   about
11 oclock we left North fork   watered our teams and
drove on 2 or 3 hours and did not find grass sufficient
to pay for unhitching   stopped ½ hour for them to
rest   had a hard shower in the afternoon   Encamped
at night at scotts bluffs and springs   had poor grass

our encampment was in a romantic place on a hollow
where there was a little stream and high blufs nearly
surrounding us covered with small cedars and pines
there was a black smiths shop near   passed 5 graves

Friday 6th   Drove 14 miles by one Oclock as our camp
master thought we should not come to water again for
19 miles   we encamped for night on the bank of Horse
creek   in the afternoon we washed   had no wood except a little that we had brought and a log found in
the creek   passed 13 graves

Saturday 7th   Drove 20 miles   stopped an hour at
noon on a beautiful stream of clear water to the right
of the road   in the afternoon we passed a trading
house   encamped at night on the river   poor grass
Passed 10 graves

Sunday 8th   Drove 17 miles   stopped an hour at noon
passed 2 trading houses   had some sandy road   forded
Larimie river and encamped at night of[f] Platts
bank 2 miles from the ford   had poor grass   We
did not go within ¼ of a mile of fort Larimaii but
saw many soldiers and plenty of indians   some came
to our camp to trade   In the forenoon we came in
sight of Larimaii peak the highest point in the Black
hills   it looked like a small dark cloud said to be 60
mile off   5 graves

Monday 9th   Drove 19 miles   Encamped at noon on
the river   in the afternoon we passed the lime killn
near is a good spring in a ravine to the right of the
road   filled our water kegs which was useless as in
five miles we came to bitter Cottonwood creek on which
we camped at night where the water was equally as
good   tolerable grass   plenty wood   to day we have

had a very crooked hilly road very sandy in the forenoon   3 graves

Tuesday 10th   Drove about 15 miles to Horse Shoe
creek   stopped an hour at noon and arrived at the
creek at 3 oclock   found the best grass we had seen
since we started   in the forenoon we passed two small
branches and in the afternoon a beautiful spring to the
right of the road   had a shower just as we stopped
hilly road

Wednesday 11th   Drove 13 miles   did not start till
noon   stopped in the forenoon to let the cattle rest
and wash   In the morning the creek had raised and
had a red hue like brick dust   The blufs above have
the same appearance   they are composed of a kind of
clay   fortunately we found a spring just above our
camp   encamped at night on the river   drove the
cattle a mile from camp and found grass nearly as
good as last night   good road most of the way

Thursday 12   about 15 miles   stopped an hour at
noon   encamped at night on a good stream of water
very poor grass   to day we have had a hard road
hilly and dusty   saw 6 graves

Saturday 14th   Drove 20 miles   grass was so poor
that we did not turn the cattle out of the corall but
hitched up as soon as daylight and drove about 5 miles
to a small creek where there was a little grass and
stopped and got breakfast   a company just ahead of
us killed 2 buffaloes and gave us all the meat we
wanted and 1 of our company killed an atelope   we
started on about 10 Oclock   in about 4 miles we came
to a small creek and 8 more to Deer creek where we
calculated to camp but found no grass   drove 3 miles

to the river where we found tolerable grass   1 cow
was found dead in the corall this morning   it was
supposed that she had drank alkaly or eaten some
poisonous weed   saw 3 graves

Sunday 15th   Drove about 15 miles   stopped 2 hours
at noon on the bank of the river in a beautiful place
where it was lined with cotton wood and bushes
encamped at night on the river   had very poor grass

Monday 16th   Drove 8 miles   stopped opposite lower
ferry   the price for crossing there was 3 dollars   a
wagon went to the upper ferry found the price 2½
a wagon and the best boat   encamped a mile from the
ferry   had good grass   in the afternoon we washed
did not cross to day as we would have to drive 12 miles
to come to grass

Tuesday 17th   Crossed the north fork   drove about
14 miles   encamped at night without water except a
little that we had brought with us which was not much
as we expected to find water   we did pass a lake of
alkaline water which we did not let our stock drink
grass was poor and no wood except wild sage   We
swam our cattle and horses across the river   Saw 2
graves one a little before we came to the river and one
after   the last was made this year June 2nd   it was
the first that we had seen buried this year   to day and
yesterday we have been in sight of a chain of mountains
to our right   snow or ice could be seen in the hollows
of them

Wedesday 18th   Drove about 14 miles   started at daylight and drove to Slew springs   come 8 miles and
stopped to get our breakfast and let the cattle do the
same   Came to willow springs in about 2 miles and

in 4 more to Crooked run where we encamped for night Had tolerable grass and water sage for wood.

Thursday 19th Drove about 14 miles did not find grass to feed at noon. Crossed greas wood creek about 4 miles from our encampment on Crooked Runn. Came to independence rock where we all encamped but the Drs folks [2] and Coollages [3] who thought they would be independent and drive by themselves. Three or four miles from independence rock are a number of sala- ratus ponds none near the road however had no water, being dried up. The salaratus seems to be pure. it is white and clear and in some places an inch thick. We gathered a basin of it which we are going to dry. Inde- pendence rock is a solitary rock some 70 or 80 feet in hight and covers some two or three or more acres. our camp was between the rock and the river Sweet water had tolerable grass good water sage and old wagons for wood

Friday 20th Our company divided in our division we had 7 wagons & 14 men & women & 6 children Drove about 15 miles stopped an hour at noon and encamped at night on Sweet water had good grass sage and greece wood for fuel to day we passed by the Devils gape where the river passes through the mountain the mountain is 3 or 4 hundred feet high with gap through the width of the river it is com- posed of rock

---

[2] The doctor was the pioneer physician, Benjamin Davenport, graduate of Pittsfield Medical College, Pittsfield, Massachusetts. There was a large family of Davenports in the 1851 migration. O. Larsell, *The Doctor in Oregon* (Portland, 1947), p. 200.

[3] Ai and Sarah Coolidge, went into the banking and merchant business in Silverton, Oregon (*Dictionary of Oregon History*), p. 61.

Saturday 21st   Drove about 30 miles   stopped an hour
at noon on the river and encamped at night near the
river and near where there are 2 roads   one crosses
the river and the other does not   to day we have had
a very sandy road   to day we have been surrounded
by mountains on our right the Sweet water mountains
of nearly solid rock and destitute of vegetation and
to the left a chain covered with a dark growth and
capped with Snow.

Sunday 22nd   Started at the long narrows   crossed
the river 3 times in a mile then left it   crossed it
again a little after noon we did not unyoke at noon
as there was not much grass but plenty of saleratus
we encamped at night about a mile and a half above
the ice springs   we found no spring but passed through
a marshy springy place where there was excellent looking grass but the alkaly was so strong that we did not
let our cattle taste it   we had tolerable grass among
the sage which was our wood and sent back to the bog
where they found ice in some places 6 inches thick
by digging down 4 or 6 inches which we used for water
to day we have occasionly seen the Wind river mountains which are covered with snow   Drove about 20
miles

Monday 23rd   Drove 18 or 20 miles   started at daylight and drove 10 or 12 miles   came to the river
stopped 2 hours and got breakfast   the grass had been
eaten of[f]   in the afternoon we crossed the river and
drove over a very hilly stony road till we struck the
river and crossed it again and followed it up 4 or 5
miles and found first rate grass and encamped for night
on the river   sage again for fuel   passed 3 graves

Tuesday 24th Drove about 20 miles stopped at noon on a little rivulet and encamped at night on Strawberry creek a branch of the Sweet water passed another branch Snow creek 2 or 3 miles from this where there was a bank of snow under the bluff in the afternoon the road wound round the bluffs it was the most crooked hilly stony road we have had it was better in the afternoon passed 5 graves

Wednesday 25th Drove about 16 miles 4 miles from our camp we crossed Sweet water for the last time 8 more we came to the top of the mountains and 4 more to the Pacific springs where the water runs west It was very cold and good we encamped for the night grass short our road to day has been tolerable good we hardly know when we were on the top of the mountain the ascent and decent was so gradual the weather is very warm in the middle of the day and cold nights passed 6 graves

Thursday 26th Drove 18 miles to Little Sandy did not unhitch the cattle at noon as there was no grass crossed dry branch about noon there was a little water but it was alkaline we did not let the cattle drink Encamped at night on the bank of the creek and drove the cattle up the creek 2 miles where they found a little grass 3 graves

Friday 27th Drove about 8 miles to Big Sandy went a mile down the creek where we found tolerable grass encamped for the rest of the day to let the cattle rest before crossing the cut off which is a distance of 40 or 50 miles with neither grass or water as yet we have not decended the mountains much it has been very cold all day to day the men have worn their overcoats

Saturday 28th   Started about noon   drove till dusk
when we stopped a few minuets to eat our supper
started again and drove till daylight when we unyoked
the cattle and rested an hour or two

Sunday 29th   Started on and reached Green river
about 4 Oclock in the afternoon   our cattle were tired
dry and hungry   the road was very rough and hilly
towards the river   we got our wagons ferried across
for 10 dollars apiece   tried to swim the cattle   got
10 or 12 across and could get no more   drove them
down about a mile where there was a little grass and
left them without a guard   left 1 ox on the desert

Monday 30th   Hunted up our stock and drove them
across the river   had but little trouble being in the
morning. Got all things in readiness for starting about
11 Oclock, drove 6 or 7 miles over the most hilly
road that we have come yet and encamped while on
Fontenells Fork where we [had] good grass and watter
at this place we found Indians and white men with
ho[r]ses and oxen for sale   Turned our stock loose
and did not guard them

Tuesday July 1st 1851   Did not move our camp   let
the cattle rest   we had willows for wood   Caught half
a dozzen speckled trout the first we had seen

Wednesday 2nd   Drove about 12 miles   did not unhitch at noon as there was no grass   Encamped at
night near a good spring in a hollow where there was
a thick growth of willows and aspen and on the hills
were the largest pines we had seen   some were 2 or 3
feet through at the bottom   drove the cattle up the
swail about a mile w[h]ere they found tolerable grass
among the hills and bushes   at night drove the cattle

into the corall where they lay down and left them without a guard

Thursday 3rd   In the morning found the cattle some scattered but soon got them together and hitched up and drove on before breakfast about 9 or 10 miles to a fork here we stopped till noon then drove 5 or 6 miles to the foot of some very steep hills found good grass and water and encamped for night left 2 oxen since we crossed Green river

Friday 4th   Drove 18 miles in 4 miles we came to Hams fork quite a stream lots of indians there with trout to swap for bread stopped an hour at noon after passing over a very hilly road in the afternoon we pass over a very level pretty road lined on either side with good grass till the 3 last miles we passed over a very high ridge about a mile up through a grove of Balsam of fir and 2 down to a beautiful rill where we encamped Had good grass Saw 7 graves

Saturday 5th   Drove about 12 miles to Bear river where we encamped for the rest of the day had good grass here high not very good water had a very hilly road

Sunday 6th   Started at 7 oclock traveled 12 miles and encamped on the river had good grass passed Owens & Wilsons trading post Situated on Thomass Fork Bear River where Father[4] bought two yokes of oxen. Crossed the fork & a slough on bridge by paying $1 per wagon saved 8 miles by doing so Our road led into the mountains which was the worst we had passed being steep and running Zigzag in all directions untill it reached the vally of bear river which we reached at dusk

4 "Father" was Ephraim Cranston, Warren's father.

Tuesday 8   Drove some 18 or twenty miles over a
smooth & level road   passed several small mountain
streams or rivulets & encamped in due time on one
of the same where have watter and grass

Wedneday 9th   Drove about 16 miles   in the morning we left the river and passed over some small hills
struck the river again at noon where we stopped an
hour then drove on and encamped near the 2 mounds
that are first seen at the soda springs   in the afternoon
we crossed a No of spring branches and one beautiful
spring on the left side of the road   had poor grass

Thursday 10th   In the morning we visited the mounds
found 1 dry   on the other water was oozing out in a
No. of places   the water is warm and has a mineral
taste   a little below the mounds is a large beautiful
cool soda spring which when put with acid made a
good drink   Soon after starting we crossed the stream
on which we were camped   just below the road we
found a good soda spring   in about a mile we cross
another spring   above this stream is a large spring and
a little below on the river bank is the steamboat spring
the greatest curiosity of all   here the water spouts up
2 feet from a cilinder formed by the crystallization of
the water   the water does not flow of[f] very fast but
the spouting is caused by the escaping of the gass
the water is warm and foams like soap suds   there
are several mounds here that have formely been springs
now dry   5 miles from the springs we left the river
which bends to the south and the road to the north
through a valley 20 miles in length and 7 in width
another road strikes across the valley that goes to calafornia   2 miles from the forks is a soda pool & 2 from
the pool a spring branch where we stopped for noon

9 miles more we came to another branch where we encamped for night grass is good on both these branches wood on the last 5 graves

Friday 11th Drove 7 miles crossed 2 small streams came to Port Neuf there was a tole bridge across it but we forded it and had the luck to upset a wagon although it was no worse place than we have crossed many times the wagon and loading were so wet and muddy that we had to lay by the rest of the day but the grass was not good and they said there was a weed or something there that poisoned cattle so we hitched up and started about sun down and drove 8 or 10 miles over the most crooked and difficult road that we had seen stopped about midnight on a little stream not much grass

Saturday 12th Drove about 13 miles stopped at noon an hour and encamped at night on the same stream that we did this morning had good road grass not very good

Sunday 13th Drove 15 miles 3 miles from camp we left the creek and crossed a plain of heavy sand 7 miles in width when we came to big springs where we stopped at noon 4 miles more and we came to fort hall on Snake river the fort is built of adobes we encamped a mile beyond the fort on a slough of the river had good grass

Monday 14th Drove 17 miles 3 miles from camp we crossed a stream 1 more crossed Port Neuf again and a bad slough then ascended the bluffs and drove 5 miles when we came into the bottom again where there was a pond near a bunch of willows here we stopped at noon there is poison here after leaving

we saw a number of dead cattle   2 miles from here
we came to the river where we camped for night   had
good grass wood and water

Tuesday 15th   Drove 18 miles   1 or 2 miles from
our camp we came to the falls, American falls in the
Snake or Lewis River which are quite a curiosity of
nature   the water comes rushing and foaming over
rocks a highth of 8 feet forming a spray sufficient to
form a rainbow   we crossed a small stream in the fore
noon   stopped at noon where there was good dry bunch
grass   crossed 2 streams in the afternoon   we encamped 2 miles beyond the last   Beaver dam creek
near the river   had the same kind of grass that we did
at noon   had some very hard hills

Wednesday 16th   Drove 20 miles   in 8 we came to
Casha [Cache] creek   stopped 2 hours at noon   had
good grass   from here it is 15 miles to next water
Marshy springs   we drove till dusk when we stopped
to eat our supper   went on 12 miles   found good
[grass?] and encamped at 12 Oclock at night   the
road is very rough between Casha creek and the springs

Thursday 17   Started before breakfast   drove 4 miles
round the springs to a little stream where we stopped
till nearly noon then drove 11 miles to the river
w[h]ere we had a tolerable camp   crossed a small
stream

Friday 18   Laid by in the forenoon to wash   in the
afternoon drove 11 miles   4 from camp came to Goose
creek   6 more to another stream where there was a
good camp   we went a mile farther to the river
a poor camp   no grass

Saturday 19th   Drove 22 miles   12 over a very stony road brought us to dry branch where we stopped 2 hours at noon   10 more to Rock creek our camp at night   had tolerable grass at both of these streams here we found a company that had been here all day 3 of their guards were shot last night by indians they think one will die

Sunday 20th   Drove 15 miles   8 to a creek where we stopped at noon and 1 more we struck the same creek again where we camped at night   this creek [has] a narrow bottom bordered with very high steep bluffs here some 30 wagons were encamped   not much grass this afternoon we had a dash of rain   it lasted but a few minuets and did not lay the dust yet it was the most we have had since leaving Horse shoe creek

Monday 21st   Drove 14 miles to the river again where we encamped for night   here the opposite side of river is lined with a high perpendicular bank   no grass near the river but got very good bunch grass by driving back a mile to the foot of the bluffs

Tuesday 22   Drove 14 miles   followed up the river 3 when we struck warm spring branch   4 more to Salmon fall creek where we stopped an hour at noon   2 more we crossed it where was a better camp   to the right of the road the water came pouring over the bluffs falling perpendicular 100 feet though in no large quantities   5 more to Salmon falls where we encamped for night   here the indians met us with salmon to swap for clothes   the largest weighed 20 pounds

Wednesday 23rd   Traveled 12 miles passing over high hills and deep ravines and heavy sand   stopped an hour at noon and encamped at night near the river

had to go down a very steep bluff nearly a mile to
get water and up a ravine the other way for grass
this morning passed the falls which is a succession of
falls all making about 15 feet

Thursday 24th Traveled 13 miles struck the river
2 miles above the ford Here we found a company
ferrying in wagon beds we unloaded two of our best
waggon beds and commenced calking them got them
finished and ferried their loads that night The next
day we finished crossing and were ready to roll out
Saturday left the river and traveled 17 miles to a small
stream encamped for the night had a good camp

Sunday 27 Traveled 15 miles 5 miles brought us to
a marshy hollow which wound to right of the direction
were traveling Traveled in this marsh 3 miles then
drove out leaving this marsh to our right one mile
from where we left the marsh and left the road were
the hot springs. They boil up in a number of places
form a small stream which when it decends into the
marsh above spokkene of is cooll and pretty good to
drink Where the water here first comes out it is
scalding hot around the spring there is a red sedi-
ment which makes the water look unfit to drink but
on trying it we found no unpleasant taste 4 from the
springs brought us to a spring branch upon which encamped 2 hours then drove 4 miles on for the night
where found good grass but no watter This day was
warm

Monday 28 Drove 19 miles 5 miles brought us to
barrel creek where no grass till 11 Oclock there being
good grass we then drove till night and camp to the
first watter since leaving barrel creek Pass a number

of dry branches   the one that we encamped on has but little watter   the road to barrel creek and for some distance very stony   the ballance was hilly being along the base of the mountains but stony

Tuesday 29th   Drove 22 miles   4 from camp crossed Charlotts creek   2 more to another branch where we stopped an hour   7 more crossed another dry branch there was water in a pool to the left of the road and excellent grass around but we drove on nine miles to Boisee river   did not reach camp till after dark

Wednesday 30th   found that we were on a slough of the river and there was good grass between that and the river   laid by in the forenoon to let the cattle rest and wash   in the afternoon we drove 10 miles and encamped on the river   had a good camp   came over one of the hardest hills we have had

Thursday 31st   Drove 16 or 18 miles   Stopped an hour at noon near the river and encamped at night on the river bank   our road to day led down the bottom till toward night we saw it led up the bluff   we turned town to the river some distance from the road to camp

Friday Aug 1st   Traveled 18 miles   2 brought us to the crossing of Boisee river a tolerable ford   stopped an hour at noon and encamped at night on Snake river at fort Boisee   no grass within 2 miles

Saturday 2nd   Got a canoe at the fort and crossed the river   carried the load of a wagon at one load and the wagon another   got across and drove 6 miles   had bunch grass   no water

Sunday 3rd   Traveled 10 miles to Malheur river   ar-

rived about noon   laid by the rest of the day   near
the crossing are several hot springs   the water is scalding hot

Monday 4th   Drove 20 miles   10 to Sulphur Springs
where there was no grass and little water   Stopped
an hour at noon and 10 more to birch creek where we
encamped at night   not a very good camp

Tuesday 5th   This morning passed a company which
camped in sight of us   one of their men died about ½
an hour before of the iricipilus and here was the grave
of one of the men shot on Rock creek who had lingered
to here   was buried yesterday   Drove 7 or 8 miles
to burnt river where we stopped 2 or 3 hours to fix a
wagon tire   went 4 or 5 more over a very rough road
followed up the river and encamped on it at night
not a very good camp

Wednesday 6th   Traveled 12 miles   crossed the river
8 times and 3 spring branches   very warm   stopped 2
or 3 hours in the middle of the day   Encamped at
night on a spring branch

Thursday 7th   Traveled 15 miles crossing several
spring branches yesterday and to day our road has
been very crooked and hilly   to day we had another
wagon tip over on a very sidling hill and a springy
miry place at the bottom   there was not water enough
to wet the things   broke the wagon bows all up   the
only damage done   got some willows and soon twisted
up some and went on   Encamped at night on a small
stream

Friday 8th   Traveled 21 or 22 miles   stopped 2 hours
at noon   the last 13 no water and at night nothing but
slough water   a slough of Powder river   good grass

had a very hilly road in the afternoon came in sight of the Blue mountains which look blue in the distance being covered with a green growth of timber

Saturday 9th Traveled 13 miles 8 to Powder river where we stopped 2 hours 2 more to the crossing 2 more to a large stream 1 more to a small one where we encamped at night a good camp these bottoms are covered with splendid grass and to our right the Blue mountains covered with timber

Sunday 10th Traveled 14 miles 6 in forenoon over a level road through a rich bottom at the foot of the mountains crossed a number of spring branches stopped an hour at noon in the afternoon we had a very rough rocky road along a long stony hill to go up and down Encamped at night in the edge of Grand round on a little stream good camp

Monday 11th Traveled 7 miles across Grand round which is a circular prairie bottom surrounded by mountains covered with timber. The river passes through the westerly part of the bottom and its course is northeast empties into Lewis or Snake river encamped at the base of a long hard hill the river being some two miles to our right Staid during the day Had good camp

Tuesday August 12th Cool and pleasant traveled about 16 miles 8 miles was up and down a spurr of the mountains (which is covered with fir and pine and most of the way with very good grass) which brought us to grand round river which at this place is hemmed in by the mountains no grass nearer than one or two miles eight miles over the mountain which is cut up by deep ravines brought us to camp or brought

us to a stop for it was dark   in the morning we found
watter in a deep ravine to our left that was runing,
a tolerable camp   This day we had to climb the hardest hills that we had climbed since we started   some
had to double teams

Wednesday August 13th   Cool and pleasant   rained
in the night   traveled 10 miles and encamped on a
small stream   called Sus encampment [?]   found
good grass to the left in the timber   The road to day
was similar to that of yesterday except but not so hard

Thursday August 14th   Cool and pleasant   rained in
the night   traveled 14 miles and encamped on the
Eumatilla   here we found plenty of indians who
brought dried peas and potatoes for which we gave
them a measure of flour for the same of peas or potatoes   had poor camp. the bottoms and hills near the
river were eat down by droves of ponies   the country
produces well   the road was very good   most of the
way down hill

Friday 15th   Traveled 12 miles down the river
stopped an hour at noon on the river   in the afternoon
crossed the river   went down a mile to where the
road left the river and encamped   had a tolerable
camp   cool and rainy in the forenoon

Saturday 16th   Traveled 16 miles across a high rooling prairie   stopped an hour at noon and encamped
at night on a slough of the river   tolerable grass but
more brush   a very warm pleasant day

Sunday 17th   Traveled 17 miles 4 to the river   the
roads fork near the river   one takes down the Columbia river   the other crosses the Eumatilla and keeps
up from the Columbia bottom   here we found a trad-

ing post and men employed in building an indian agency the information that we could get was that the
left hand was much the best road and grass but water
scarce 2 of the wagons of our company chose to go
the Columbia road the rest of us crossed the river
eat dinner and went 10 miles to Butter creek where
there was a plenty of good cool water and good grass
where we encamped the road was some sandy a
pleasant day

Monday 18 Traveled 20 miles stopped an hour at
noon encamped at night at the well springs here
are 2 springs about a quarter of a mile apart to the
left of the road 1 is good drinking water at the
other they watered the cattle by dipping it up no
grass near a warm pleasant day our road lay over
a roling prairie very dusty

Tuesday 19th Traveled 15 miles stopped an hour
at noon and encamped on Willow creek to the right
of the road had good water and grass road much
like yesterday warm and pleasant

Wednesday 20th Very warm and pleasant drove 22
or 23 miles stopped 2 hours at noon passed sulphur
springs took the left hand road which strikes a creek
2 or 3 miles from the springs and followed it down to
John Days river the right hand road leads over the
bluff directly to the river 5 miles from the springs
Did not reach camp untill after dark Plenty of water
not very good grass and about the same as yesterday
very dusty

Thursday 21st Traveled only 8 or 10 miles 5 down
the creek to John Days river where we stopped till
about 4 Oclock crossed the river drove on till dark

encamped on the prairie without water   the road leaving the river follows up a crooked rocky ravine to the top of the bluff

Friday 22nd   Traveled about 20 miles   started before breakfast intending to go the Well springs which we supposed to be not more than 9 miles distant   went that distance and learned they were still ahead and there was not water enough to water the cattle so we stopped and got something to eat then drove to the Columbia 5 miles from the springs and encamped had tolerable grass on the bluffs   here the river is lined on the opposite side with very steep high bluffs and on this with huge sand drifts which are blowing about

Saturday 23rd   Drove down in sight of the ferry across Dishoots [Deschutes] river 2 miles from our camp found so many wagons there that we could not cross to day and on the Columbia had a tolerable camp

Sunday 24th   Crossed the river in safety though the ferry was not very good and the river was very swift and full of rocks   drove out 6 miles to a creek and encamped   had a tolerable camp

Monday 25th   Did not leave camp as some of our company were not well and to wait for the two wagons that went the river road   they came up in the afternoon

Tuesday 26th   1 wagon of our company left for the Dalles intending to go down the river   we traveled 8 miles to another creek and encamped   Had a good road since leaving the river

Wednesday 27   Traveled about 8 miles up the creek and encamped   the two last camps have been tolerable

A Letter to Mother

❦ Lucia Loraine Williams

INTRODUCTION

We would like to use the introduction to the Lucia Loraine Williams letter — which contains quotes from her diary — to describe what we think to be an innovative method of research.

A good part of research is search: that is the seeking out and locating of primary documents in unlikely places. This is where the historian becomes like Sherlock Holmes, a detective seeking evidence. The search for these documents in this series was an experience very close to my heart — both figuratively and literally. In recuperating over a number of weeks after having open heart surgery, I napped in the daytime (still do), which meant I often lay awake at night in the wee small hours. I learned to tune in to radio station KGO, San Francisco, which is a powerful talk station with radio waves reaching all up and down the Pacific coast.

One night on a whim, I telephoned the station and the announcer gave me several minutes to tell of this project of collecting and publishing the diaries and letters of women who crossed the plains in covered wagons. I asked listeners if they had such documents in their possession and to let me know so that they might also be included in our project. As a result of this call and some ten others, we have received ten manuscripts of diaries or letters sent in by persons who are most happy to let us have the use of their precious family treasures. Such documents have been passed on from generation to generation, stored away in dresser drawers or closet corners, taken out only for special family occasions.

The Lucia Loraine Williams letter/diary that follows is one of these. It was written immediately after she arrived in Milwaukie, Oregon, on September 16, 1851.

Word of this document came to me in a letter postmarked Tacoma, Washington, dated October 22, 1979. It was from Mrs. Helen Stratton Felker, who wrote, "I have a diary of my great-grandmother's." So as a result of several telephone calls and some letters back and forth, we have this precious record of an overland journey during the season of 1851. It is with deep appreciation to Mrs. Felker that we publish it here.

Now to Lucia's own life: She was born Lucia Bigelow on April 29, 1816, somewhere in Vermont. This means that she was 35 years old when she crossed the plains with her husband of a few years, Elijah Williams. They had been married in Ohio. Lucia was Elijah's second wife; the first was Sarah Ann Watson Williams. But let Elijah tell of his married life himself in his own words. There is a letter of his in the Oregon State Library giving a "History of Family," in which he says, "I took $100 and entered 80 acres of land at Findlay, Hancock County, Ohio . . . and there I got married to Sarah Ann Watson lived some 9 or 10 years with her and she died and then I married Lucia Lorain[e] Bigelow, and emigrated to Oregon. . ." He had originally come from Luzerne County, Pennsylvania, when he made the above land claim in 1832.[1] Over the years, he read law and became a practicing attorney, and also engaged in business enterprises.

There were two boys who were left motherless when Sarah Ann died: Richard and George. Richard,[2] the oldest,

---

[1] "Elijah Williams," *Oregon Native Son* (Portland, Ore., 1899), p. 347.

[2] H. K. Hines, *An Illustrated History of the State of Oregon* (Chicago, 1893), pp. 813-14.

had been born in Findlay on November 15, 1836; George [3] on April 5, 1839. They were respectively 22 and 15 years old when they crossed the plains with their father and their new mother, Lucia Loraine, in 1851. They both grew up more to become lawyers, educated at their parents insistance, in the pioneer Willamette University Law School in Salem, still a dynamic institution.

Elijah and Lucia also began their 1851 overland journey with two small children of their own: John, 10, and Helen, 3.[4] The tragedy of the death of little John is told in Lucia's letter. It is also dramatically described in another primary source, the reminiscences of Esther M. (Mrs. Freeman) Lockhart, which were taken down as a kind of "oral history" and published in a book by a daughter, Agnes Ruth Sengstacken, the title of which is *Destination West!* (Binfords & Mort, Portland, 1942). Although Esther Lockhart's record of the journey is a reminiscence uttered many years after the event, we are making an exception and, with the permission of Thomas Binford, are reprinting the pertinent story of the overland journey as an Epilogue to Lucia Williams' letter. Esther Lockhart tells about the same series of events and mentions many of the same persons taking part in the journey. However, it is like using binoculars instead of a single spy-glass, in that the double vision gives perspective to the story. The Freeman Lockharts became pioneer settlers on the southern Oregon coast, in the Coos Bay area.[5]

Lucia and Elijah Williams had another child added to their family on February 15, 1853, in Salem, Oregon. Emmet B. Williams [6] grew up to study law at the Wil-

---

[3] Hines, *op, cit.,* pp. 1255-56.

[4] Helen S. Felker, telephone conversation.

[5] Emil R. Peterson and Alfred Powers, *A Century of Coos and Curry* (Portland, Ore., 1952), pp. 272-73; Orvil Dodge, *Pioneer History of Coos and Curry Counties* (Salem, Ore., 1898), pp. 349-56.

[6] *History of the Bench and Bar of Oregon* (Portland, Ore., 1910), p. 245.

lamette University and to become a practicing lawyer in
Portland in his later years.

The Williams family settled in Salem where Elijah practiced law and was an active business man. Lucia dedicated
much of her spare time to being one of the founders of the
First Congregational Church of Salem. In the downtown
church building today, there is a stained glass window
commemorating her part in the founding of the church.

The Williamses lived in a house that was built right
across the street from the state capitol. Mrs. Felker re-
members visiting the house as a little girl.[7] It was in this
house on November 9, 1870, that the daughter, who at
age three had crossed the plains, was married to Milton
A. Stratton of Clackamas, Oregon.[8]

The last few weeks of Lucia Williams' life are told in
several editions of the *Daily Oregon Statesman* newspaper
of Salem early in 1874. On Monday, February 2, the following appeared:

> In Failing Health — Our fellow citizen, Hon. Elijah Wil-
> liams, received a telegram Saturday, from his wife who has
> been for some time at Santa Clara, Cal., for her health, stating
> that she is not as well as when she left home. Mr. Williams
> will start by the Ajax [steamship] to-morrow, for the purpose
> of bringing his wife home if she is well enough to endure
> the trip.

Then on March 2, 1874, there appeared another item,
dateline Portland:

> Returned, — Hon. Elijah Williams and wife returned by the
> steamer Ajax, arriving in this city yesterday, from Santa Clara,
> Cal., where Mrs. Williams has been spending several months
> for her health; which we regret to learn, has not been so much
> improved by her sojourn there as her friends had hoped.

---

[7] Helen S. Felker, typescript on the Williams family.

[8] Jean Carter and Daraleen Wade, *Marion County, Oregon, Marriage
Records, 1849-1871* (Salem, Ore., 1979), p. 87.

Then on Saturday, May 23, there appeared the final sad message:

> Died, — In Salem, May 22d, 1874, Mrs. L. L. Williams, wife of Elija [sic] Williams, Esq., aged 58 years. The funeral services will take place at the Congregational Church to-morrow at 10½ o'clock A.M. Rev. P. S. Knight will conduct the services, there at that hour.

THE LETTER OF
LUCIA LORAINE WILLIAMS

Milwaukee, [Oregon] September 16, '51

Dear Mother:

We have been living in Oregon about 2 weeks, all of us except little John, and him we left 12 miles this side of Green River. He was killed instantly by falling from a wagon and the wheels running over his head. After leaving the desert and Green River, we came to a good place of feed and laid by a day for the purpose of recruiting our teams. On the morning of the 20th of June we started on. John rode on the wagon driven by Edwin Fellows.[1] We had not proceeded more than 2 miles before word came for us to turn back. We did so but found him dead. The oxen had taken fright from a horse that had been tied behind the wagon preceding this, owned by a young man that Mr. Williams had told a few minutes to turn out of the road. Two other teams ran also. John was sitting in back of the wagon but as soon as the cattle commenced to run he went to the front and caught hold of the driver who held him as long as he could but he was frightened and

---

[1] Edwin B. Fellows lived out his life in the Oregon Country and became one of the most able river boatmen on the Willamette and Columbia rivers.

did not possess presence of mind enough to give him a little send, which would have saved him. Poor little fellow, we could do nothing for him. He was beyond our reach and Oh, how suddenly, one half hour before we had left him in health as lively as a lark, and then to find him breathless so soon was awful. I cannot describe to you our feelings. We buried him there by the road side, by the right side of the road, about one-half mile before we crossed the Fononelle, a little stream. We had his grave covered with stones to protect if from wild beasts and a board with his name and age and if any of our friends come through I wish they would find his grave and if it needs, repair it.

Helen [2] has been sick nearly all of the way and at the time that John died she was getting a little better so that she could be around a little. It was impressed on my mind that we were not all to get through, but I thought it would be Helen that we would leave for she was continually sick. We think that she had scarlet fever on the road. The night that we passed Ft. Laramie she was very sick. She came out with a fine rash accompanied by a high fever. She would not be satisfied unless I was rubbing her all of the time. Her throat was sore and she vomited blood several times. After she had partially recovered she was tolerable healthy and enjoyed herself well. She could talk to the Indians and throw the lariat with a great deal of glee. An old squaw and a young one with a papoose came and sat on one side of the fire, the papoose tied to a board. (There were snakes) and commenced talking to Helen. She would jabber back and laugh then they would talk and laugh, until they got into quite a spree.

---

[2] Helen L. Williams was the three-year-old daughter of the Williams'.

The mother of the papoose wanted to swap her papoose for mine but I told her "no swap." I believe she would have done it as she seemed quite eager to trade.

After we passed Ft. Laramie I wrote a letter home and sent it to the Fort by a mountaineer calling himself the mail carrier but have since learned he was an imposter and that the others were in pursuit of him, so you may not have received that. I will mention some thing over again covering our journey.

After crossing the mountains our company was so large we separated, making two, one bound for Oregon and the other via Salt Lake. In one company were 14 wagons and 2 carriages. One Baptist preacher from Iowa,[3] one family from near Norwalk, O. The gentleman's name was Lockhart.[4] Mrs. L's sister accompanied them.[5] The ladies are sisters Hannah Adams' stepmother. Judge Oleny [6] from Iowa also two other families, one a widow with five small children. They elected Mr. Williams captain in which honorable office he

[3] The "Baptist preacher from Iowa" was the Rev. Robert Crouch Kinney who, with his family, had been living in Muscatine, Iowa, since 1838. He later served in the Oregon legislature and was a member of the state's constitutional convention. When he died in Salem on March 2, 1875, he was honored by the suspension of business all over town for several hours. C. H. Mattoon, *Baptist Annals of Oregon,* I (McMinnville, Ore., 1905), pp. 66-67.

[4] Freeman Goodwin Lockhart and wife, Esther Mehitable. It is Esther Lockhart's story that is told by her daughter, Agnes Ruth Sengstacken, in the reminiscent book, *Destination West!* (Portland, Ore., 1942). This book should be read as an adjunct to the reading of the Williams letter. It tells about the same wagon train. Selections from it are printed herewith as an "Epilogue" to the Williams letter.

[5] Laura Selover was Esther (Selover), Lockhart's unmarried sister. (*Destination West,* p. 37).

[6] Cyrus and Sarah E. Olney were members of this emigrating company. He later practiced law in Oregon and became a Justice of the Terriorial Supreme Court in the mid-1850's. He also served in the legislature. He died in 1870. Howard M. Corning, *Dictionary of Oregon History* (Portland, Ore., 1956), p. 179.

served until we crossed the Blue Mountains and were out of danger from Indians. The first tribe we passed was the Omaha. They are a beggarly set. The next came the Pawnee, they are the tallest, strongest and most savage, also the noblest looking of any of the tribes I have seen. While we were camped at Shell Creek several of them came and stayed with us. They were nearly starved, their hunting excursion the fall previous having not proved successful and most of the warriors – some 300 – had gone into the disputed to hunt (between them and the Sioux). The day previous to our arrival at Shell Creek the Pawnees had taken two cows from a company, exacting them to pay for passing through their country and their captain being afraid, dared not refuse. They wanted some cattle of us but did not get any. Smith [7] came up and camped with us and Joe Williams' [8] company from Ill. Also, several other companies who all united in constructing a bridge over the creek. The next day, the 13th of May, about noon companies commenced crossing. Some 80 wagons all in a heap. The bridge was constructed of brush and logs on the top. We soon swam the cattle and crossed a little before sun down, went through a sea of water on to an island and camped without wood. In the morn the wind arose and blew the carriage over with Helen and myself in it, Mr. Williams

[7] Hiram Smith had already crossed to Oregon in 1846 and had returned east. Now he was taking with him a large herd of cattle and horses and some high quality Merino sheep. He became a farmer, merchant, and saw mill owner in Lane County. In 1851, he was accompanied by his wife of three years, Mary (Fleming). *Dictionary of Oregon History,* p. 227.

[8] Joseph Williams of Springfield, Illinois, with his six sons, traveled to Oregon in 1851. The Oregon City *Spectator* newspaper reported on Thursday, July 3, 1851, a story in the Springfield *Journal* that listed him among several who "Left this spring for Oregon." There was no mention of a wife.

standing upon the wheel to keep it down. However, they got us out without serious injury to us, but the carriage top was broken short off for the wheel stood uppermost for two hours. I never saw it blow harder. Mr. Lockart's wagon started towards the river and 3 men could not stop it until they succeeded in running the tongue into the ground. Mrs. Olney's bonnet, a leghorn,[9] was blown off, the boiler of my stove, tin pans, hats, pillows, buckets etc. Nothing recovered but the pillows belonging to Mr. L. and the cap. All our cattle gone but we succeeded in finding all but one cow that was given to Mr. Williams by the owner of the ferry on the Missouri.

On the 28th we came up with Kinney. He had found one-third of his stock. While here we had buffalo meat. We did not like it very well. It is much coarser than beef. We saw herds of them. The antelope and this country abounds with them and is most excellent. Also mountain rabbit. Passed several prairie dog villages. W. and myself went among them but they ran, barking to their houses, which are holes in the ground. They are as large as a half-grown kitten.

[May] 31st. Camped near the Lone Cedar Tree. Received visits from seven Sioux Indians. Prepared supper for them.

1st of June. Passed the Sioux village. Their wigwams are made of buffalo skins (the Pawnees were mud.) They seemed to be a much wealthier tribe than any that we have yet seen. The squaws were dressed in antelope skins, ornamented with beads. The men were

---

[9] Mrs. Olney's bonnet, a leghorn, would have been a plaited wheat straw broad-brimmed hat. The wheat was cut green and dried as was the practice in Italy.

also clothed with skins or blankets. They owned a great many ponies. On one of the wigwams were several scalps hung out to dry, taken from the Pawnees. They were friendly. I saw some beautiful bluffs apparently not more than one-half mile off and wished to visit them. W. consented to go with me but said that it was farther than I anticipated. We walked four miles, I should judge, crossing chasms and bluffs before we reached the road and after all did not ascend the one that we set out for. Camped by the Platte. No wood but buffalo chips, which we have used for a long time.

4th. Passed Chimney Rock and camped under Scott Bluffs near two wigwams. They came over to eat with us. I helped to get supper for two Indians. We gave them a knife and fork. They took the knife but refused the forks. They were well dressed in blankets, which a hood to come over the head. They were very careful to take all from their plates and tie up in a corner of their blankets. They belonged to the Cheyennes.

On the 7th we arrived at Ft. Laramie and on the 8th commenced crossing the Black Hills. Some of them were steep. Laramie Peak to the left covered with snow.

9th   crossed the Red Hills and camped by a lake.

17th   traveled over twenty miles and camped by the Devil's Hole, or Gate. In the morning two young ladies and myself visited it. The rocks on each side were perpendicular, 400 ft. high and the narrowest place was about 2 ft., where Sweet Water came tumbling through. The road leading to it was crooked and thorny, but we found all kinds of beautiful flowers blooming beside the rocks. It was the most sublime spectacle that I ever witnessed. I must not forget Independence Rock which we passed yesterday. I did not ascend it but read several names of friends. We are in the Sweet Water Mountains which are plentifully besprinkled with snow. The wind which comes is very cold — a shawl is not uncomfortable any of the time, excepting when the air is still. Then it is uncomfortably warm. Gathered several lbs. of Salerates, very nice, from a lake that dried up. We have to take particular care that our cattle do not drink at any of these alkali springs and lakes. Carcasses of cattle are plenty along here. Crossed Sweet Water seven times and passed the Wind Mountains where it blew a perfect hurricane all of the time.

19th. Can see the Rocky Mountains, a distance of some 60 miles. The tops were covered with snow and from here they looked like fleecy clouds. Camped near two snow banks in a beautiful valley.

22nd. [Sunday] Pased between the Twin Mounds and over the South Pass of the Rocky Mountains. We could hardly tell when we were on the summit, the ascent had been so gradual, although we were nearly 8,000 ft. above the level of the sea, but a little to our right are ranges that are covered with snow and nights and mornings we almost suffered with cold. Camped at the Pacific Springs.

25th. After laying by a day on Big Sandy, started on to the desert. At about two o'clock p.m. found it a barren sandy plain. No vegetation except stunted sage. Drove all night. Towards morning found it more hilly until we came down to Green River, which was high and rapid. Paid $10.00 per team for passage.

Then we found several white families living in wigwams. They were Mormons and soon going to Salt
Lake. Also, some white men having Squaws for wives.
Snake Indians, the most of their tribe with Mourner
their Chief, had removed to Bear River a few days
previous.

July 1st. [Tuesday] Crossed Bear River through an
Indian village and were guided by them across the
water. Passed some traders, paid them toll for crossing a bridge over a slough and Thomas Fork. Camped
on the Platte. Last night we were awakened by sere-
naders. Five horsemen circled around the carriage,
singing Araby's Daughter. It was a beautiful night.
We were surrounded by bluffs in a little valley and
on being awakened by their song, seeing the panting
steeds and looking around upon the wild country it
seemd as though we were transplanted into Arabia.
They were beautiful singers from Oregon. Said they
were exiles from home. Mr. Williams arose. They
sing Sweet Home and several others. Invited us to
stay and celebrate the 4th. Said they would make us
a barbecue, but we were anxious to get on and the
affliction that we had just suffered unfitted us for
such a scene. Jo Williams and company remained.

5th   Came to the Soda Springs about noon. The water
oozed from between the rocks, the surface of which
was red as blood. The water was warm. A little farther on we came to the Cold Spring, which was in
the bank of Bear River. There were two close together,
one in a rock. The water boiled up as it would have
done in a cauldron kettle and was very cold. When
sweetened it tasted like small beer. I was fond of it.
Took a canteen and started on but the gas escaped

soon and was not good. There were two white families at this place. A mile farther we came to the Steamboat Spring where the water rises about 2 ft. foaming from the middle of the rock. The water was soda and warm. The rock was also warm for several ft. around the basin. The noise resembled the puffing of a steamboat. Plenty of Snake Indians begging for bread or skirts or any kind of clothing. We could get a pair of moccasins for a bit of bread. At night we camped beyond a pool of soda water which is said not to be good at this place. There were two traders living with squaw wives. I took Helen and called upon them. They were going to Ft. Hall with a band of ponies to sell.

6th [Sunday] Lockhart and Rexford,[10] the Baptist preacher remained in Camp to recruit their cattle. The rest of us moved on to a creek. Plenty of willows for fuel and fish. We bought some salmon trout of an Indian for a couple of pancakes.

8th. Traveld twenty miles, most of the way sandy. Camped on a branch of Snake. Two Indians came to camp. Mr. W bade them stay all night as they looked rather suspicious. About midnight one of them arose cautiously and crept in the direction of one of our horses. On seeing the guard was watching him he laid down again. This time he tried again but with no better success.

9th. Arrived at Ft. Hall, a desolate place and filled with thieves. We saw one man (emigrant) that had lost nine horses. He offered $100 reward. The Indians

---

10 The Rev. John Rexford was a Canadian born Baptist minister, who traveled from Illinois to Oregon in 1851. He helped to organize several churches in Oregon before returning to the Middle West, where he spent his later life. Matoon, *Baptist Annals*, I, p. 16.

brought four back. He then offered as much more. The Indians then started again. In all probability they were the ones that took them. The white men (traders) are worse than the Indians. We heard of a great many emigrants who had lost horses and one company who had lost twenty-four head of cattle near this place.

10th.   Heard that Lockhard and Rexford wanted us to wait for them. Accordingly laid by near a pond where was excellent grass. At night they came up, minus two horses. One they recovered belonging to a hand. The other belonged to Mr. R. which he did not recover, making the second that he had lost. The first was taken from him while in Canesville.

11th.   On starting found that two head of stock were staggering from the effects of alkali which they had eaten with grass. The ground in some places was white with it under the grass. Mr. W. fed one fat pork and lard and left it with a couple of men. The other cow soon fell. He gave them alcohol and left it. At night the ox was driven in but the cow was dead. The last one that gave milk.

14th. [Monday]   Drove twenty-two M. Camped on Spring Run. An Indian half breed[11] camped within a few rods of [us] with several horses, going to Oregon. On one side of us was quite a patch of rushes, six ft. high. At night there seemed to be considerable fuss in the rushes. A duck was scared up, the mules were frightened and ran the length of their lariat. From

---

[11] Esther Lockhart remembered in *Destination West* (p. 71) that this was a group of 35 or 30 friendly Indians under the leadership of Dick, "an intelligent half-breed." They were of some unnamed Missouri River tribe returning home from California.

the rushes our guard kept up a vigilant watch. In the morning one of Indian Dick's horses was gone. His squaw and papoose started on with us, but he went in pursuit of his horse.

16th. Dick, the Indian came up. He had recovered his horse. Said he traced his horse behind the bluffs where he saw his with three more American horses and three Indians. One of the Snakes shot an arrow at him which he dodged. He then shot another which he also dodged. It was then Dick's turn, who fired his rifle loaded with three balls. One of the Indians dropped. The others ran. He seized his horse and another one and started back, but an Indian shot the other horse. He belongs to the Nez Perces and hates the Snakes as bad as a white man does.

17th. Last night at twilight we had quite a fright. Dick camped by us again. Williams was at his fire when he discovered four Indians creeping along the brow of the hill. Dick caught his rifle and ran crouching about two hundred yards and fired. One of the Indians hallowed in a manner that I never shall forget and they all ran. Our folks ran back to camp for weapons. Those that had no rifles armed themselves with axes, clubs or anything that they could get hold of. We did not know but there was a body of them at hand thought best to be prepared for the worst. We were unfortunately camped near a thick body of willows on the other side of which was a small creek whose banks were rather steep. Mr. W. told myself and children to get into a wagon and lay down in the bed. I was preparing to do so when Mrs. Rexford sent for me to come and stay with her. We did so and sat watching the willows for a long time. Sev-

eral times we thought we heard splashing and saw
an Indian peeping out of the willows, but alas! sadly
to the disappointment of some who wished to have a
round with them, we were not disturbed again.

18th.   Traveled about fifteen M. over a sandy bottom
and camped on Snake. Descent to water 100 ft. On the
opposite bank was a boiling spring. Powell's [12] company camped at the same place. They had a horse
stolen last night. Fired at an Indian without effect.

[July] 28.   Came to the Hot Springs. There was a
little stream or drain running across the road about
one-half mile from the spring. It was such a beautiful
water that several of our comany alighted to drink
but on a near approach they were satisfied with jerking their hands away. Some complained of burning
their lips and those that were at first deceived tried
in their turn to deceive others. Camped near. Visited
the springs. There we found the water hot enough for
cooking. The ground a few feet from the spring was
covered with saleratus and those of the company who
were short of the same replenished their storage.

31.   Camped on the Snake, Indians came with salmon
to sell. I let them have Helen's apron with a needle
and thread and bought salmon enough for several

---

[12] There was a whole host of Powells with the 1851 company to Oregon.
The leader was the Rev. John A. Powell, and there were several of the
sons and daughters of this man and his wife, Savilla, who accompanied
them west with their families. They became quite instrumental in the growth
of the Disciples of Christ (Christian Church) in their new homeland. They
were also important in the establishment of the "Christian College" in
Monmouth, Oregon. This later became Oregon Normal School, then Oregon
College of Education, and now Western Oregon State College. Their story
is told in great detail in a book about the family, *Powell History* (1922) by
James Madison Powell.

meals. I wish you could eat with us. Certainly never tasted any fowl or fish half so delicious.

Aug. 1st. [Friday]   Last night J. Williams came up and camped on one side. On the other a very large Hoosier company. The night before the Hoosier company camped on Rock River (the banks of which are very steep and high.) Some five or six Indians came into camp in the morning to sell salmon. While they were trading one of the Indians jumped on to a valuable horse and made toward the bluffs. The Indian then showed fight and some twenty or more came up the river bank and dared them to fight. Williams had a man from Ill. that had [been] shot the week before in the same place where we came so near to fight. This young man was on the last guard standing before the fire. An Indian shot him through the body and he fell and rose three times. Cried "O God! I am shot." Think of leaving him at Ft. Boise.

2.   Reached Fort Boise. Quite a pretty place situated on the other side of the Snake. Did not visit it.

5.   W's company came up. That young man considered to be dying. He had hopes of getting well, poor fellow! I did not go to see him.

6.   Camped on Burnt River. W's company came up. The young man is dead and burried. He had one brother with him.

7.   Left a cow that gave out. Traveled about twenty-five miles. Country improving.

8.   Came to Powder River. The sand and mud were full of shining particles which some took to be gold. There were some so eager to wash gold that they could

not eat. It is called the Grand Rond. It resembled an enchanted valley. As we wound around the hill before descending into it found plenty of Cayuse Indians.

10.   Moved at the foot of Blue Mountains. Paid an Indian three shirts for passing over a few miles of new road and avoiding a hill. Plenty of pine timber. Camped at the first creek. No food. A gentleman from Puget Sound, Oregon stayed with us. Going to meet his wife from whom he had been absent about three years. An Indian, also to whom I gave supper. He ate a plate of beans and one of bread, an apple dumpling, meat & c & c.

11.   Powell's daughter [13] was brought into camp dead. We passed them at noon and inquired for her. They thought she was a little better. She left a husband and two children, the youngest a few weeks old. She was confined on the road. Powell is a Baptist preacher.[14] In his company are twelve wagons and all connected save two. Bought potatoes and peas of Cayuse Indians (squaws.) This tribe dresses like white people.

13.   Parted into three companies on account of grass being scarce. Are out of danger from Indians now. Two Indians moved with us. One of them showed how he had killed a Snake Indian. His arrow was bloody. Told where he shot him and how he tore off the scalp. I could not help but shudder. We are alone.

14.   Camped on the Umatilla. Found traders. One old

---

[13] The Powell daughter who died was Theresa, the wife of William McFadden. She had given birth to a baby boy, John, on June 27, 1851. She died on August 10. The baby was cared for by the other Powell women, but he died not long after his mother. *Powell History,* pp. 37-38.

[14] John A. Powell was not a Baptist but a minister in the Disciples of Christ, or Christian Church.

gentleman married to a young squaw. She called at the carriage. I took Helen and visited her wigwam. Also several others. We found a Mr. Johnson [15] from Iowa, Presbyterian preacher. He had been staying by for a few days in order to recruit his cattle and in hopes to hear from his cattle that went of in a stampede with Kinny's.[16] He has a wife and several children Two young women grown appear well.

[August] 17. [Sunday] Camped on John Day River.

[August] 25. [Monday] Started on to the Cascade Mountains. Bad road. Camped on a muddy creek. No feed but plenty of browse, maple and alder.

26. Left an ox. Commenced raining. Cold – very cold. We arc ncar Mt. Hood whose top is covered with snow and above the clouds. Two other lofty peaks, one on each side of Mt. Hood are equally as white and apparently as tall. Towards night found a patch of bunch grass. Turned out but the cattle would not eat it. Yoke up again and started on. Arrived within a mile of the prairie. Several bad hills to descend. I took H. and walked, got mired. W. had gone ahead to find a camp. Word soon came from him to come back to the carriage. One of the wheels needed repairing. Could get no further. Unhitched the mule and oxen and left the wagons on the other side of the slough. Drove them to the prairie. It was raining and I could not see to return to the wagons, so kept on to where there were several companies camped. I was cold and wet. Helen was not well. I drew near the fire and seated

---

[15] The Rev. Neill Johnson was a minister in the Cumberland Presbyterian Church who became a resident of McMinnville, Oregon. *Dictionary of Oregon History*, p. 129.

[16] See foonote 3, above.

myself on the root of a tree. I looked around and discovered two families that had traveled with us a few days. Their names were Allen [17] and Sanders.[18] Mrs. Sanders was the old man's daughter. They shook hands with me and sat down to their supper, never inviting me. H. was crying for bread but I tried to quiet her. Soon a lady from another wagon came to me, gave me a seat before the fire and went to get me some supper. Mr. W came up at that time and thinking that I was going to fare hard, asked Mrs. Woodard [19] to give me some supper. Said he would pay them. They gave me a cup of tea and some bread and c. but my heart was full and I could not eat. The husband of this lady, a fine looking man came up and introduced himself as Mr. Chandler.[20] We had often heard of them en route. He is a Baptist preacher, formerly president of some college in Indiana and going to Oregon City to found some college or school. They are fine people. Mrs. Allen let us have a tent, cloth and pillow to make our bed in the rain, but Mrs. Chandler went to work and made us as comfortable as she could

---

17 Nathan W. Allen from Trimble County, Ohio, became a settler in Umpqua County, Oregon. *Genealogical Material in Oregon Donation Land Claims,* III (Portland, Ore., 1962), Claim #583, p. 39.

18 This was John Simpson Sanders, a Missourian who settled on a land claim on the border of Lane and Benton counties south of Corvallis. *Genealogical Material,* III, Claim #1605, p. 115.

19 Elizabeth Woodward was the wife of Luther L. Woodward. They settled in Linn County on Claim #2122. She and Luther had been married on August 16, 1849, in Vermillion, Indiana. *Genealogical Material,* I, p. 89. They were very active in Methodist work in Oregon. Read Bain, "Methodist Educational Effort in Oregon to 1860," *Ore. Historical Qtly.,* XXI, No. 2 (June, 1920), pp. 85-86.

20 This was the Rev. George C. Chandler who would also become a prominent Baptist educator in Oregon as the first President of McMinnville College, now Linfield College. Kenneth L. Holmes, ed., *Linfield's Hundred Years* (Portland, Ore., 1956), pp. 4-5.

under a tree. It rained all night and W. got up before day and made a fire close by the bed. Mrs. C. gave us some breakfast. The next day we were able to return their kindness in some measure. Their horses gave out and could not pull their carriage. He helped them up several hills, took Mrs. C and 2 children into our wagon. They are Vermontans. Allens are from the reserve.

[August] 27. [Wednesday] I cannot describe these mountains. They have been a scene of suffering. The snows set in next month and falls to the depth of 50 ft. The road is strewn with bones of cattle, horses, wagon yokes and in short a little of everything. Descended one hill where we had to tie trees behind our wagons. Crossed Laurel Hill, the worst hill of all. I never could give you a description of it, if I should write all night so will close my narrative soon.

Sept. 1. [Monday] Camped within a mile of a house. Bought some potatoes at $1.00 per bushel. Had several calls from white men.

Sept. 2. Came in sight of a house. H. clapped her hands, laughed and called me to see. It was a long log house with a stick chimney at one end and soon we saw another house painted white. She then changed her mind. Called that a house and the log house a steam boat. "Ma Ma we will go in and live in that house, and see there are chickens and pigs."

Sept. 3. Arrived at Milwaukie. Went into a house to live again. The first one that I had been in since we crossed the Missouri. H. nearly nearly wild with joy. Did not want to camp out again.

Sept. 27. [Saturday]   You will see from the date that
I have been a good while writing. I cannot tell you
much about the country as I have seen naught, but
this place is situated on the Willamette. Steamboats
and vessels from the salt water come here but cannot
go to Oregon City at all times. We are eight miles
below the city and six from Portland and has the best
harbor in the world. It is 18 months old, has three
taverns and three stores. Provisions are high. Butter
from .50¢ to 1.00, chickens $1.00, wheat $1.00 per
bushel, beef .18¢ per pound. Labor is high though
not as high as formerly. From $2.00 to $10.00. A girl
can get $1.00 per day. Most of the house girls, how-
ever, are men and boys. Girls are foolish that they
do not come to Oregon Territory to marry. There
is no end of bachelor establishments. Several in this
place who board themselves and others hire a cook.
Tell Mrs. Marian that I have a rich merchant picked
out for her. Jane Wilson too.

The soil is very productive. They raise three crops
from once sowing cabbage, three years from one stump.
I saw some stumps the other day that had five heads
on one stalk. Our stores have not come yet. Mr. Smith
is expected daily. It is a great place to make money.
Everything will count. I could have taken a school
this winter from $5.00 to $8.00 a quarter, but would
not.

Sold one set of harness for $50.00 that had been
used considerable. One wagon for $150.

EPILOGUE

Ordinarily it would be against our policy to publish reminiscences written long after the fact of any one of the overland journeys. However, such a reminiscence told by Esther M. Lockhart gives her version of exactly the same journey described by her friend, Lucia Loraine Williams, and in such a way as to add depth and understanding to the event. She tells page by page the same journey and person by person of individuals described in the Williams story. Due to these special circumstances, this time we are publishing a reminiscence recorded long after the fact. That is what the story, *Destination West!*, is all about.

Late in life, Esther Lockhart told her daughter, Agnes Ruth Lockhart Sengstacken, of the journey. Agnes' written version of the events described was published in 1942 by Binfords & Mort Publishers of Portland. Today it would be called an "oral history." The Lockhart story parallels much of what Mrs. Williams described in her letter. Many of the same persons are named, and another spotlight is thrown on them and on the events of the journey.

We have selected, with the permission of the publisher, certain passages of Esther Lockhart's reminiscences that relate to the 1851 crossing. Besides giving insight into certain practices and episodes not touched on by Lucia Williams, Esther Lockhart comments with added depth on events told of in the letter, especially the accidental death of little 10-year-old John Williams.

The selections below are taken from pages 35 to 67, inclusive.

It was Christmas Day, 1851, in Ohio. My little house was full to overflowing with relatives who had come from near and far to share the holiday festivities with us. Nobody knew when we would all be together again on another Christmas day, for Freeman and I, with our year-old daughter, were going far away. It was sometimes difficult for me to realize that we were about to make such a momentous move. But it was actually true. We had decided to go west, to cross the plains to Oregon Territory. It had all come about rather suddenly. Some of our neighbors who had gone to California following the gold rush of '49, had now returned for their families. . .

From the first my husband was eager to go. At that time he was twenty-seven years old, with an adventurous, somewhat rebellious spirit that often chafed under the restrictions placed upon the younger men by the stern, staid, old-fashioned settlers of his neighborhood and time. As my brother Isaac had said before he left New York state for Ohio, Freeman declared that there were fine opportunities for strong, willing young men in that great western country. He said he was weary of slaving through the hot summer to save money that must be spent during the long, cold winter that followed. Besides, this would take him away from farming, which he despised. . .

Finally, after many vexatious delays, our arrangements were completed and we left our home on March 18th, 1851, bound for a destination more than two thousand miles away. "Fools rush in where angels fear to tread!" I had many a heartache for the dear home and friends we were leaving. Although we had not forgotten our New York days, I had grown to love my adopted state, and to me it was and ever will remain "Dear old Ohio."

My baby daughter was but fifteen months old, and I did not know how she would stand the long, hard journey. My unmarried sister, Laura, had chosen to cast her lot with ours. So I was not entirely alone. At Council Bluffs we were to join a large emigrant company, bound for Oregon Territory. . .

When we were within a mile or so of Council Bluffs, we noticed a man walking briskly toward us. As we reached him, he halted, addressing us by name and saying that we were expected. He then climbed into our wagon and introduced himself as Hiram Smith, our captain.

He gave us all the news concerning his company, told of his arrangements for the trip and his desire to be off soon. He made my heart glad by telling me that his niece, Harriet Buckingham, my old friend and schoolmate at Miss Flanders' Academy, was to make the long journey with us. Her spirit longed for adventure, too, it appeared. This was to be Mr. Smith's third trip across the plains. Years later Miss Buckingham became Mrs. Samuel A. Clarke, of Salem, Oregon. Mr. Clarke was famous as a writer and historian. We found Council Bluffs a tented city, literally, and not a very large one at that. Not a house of any description was to be seen. About a hundred tents and nearly as many covered wagons gave the place a picturesque, if primitive, appearance. Here we remained for a week, waiting for a few belated fellow-travelers, adding to our supplies and trying to get everything in perfect condition before starting into the wilderness. While we waited at Council Bluffs for our captain to conclude his arrangements, I spent some enjoyable time observing the different characters and personalities that came under my immediate notice. The entire scene might have been well described as kaleidoscopic. It was all new and strange, and it thrilled me with its novelty and picturesqueness. A certain glamor of romance hung about this party of Argonauts, going forth valiantly into untried and unkown lands so far away.

They knew not, neither did they seem to care, what adventures awaited them there, but they looked forward with eager anticipation to whatever might befall. It seemed as though all sorts and conditions of people had gathered in that little crude border settlement, all animated by the same purpose, "Destination, West." It was a motley assemblage, indeed. I never tired of watching it, studying it, wondering about it. It fascinated me. Despite the diversity in tastes, temperaments, education and character, there was no friction among the crowd. Everybody was good-natured, though some of the women I met were sad and lonely, grieving for the home and friends they had left and fearful of the uncertain future that lay before them.

As a rule, however, all were satisfied and eager to get started westward. Some, like ourselves, were going because of the opportunities offered them for acquiring wealth and honors. Others, who had suffered from ill health for years, and to whom life had become a burden, expected to regain health, if not on the journey itself, surely after reaching the far west, with its reputed mild and healthful climate. Still others had wearied of the hot, disagreeable summers and the frigid winters and longed for more congenial climes where existence might be a little more comfortable with less exertion. Some were actuated merely by the spirit of adventure. Life was too prosy and tame in their old environments. They wanted more action, more diversity, more thrilling experiences with man and beast.

I especially enjoyed the evenings, for it was then that the actual spirit of the company seemed manifested. Campfires burned cheerily in the darkness, groups of congenial people sat aroung the blaze, the men "swapping yarns," the women usually quiet and serious, sometimes knitting industriously in the half light, the children hiding and playing in the gloom before their early bedtime. The sound of many "fiddles," banjos, flutes and jewsharps made music on the air. Occasionally the gay laughter of some happy young people would ring out between the pauses in the music and the story-telling and remind us that youth was ever carefree and light-hearted. The sun beat down fiercely at Council Bluffs almost every day while we were there, though we had frequent heavy showers of rain.

Our "slatted sunbonnets" were comfort and a protection as well. Most persons today probably do not know what a "slatted" sunbonnet is, for they are among the things of the past now. For the long, hot, dusty trip across the plains, with its variable weather, the women were advised to wear sunbonnets. Many of them wore sunbonnets at home, especially in the rural neighborhoods. The sunbonnet kept the head from direct exposure to the heat and dust, protected the face and neck from tan, sunburn and freckles. They were a boon to women with delicate skin, like my own. These head coverings were by no means beautiful in those days. They were usually made of gingham or seersucker or other serviceable materials in some inconspicuous shade of brown or gray, though many were made of black. Rarely did we see any bright colors, even on rosy-cheeked young girls. Flaming colors would not have been considered modest then. These sunbonnets came well over the face, the entire front portion being made of a double thickness of cloth which was stitched tightly in strips an inch or less in width and as long as the front part of the bonnet itself. This was ordinarily about eight or ten inches. In these small stitched compartments, always of uniform width, thin strips of light wood were inserted. This made the entire front very pliable, so that it might be folded up between every strip. Naturally, these strips or "slats," were removed when the bonnet was laundered, which was not very often. A cape of the material used for the bonnet extended around the lower portion, thus protecting the neck and the upper part of the back. These old-fashioned sunbonnets may not have been beautiful, but they were a godsend to women on that long journey. . .

We now traveled for hundreds of miles close beside the North Platte River, over wide, treeless and grassy plains where our cattle kept in fine condition. In many respects the North Platte River is an interesting stream. It waters, or drains, a large territory, but it is shallow and full of dangerous quicksands. In many places it is nearly a mile wide, and only a few inches deep, so shallow that it will not even float a canoe. It looked very beautiful when we first saw it, where it joins the broad Missouri, with here and there a small green island and the great plains stretching away on either side as far as the eye could reach.

As we approached nearer its source it seemed as though we might venture to walk upon it, so thickly was its surface incrusted with sand. But woe to the unfortunate creature that was tempted to set foot upon it! The treacherous quicksands would quickly clutch him in their powerful grasp, and without immediate and very material assistance, he could not hope to escape that deadly foe.

One night, while we were still following the devious course of the North Platte, we camped on a grassy rise of ground with the silvery river flowing serenely along just below us. We slept soundly until nearly morning. Then we were suddenly awakened by a furious storm of wind and rain. Looking out, we discovered to our alarm, that we were on an island, with madly-rushing waters swirling all around us. Immediately, all was confusion in the camp. Women and children were screaming, dogs barking and whining, horses whinneying in fright, cattle bellowing and men shouting orders. It was evident that we were experiencing one of the tornadoes for which that region has since become famous.

Everything that was not securely fastened down blew into the water. All the tents were thrown to the ground. Our blankets, pillows, mattresses, tubs, buckets and tin pans floated away and were rescued with difficulty. Several serious accidents were narrowly averted. The carriage in which Mrs. Williams and her three children rode was overturned and its occupants slightly injured. My sister, my baby and I were in our wagon. Suddenly it was caught by a fierce blast and whirled rapidly down the incline. Just as it was about to plunge into the eddying waters, it was caught and held by several strong men. Later, an old lady who was badly frightened came over to our wagon and asked permission to ride with us for awile. She said, "It looks like

you gals never git scairt. You jest set thar with your
sewin' or your knittin' just as though nothin' had
happened." Of course we could not refuse her simple
request to ride with us for the remainder of the day.
Gradually, the high waters receded. The wind calmed
down and the sun shone out warm and bright and we
partially dried our wet clothing and bedding. Horsemen rode through the water to ascertain its depth.
Although it reached the hubs of our wagon wheels,
we resumed our journey about two o'clock that afternoon. We could not afford to linger longer than was
absolutely necessary. . .

In the company I recall five families that associated
together intimately and thoroughly enjoyed each others' companionship. These families were Judge Olney's
– Mrs. Olney had been a friend of my old Norwalk
principal, Miss Flanders – Hiram Smith's, E. N.
Cooke's, Elijah Williams's and our own. Though for
many, many years our paths have been widely sundered, as long as memory lasts, I shall look back
with keen pleasure to the months we spent together
in that wild and practically unknown wilderness. And
it was truly a wilderness. We were linked together
not only in ties of comradeship and congeniality, but
also by the common danger that surrounded us all.

In our company was a certain Methodist minister,
a Mr. Allen, brother of the young clergyman who had
been obliged to leave us at Weston because of health.
All along there had been considerable discussion, for
and against, about traveling on Sundays. No decision
regarding this matter had yet been reached. Originally,
the general desire and intention had been to travel seven
days a week, if possible, and thus shorten the time con-

sumed in making the long journey. From the first, Mr. Allen had strenuously objected to the Sunday travel. Finally, the question of resting on the Sabbath was submitted to the entire company. By a large majority vote, it was decided to make no stops except those necessary for repairs, accidents or other unforseen circumstances. As a result of this decision, Mr. Allen, with his wife and children and several other families of the same opinion as himself, withdrew from our company and we saw them no more during the journey. However, it is interesting to know that Allen's party, though resting every Sunday, reached Oregon Territory two weeks earlier than we did, with all their cattle in fine condition, while ours were either starving or dead. . .

We crossed successively the Little and Big Sandy Rivers, and when we were about twelve hundred miles from Council Bluffs, the families of Hiram Smith and E. N. Cooke left us for Salt Lake City. Mr. Smith took with him four big wagon loads of merchandise to sell to the Mormons. He had already shipped forty thousand dollars' worth of goods around the Horn, bound for the same destination. It would be well-nigh impossible for me to express how deeply we regretted losing these two families and how we missed them continually. Separation from them was really a personal grief, as we had become greatly attached during the long months of our association. Much later, these two families came on to Oregon, where they lived for years, being considered among the most highly respected people in the state. Upon Mr. Smith's departure from our company, Elijah Williams was elected captain, and a very excellent leader he made, too.

In respect to evil happenings, our company was singularly fortunate. Only one tragedy threw its dark shadows over us during the whole trip and that was caused by an accident in our own ranks. Elijah Williams, our newly-elected captain, had with him his wife, three young sons and a little daughter. He had brought his carriage along for the family, and ordinarily they all rode in this vehicle. On this particular day, however, Johnny, a bright lad of ten years, had asked and obtained permission to ride in the baggage wagon with the driver. This was considered quite an adventure by the boys, something not quite as prosy as riding day after day in the more comfortable carriage. Just exactly how the dreadful accident occurred, we never knew definitely. The supposition was that the driver fell asleep, the day being very warm, and that the oxen, finding themselves unguided, took fright and ran away, throwing little Johnny out of the wagon. We were traveling just ahead of Mr. Williams' wagon that day, and as the team ran wildly past us, the driver, his face white with terror, cried out, "I'm afraid Johnny's killed!"

The entire train was immediately stopped. We were the first to reach poor little Johnny, and we saw at once that he was beyond earthly aid. The heavy wagon wheels had passed directly over his forehead and face, and death must have been instantaneous. The innocent victim never knew what had happened to him and when Mr. Williams, who was an extraordinarily devoted father saw the lifeless form of his child he was beside himself with grief and anger. He ran for his gun and was about to shoot the unfortunate driver when four men overpowered him and took his weapon away. Later, when reason and calm judgment returned to the distraught father, he was thankful he had been restrained from committing a heinous crime.

The driver was broken-hearted over the tragedy. He did not recover from the effects of this deplorable accident during the remainder of the journey. A rude casket was improvised from a large trunk belonging to Mrs. Williams, and the body of the dear little lad who had been a merry companion a few hours before, and loved by everybody, was tenderly buried near the scene of the accident. After some hymns had been sung and a few prayers said, a wooden marker was placed at the head of the grave. The parents wished this to be done, as they felt that we were now in a neighborhood where the Indians would not disturb such places. On the headstone was written the little lad's name, his age and the brief circumstances attending his death. Then, with many regretful tears for the promising young life so suddenly and cruelly cut short, we drove sadly away, leaving him alone in the wilderness, in his last long sleep. For many days we could not forget this agonizing experience. It hung over us like a black shadow. It took all the joy out of our lives, it had been so sudden, so unnecessary, so full of all that was sad and tragic.

Journal of a Trip to Oregon
⸮ Elizabeth Wood

INTRODUCTION

Elizabeth Wood is a person to whom we draw tantalizingly close without really reaching her. She traveled west as a single woman at age 23,[1] a most unusual occurrence.

So far all we know of her early life comes from the 1850 Federal Census of Illinois (Tazewell County):

Elias Wood	27	m	farmer	b.	Ohio
Nancy	25	f			"
Emily	24	f			"
Elizabeth	22	f			"

Now, there are two possible ways to interpret this data: One would be that Elias and Nancy Wood were husband and wife, and that the other two women were Elias' sisters living with them. The other would be that the four persons were a brother and three sisters. The second interpretation seems to have more logic to it, but history is often disdainful of logic.

The source of our Elizabeth Wood diary is the *Quarterly of the Oregon Historical Society* for March, 1926. It had been submitted by a young scholar named David Duniway, who had been perusing the old files of Illinois newspapers. He had located the diary in the *Peoria Weekly Republican* of January 30 and February 13, 1852. David Duniway later became the highly respected Archivist of the State of Oregon. The published part of Elizabeth Wood's "Jour-

---

[1] The age is estimated from the herein published 1850 Federal Census figures.

nal" covers the trip from west of Fort Laramie to somewhere in the country of the Walla Walla Indians in eastern
Oregon, June 29 to September 15, 1851. So our record is
truncated at the beginning and at the end.

The first mention of Elizabeth in Oregon is in marriage
records in the Marion County Courthouse in Salem:

> MORSE – WOOD   Rev. W. B. Morse & Elizabeth Wood,
> m 23 June 1853 in the city of Salem; Thomas H. Pearne, M.G.
> [Minister of the Gospel]

William B. Morse was a Methodist clergyman who had
been assigned to the Puget Sound Mission of the Methodist Church the previous March, immediately after the
formation of the northern part of the vast Oregon Territory into Washington Territory. He was serving the tiny
seedling churches at Whidby Island and Port Townsend.

Kate Blaine, wife of a ministerial cohort of the Morses,
remembered the following:[2]

> Middle of March, 1854, Rev. Wm. B. Morse came to Seattle
> during the winter of 1853-4 and during his residence here, con-
> tinued to supply the work of Whidby Island. Mrs. Morse gave
> birth to a baby about the middle of March 1854. Rev. Morse
> also did what he could at Port Townsend and Port Gamble.

A year later in a letter written on March 2, 1855, Kate
Blaine reported the addition of a second child to the William Morse family:[3]

> I have suceeded admirably, not only doing all my housework,
> washing and all, but I have managed to keep my sewing done
> up, and in addition to all this, I am helping take care of a
> sick neighbor. Sister Morse, the wife of the minister who for-
> merly lived on Whidby Island, but is now here studying with
> Mr. Blaine, was confined last week. I was present at the party

---

[2] Richard A. Seiber, *Memoirs of Puget Sound* (Fairfield, Wash., 1978) 9.
Permission to use quotes granted by Pacific Northwest Conference of United
Methodist Church, Rev. Richard A. Seiber, Archivist.
[3] *Ibid.,* 133.

which consisted of a woman experienced in such matters, and myself. No doctor, I tell you I was thankful for what knowledge I had acquired of such matters by reading and otherwise. She got along very well. I stayed with her the first night; since her husband has taken care of her and the child night and day, with what assistance I can render. I have washed and ironed and baked some for them and wash the baby. I closed school for two or three days on her account, which, together with the time I lost while at Steilacoom, puts me back nearly two weeks in my school.

According to the conference minutes of the Methodist Church, the Morses were stationed at "Whitbys Island and the Skagit Mission" in 1855.[4] They were stationed at Seattle from 1856 through 1858.[5]

We learn that they had moved to California by 1860, when they were stationed at Petaluma according to the Methodist paper, *The Pacific Christian Advocate,* in its issue of October 6, 1860.[6]

Over many years later the Morses served Methodist churches in northern California. There is a fascinating letter in the Oregon State Archives in Salem dated many years later regarding their experience:

Cloverdale, Cal. May 8th 1901
Recorder of Marion County Oregon   Salem, Oregon
Dear Sir: — At the request of Rev. W. B. Morse I write you in regard to the recording of the enclosed marriage certificate. The original certificate was lost and Rev. Morse tells me that the record of the marriage was destroyed by fire many years ago. Within the past year he has secured a new certificate from the minister who performed the marriage ceremony which he wishes to put on record. Rev. Morse [is] an old war veteran, and he wants the document recorded believing it will facilitate

---

[4] *Minutes of the Oregon Annual Conference of the Methodist Episcopal Church for the Year 1855* (Salem, Oreg.) 25.

[5] *Minutes of the Fourth Session of the Oregon Annual Conference of the Methodist Episcopal Church at Portland, O.T., Convened September 1856* (Salem, 1856) 7. Same title for 1857, p. 3.

[6] Volume VI, No. 39, p. 1, col. 2.

matters in getting a pension for his widow when he is gone.
Please put it on record and then return to me with your bill
of cost and I will immmediately forward you the money.

> Very truly yours
> I. B. Lewis Notary public in and for
> the Co of Sonoma, State of California

Recorded Aug. 16, 1911   U. S. Boyer, County Clerk.[7]

The final word on Elizabeth Morse is to be found in the
San Diego *Union* newspaper for July 14, 1913, under the
headline: DEATHS

> MORSE — In this city July 12, 1913, Elizabeth Morse,
> grandmother of Miss J. M. McCabbe of this city; a
> native of Illinois, aged 85 years.

The remains were to be embalmed and "forwarded to
Sacramento for funeral services and interment." [8]

THE JOURNAL OF ELIZABETH WOOD

We have received for publication, a long correspond-
ence, or rather a journal, of a trip to Oregon, kept by
Miss Elizabeth Wood, of Tazewell County, who went
out with the emigration last season. It is very lengthy,
though perhaps one of the most faithful graphic accounts of the adventures "by flood and field" to that
far-off country of any that has been sent us for publication. Accounts of "Trips to Oregon" have been so
often published that they are now getting to be an old
story and do not possess the interest which they did
but a short time since when emigration first commenced

---

[7] Jean Custer and Daraleen Wade, eds., *Marion County Marriage Records*
(Salem, 1979) 35.

[8] This quote was sent by Rhoda E. Kruse, Senior Librarian, California
Room, San Diego Public Library.

to that region; and the following is inserted more for the reason that it is the communication of a young lady, while most of the contributors of this nature have been furnished by the other sex. We omit all that portion of it relating to the journey from the States to Fort Laramie, where we commence the journal and coninue it over the mountains (Peoria, Illinois, *Weekly Republican,* January 30, 1852.).

June 29. – This morning we start with a company of 25 wagons, and commence the ascent of the Rocky Mountains; we go up some very high hills, called the Black Hills, which are very handsome to look at, as they have shelves of rock around them, between which are cedar bushes growing, which adding to the beauty of their appearance and looking as if they were fashioned by the hand of art. The water is so bad here, and the milk from our cows so strongly impregnated with alkali, that I have substituted coffee as a beverage. The ground is white with alkali, and the cows get it by feeding in the grass. This substance made some of our company sick before they knew what was the matter.

July 4. – We have been traveling among the hills and the monotony has been relieved by the ever varying beauty of the scenery and the pleasantness of the weather. Today we traveled till noon, and then stopped to get a Fourth of July dinner and to celebrate our nation's birthday. While making the preparations, and reflecting at the same time of what the people of Morton and Peoria were doing, and contrasting my situation with what it was this day last year, a storm arose, blew over all the tents but two, capsized our stove with its delicious viands, set one wagon on fire, and for a while produced not a little confusion in the camp. No serious injury, however, was done. After the storm was over, we put up the stove, straightened up the tent and got as nice a dinner as we had upon the "Glorious Fourth" in Morton last year. We then took care of our game, consisting of 5 black-tailed deer, 1 antelope and 3 buffalo. Last of all we went to hear an oration delivered by Mr. S. Wardon.[1] For your amusement I will give a description of my dress for the occasion: A red calico frock, made for the purpose in the wagons; a pair of mockasins, made of black buffalo hide, ornamented with silk instead of beads, as I had none of the latter and a hat braided, of bull-rushes and trimmed with white, red and pink ribbon and white paper. I think I came pretty near looking like a squaw.

July 5. – We found a squaw, which we suppose had been up a tree,* perhaps alive, as it was lying at the foot of one, and had been, probably, placed there several months previously. She had $5. worth of beads about her.

July 6. – Every week we find different soils, different weeds and different grass. Here the grass is parched up with the sun, and looks as if nothing could live upon it; but it almost as good for the cattle as oats. We find wild pepper, camomile, and a great many things I didn't expect to see. We are now a hundred miles from the fort [Laramie], and we find three cabins with white folks living in them. It seems strange

---

[1] S. Warden (or was it "Worden?") is so far unidentified.

* It is a custom of Indians to deposit their dead in a tree. (Ed.)

to meet any person living here, away from civilization, among the Indians, wild beasts, and the Sand Hills, where nothing can grow for man's sustenance.

July 7. – We have got where the horny toads are, and they are very poisonous.[2] They resemble the toad, except that they have a tail as long as one's finger and horns upon each side as thick as saw teeth.

July 25. – Since last date we camped at the ford where emigrants cross from the south to the north side of the Platte. On the south side there are a great many graves, as if whole families had been swept off at once, and the wreck of every description of property taken out by the emigrants. We stopped near the Red Buttes, where the hills are of a red color, nearly square, and have the appearance of houses with flat roofs. We have left the Platte, which we followed for 500 miles; traveled over the Sand Hills, where the wind blew the pebbles against my face almost hard enough to fetch the blood; camped by a spring almost cold enough to freeze your face and hands if you washed in it; passed over the sage plains; came to the Sweet Water River, and it did look sweet, too, after traversing a country of nothing but sage, without a spire of grass or a drop of water. We also passed Independence Rock and the Devil's Gate, which is high enough to make one's head swim, and the posts reach an altitude of some 4 or 500 feet. We found dead oxen, of which our company lost several, and any amount of wagon wheels, strewed all along the road. One of the strangest sights to me, in the month of July, was the snowy mountains,

---

[2] We, as children, called the horned toads "horny toads" in Southern California. It is not a toad but a lizard, and is not poisonous.

covered with their everlasting snows. On Saturday, July 19, we reached the top of the mountains, and found the roads as level as the streets of Peoria. Passed the Pacific Springs, and commenced the descent, which was here so gradual as barely to be perceptible. Came to bad roads after a while and found worse hills going down the Rocky Mountains than when ascending. We had hills to climb so steep we could hardly get up, and so sidelong that we have to tie a rope to the underside of the wagon, let it extend over the top, and then walk on the hill above and hold on to the rope. When we gain this summit, we then have to go down one a great deal steeper; everything that is not tied in the wagon falls out, and it would be amusing for a disinterested person to stand at the top with a spy glass and witness the descent of a train down one of these terrible looking hills. You would see the women and children in advance seeking the best way, some of them slipping down, or holding on to rocks, now taking an "otter slide," and then a run till some natural obstacle presents itself to stop their accelerated progress, and those who get down safely, without a hurt or a bruise, are fortunate indeed. Looking back to the train, you would see some of the men holding on to the wagons, others slipping under the oxen's feet, some throwing articles out of the way that had fallen out, and all have enough to do to keep them busily occupied. Often the teams get going so fast down hill it is difficult to stop them to double lock, and when, at a still steeper place, there is no stopping them at all, the driver jumps on the near wheel ox and the whole concern goes down with a perfect rush until a more level place is reached. So you see we have some "hair breadth" escapes, and a jolly time of it if we could only think so.

July 29. – The road goes between high hills and rocks, and we have to drive over rocks so large it seems as if the wagons would break, and they would if they were not good ones. If we were the first that ever went along here, I should think we had come to the end of the road, for we can see but a short distance before us, and it seems as if the high mountains ahead had to be climbed but could not.

August 2. – Cold weather; the leaves on the trees are killed with frost.

(To be continued)

[From the issue of February 13, 1852.]

JOURNAL OF A TRIP TO OREGON

The long financial report which we published in our last crowded out the continuation of Miss Wood's "Journal of a Trip to Oregon," commenced the week before. We continue its publication this week, and will give the conclusion in our next.

Oregon, August 3. – Snakes and grasshoppers rule here; of the former I mean the Snake Indians instead of the genuine serpent – This morning, by way of variety, we were treated with an Oregon blow, the wind coming in such furious blasts that we had to hold the plates fast to the tables, and make our repast the best way we could. Though it is now August, "dog days" with you, yet here it is quite cold and "winter is coming." The weeds are as dry and brown as they are in Illinois quite late in the fall. – One of our company

is doubling his money on his goods. Cloth that can
be bought for 16 cts. in Peoria he sells for 75 cts. per
yard; coffee 50 cts. per lb., and tea that cost him five
bits a pound he readily sold for $2. As money-making
is the "order of the day," I engaged in some profitable
speculations in a small way, and realized quite a handsome profit comparatively to the cost of the articles
sold. For instance, I disposed of a worn and faded
dress to the Indians for $3.50, which was purchased
when new, in Peoria, at 10 cts per yard – other things
in the same proportions. – Here the roads were so bad,
as we went over the steep hills and clambered over
the rocks, I could hardly hold myself in the wagon.
Sometimes the dust is so great that the drivers cannot
see their teams at all though the sun is shining brightly,
and it is a great relief to the way-worn traveler to meet
with some mountain stream, meandering through a
valley, after traveling for miles over these rough and
dusty roads, through a country where every blade of
grass has been dried up, with the drouth that generally
prevails here at this time of year, except in the bottoms along the river banks, where we can yet get feed
for our cattle. – One day we only made seven miles
through a very deep sand. – On Wednesday, August
6th, we passed Fort Hall; met a company of Indians,
moving; they had their ponys packed with their goods
until one would suppose nothing else could be got on
them; but on the top of their "plunder" the little
papooses were tied, to keep them from falling off.
Some of the ponys were rode by the squaws, with a
papoose lashed to their backs, and in some cases one
or two at their sides, or if one, something else to keep
up the equilibrium. There were about 20 families of

these Indians, seeking for winter quarters. — One
morning at the break of day I was awakened by a
disturbance among the cattle, which had got frightened at the barking of a dog. They run against the
wagons, broke the wheels and tongue of ours, and
bawled and pitched around till they finally got loose
and run off in an estampede. For a while all was
confusion in the camp, and we expected to lose some
of the cattle. They kept on running until something
in the distance frightened them back again, and they
returned as furious as they went, when the men with
great difficulty managed to stop them. The captain
ordered all the dogs to be killed, and in obedience
to his commands, our faithful "Tray" was shot. Some
of the company were not disposed to comply with this
sanguinary, though I believe necessary, decision of the
captain's, and threatened retaliation in case their dogs
should be killed. So, after repairing, we started on
our journey with the expectation of having another
run-a-way scrape; an expectation which was shortly
realized. We had not gone far when the train commenced running. I was on the pony, and he did not
seem disposed to lag behind, but made every exertion
to come out "first best" in the race; as I had nothing
but a man's saddle I jumped off, after getting in advance of the train, and you may imagine my position
with the whole train coming towards me, and the
clouds of dust so thick that I could not see them.
The last I did see of them they were running three
or four teams abreast and making as much confusion
as only such "critters" can when they get frightened.
Cattle here are as different from what they are in the
states as day is from night; and I think a little as

Mrs. W— says, that they are paying up for the abuse
they received at the start. They have been maltreated,
cursed and hallooed at all the way, but now the men
durst not speak loud to them they are so easily frightened. – We are waiting for our cattle to be found;
hunted till the afternoon, and have lost our best yoke.
The two Wilson families [3] lost so many they had to
join teams and go on with one wagon. While hunting
for the cattle one of the company was shot at by an
Indian, who missed his mark. This afternoon we traveled four miles to another campground and had another frightful runaway before stopping. The dogs,
now, are all killed; but the cattle get frightened at
any thing, and sometimes at nothing. We dare not
ride in the wagons, for the cattle are perfectly wild –
and I believe the people are too, for they don't know
what they are doing. – Saturday the 9th, started and
drove all the loose cattle ahead; the men, women and
children also go ahead of the teams, or far enough
behind, so as not to frighten the cattle. In this wild
region we cannot milk our cows any more than so
many untamed antelopes. Perhaps they smell the wild
animals, or scent the Indians; though the dogs frightened them in the first place. Dogs are of no use on
this road, "no how," and I would advise all who emigrate to Oregon to bring none of these animals with
them; ours is not the only company who have had to
kill them off. After experiencing so many hardships,
you doubtless will think I regret taking this long and
tiresome trip, and would rather go back than proceed
to the end of my journey. But, no, I have a great

---

[3] Oregon land records list four Wilson families arriving in September
and one in October, 1851.

desire to see Oregon, and, besides, there are many things we meet with – the beautiful scenery of plain and mountain, and their inhabitants, the wild animals and the Indians, and natural curiosities in abundance – to compensate us for the hardships and mishaps we encounter. People who do come must not be worried or frightened at trifles; they must put up with storm and cloud as well as calm and sunshine; wade through rivers, climb steep hills, often go hungry, keep cool and good natured always, and possess courage and ingenuity equal to any emergency, and they will be able to endure unto the end. A lazy person should never think of going to Oregon. – Our cattle, by treating them kindly and speaking to them gently, are beginning to get a little tame, and we can now venture to ride in the wagons. – Here we have very little grass, and have great difficulty in finding enough for our stock; what there is, is dried up, but the cattle eat it.

August 15. – We have found some good grass, and the cattle are into it up to their eyes; it looks like timothy, off at a distance, just ready to mow. – At one place here we have had to drive our cattle down 2000 feet to water; in doing this we were obliged to leave a cow, which had no strength to walk after the fatigue of going down and up this mountain of a hill. – Again, there is no grass, but the soil is of an ashy nature, very mellow and consequently dusty, and produces nothing but sage brush. – On further we came across warm springs (not the boiling springs) oozing out of the top of the ground; a cold spring is near by. On the opposite side of the river from us is a spring flowing out of the wall of a rock, large enough to turn a mill; it is a very beautiful stream, clear as crystal, and runs so rapidly that it looks white as ice as it flows over the rock, and roars like a mill race. We got some salmon of the Indians here. – Monday the 18th we passed the Salmon Falls, at which place Capt. Taylor's [4] company caught up with us; one of his women had got her arm broken going down a steep hill, where the road was only wide enough for a wagon, at the side of which was this woman. I wonder she was not smashed to pieces. –

Tuesday, 19th – This morning we expected a fuss with the Indians; one shot from across the river and killed a cow, and then snapped his gun many times at the men, some one of whom had killed the Indian's dog. This, in my opinion ought not to have been done. It is not always that the Indians are the aggressors; when they are it is well enough to chastise them, even with severity, but it is certainly a wrong policy, and results in much mischief, very often to unoffending people, to molest these ignorant and revengful savages even by killing a dog.

August 21. – We forded the Snake River, which runs so swift that the drivers (four to a team) had to hold on to the ox yokes to keep from being swept down by the current. The water came into the wagon boxes, and after making the island we raised the boxes on blocks, engaged an Indian pilot, doubled teams, and reached the opposite bank in safety. It is best in fording this river to engage a pilot. – The "Telegraph Company," as we call them, who passed us in such a hurry on the Platte, have left their goods and wagons

---

4 Too many Taylors for identification.

scattered over the mountains. We find them every day. Their cattle have given out, and I have seen several head of them at a time which had been left dead at the different camping places on the road. We drove too slow on the Platte, and the "Telegraph" hurried too fast, and while our cattle are comparatively strong and in good condition, and will enable us, if we have time before the setting in of winter, to reach our destination, theirs are so worn out from hard usage that it is doubtful if they get through at all this season. We have met some "packers," and they inform us that we are too late to cross the Cascade mountains this season.

August 25. – Palmer's company [5] found a dead man, shot through the heart, supposed to be one of the returning packers.

Tuesday, 26th. – A poney was stolen by the Indians last night. We are now camped with three companies, and an encampment of Indians is near us; but we are not afraid of them when they come in sight. It is only when they keep out of sight, and hid in some secret place, near enough to see us, that they are to be feared or will commit mischief, if they can. The Indians we have met with here are more savage, cunning and treacherous than any we have yet seen. At one place they had cut a road through the willows, so that they could come up to camp after night undiscovered. The willows were not cleared quite up to the road, but a short space was left to hide in ambush, so that the enemy could attack us by surprise.

---

[5] This is not the same as the Palmer whose journal she mentions later on. This one remains unidentified.

They know where we have to camp, and often see us when we are not aware of it. If a company is large enough they are too great cowards to attack it, but watch an opportunity to steal. – Our captain has at last resigned,[6] and had sufficient cause for so doing. It is our desire to travel with a captain, and not with a tribe whose insubordination will not allow of one. – Here we find balm of giliad trees, which when dry, make very good fuel. Some of them are large enough for saw logs, and it is very pleasant to see trees again after traveling hundreds of miles over the sage plains. – We have forded Boisee River, passed the Fort of that name, and the second time forded Snake River, which we have left never to return, and on Thursday the 4th of September pitched our tents upon the top of a high mountain; but away up above us are mountains still higher. These are the Wind River Mountains. Here we left Dr. Perkins,[7] of Indiana. His team gave out, and he waits for another company. – This is a dismal morning, as it has been raining; the hills are very slippery, and before us is a mountain that looks as if it could not be climbed. We are at one of those places where the way cannot be seen twenty steps ahead, but as we proceed openings are found to let us through, and where others have been we can go. It is snowing in the mountains while it is raining in the valleys. Here we got a pheasant for dinner; their size is between the turkey and common fowl, and they resemble the prairie chicken, only their breasts are black. Monday the 8th we descended a very

---

[6] Nowhere has she given a clue to the name of the captain.

[7] John N. and Deressa A. Perkins settled in Linn County on Donation Claim #4643 on November 7, 1851. *Genealogical Material in Oregon Donation Land Claims,* II (Portland, Ore., 1959), p. 106.

steep hill, which took an hour to get down, into a valley called the Grand Rounds. This valley is one of Nature's beauty spots, and at the foot of the hill we were met by a great many Indians waiting to see the emigrants. This valley is very fertile, its area is about 10,000 acres, fenced in with very high mountains, covered with fine trees. Its fertile soil produces several kinds of luxuriant grass – blue grass, timothy, clover, red top, and "broom corn" grass, that looks like oats, only the head is not heavy enough. As we ascended the high hills upon leaving this delightful valley, we found that the trees, which looked like bushes before, were of the very largest and tallest growth. Some of them I was told would make 300 rails, and they would, evidently, the best kind of saw logs. A large number of Indians followed us here, for the purpose of trading with the emigrants. They will exchange a good pony for a good cow, or give a squaw for a pony! or a pony for $100. The hills here are all covered with fine timber. Some of them are awful steep, however. We went up one today and it took twenty-two head of cattle to haul up one wagon, and there was not much in the wagon either. Emigrants will therefore see the necessity of kind and careful treatment of their teams at the outset and indeed through the whole of this long journey, to reserve their strength for these difficult places. We came up here with Mr. Noosam,[8] who is keeping a journal, with the intention of having it published for the benefit of the future

---

[8] David Newsom was reported among Peorians on the way to Oregon by the Springfield, Illinois, *Journal,* as quoted in the *Oregon Spectator* of Oregon City, on July 3, 1851. David and Mary Newsom and several children settled in Marion County. There is no record of the publication of a guidebook written by David Newsom.

emigration. It is the best guide I have seen, shows the road much better than Palmer's,[9] gives more in detail the particulars, and its statements are to be relied upon.

Sunday, September 14. – This is a beautiful, clear day, and we are traveling over as nice a rolling prairie as I have ever seen and along a clear and beautiful stream of water. There are no sloughs like those in Illinois.

Monday, 15th. – Pleasant weather and good roads; passed a tastefully built frame house, the first we have seen. Mount St. Elias is in the distance, and is covered with snow, so you can imagine somewhat the beauty and grandeur of the scene. We are now among the tribe of Wallawalla Indians, the same who murdered Dr. Whitcomb [Whitman] and family. You have doubtless heard of the circumstances before. While we are getting supper tonight a squaw is near us engaged in picking vermin off from her papoose's head, and eating them, and while she is engaged in this dainty repast, I will repair to my tent and write to friends at home and far away.

(To be continued)

NOTE. [by David Duniway] – Contrary to the promise to print the conclusion in the next number of the *Republican,* it did not appear then nor in later issues of the paper.

---

[9] This was Joel Palmer's *Journal of Travels over the Rocky Mountains* (Cincinnati, 1847), which was republished by the Arthur H. Clark Company in Reuben Gold Thwaites, *Early Western Travels, 1748-1846* (Cleveland, 1906), xxx

Journal of Our Journey to Oregon

§ Eugenia Zieber

INTRODUCTION

Eugenia Zieber learned that she would be going on a long overland journey to Oregon when she was a student at the Moravian Seminary for Young Ladies in Bethlehem, Pennsylvania. A letter came from her father in Peoria, Illinois, dated December 23, 1849, telling her about the prospect. Her father's idea was to move the family to Oregon to be in a more healthy climate.[1]

It was on April 17, 1851, that she sent a short note to a friend, Elizabeth Skirving, saying, "Dearest Lissie, We leave this afternoon for Oregon, are as busy as bees and a little busier." [2] Then on April 27, ten days later, she wrote the first entry in her diary on "the second Sabbath of our journey."

Eugenia was 18 years old during the 1851 wagon trip. Her parents were John Shunk and Eliza Sloan Zieber. The other children were Ella, 15 years old; Octavia, 13; John, 10; and Zulette, 7. The first three girls had been born in Princess Anne, Maryland; the other children were born in Peoria.[3]

John Zieber was a printer and a newspaperman. He had learned the trade as a teen-ager and then worked for sev-

[1] Bush-Zieber Archives, the Bush House. Letter written from back home in Peoria, by her father John S. Zieber to Eugenia Zieber, who was in school in Philadelphia. This letter is also mentioned in a fine article about the Bush House in the Salem, *Oregon Statesman-Journal* of August 16, 1982, by Ellen Foster.

[2] This note is also in the Bush-Zieber Archives in the Bush House.

[3] Information gathered from the Bush-Zieber Archives.

eral years for others. Born in Pottsdam, Pennsylvania,
he had received his training in Philadelphia, started in the
newspaper business in Baltimore, and then on to Cambridge, Maryland, where he met Miss Eliza Sloan. They
were married on February 1, 1825, and the two lived
together for 53 years before her death. They moved to
Princess Anne, Maryland, where on April 3, 1827, they
started a newspaper, the *Village Herald*. Zieber was the
publisher of the newspaper for eight years. The next
newspaper Zieber founded was the *Democratic Press* of
Peoria, Illinois. He entered politics in 1844 and was elected
to one two-year term in the Illinois Legislature. He sold
the newspaper in 1845, and the family began making plans
to go West.[4] It was not until 1851 that they were ready,
and it is the story of that journey that is told in Eugenia's
"Journal," as well as one kept by her father. Zieber's
career in Oregon involved printing, surveying, and farming. Their farm was four miles north of Salem.

Because he was a newspaperman, Zieber got much more
attention from the press on arrival in Oregon. The pioneer
newspaper, the *Oregon Spectator,* announced in glowing
terms the arrival of the Ziebers in its October 21 issue:

> Mr. John S. Zieber, of Peoria, Ill., arrived here some eight
> or ten days since with his family, who are all in good spirits, and
> is residing for the present in Linn City. They encountered many
> severe trials on the road, having had all their team stolen from
> them some 500 miles from this place, where it was impossible
> for them to make an arrangement for the conveyance of them-
> selves and goods, other than what could be made with their
> company. We are happy to learn that he was fortunate enough
> to be cared for by some of the company until he reached the
> Dalles. . .

It was in Salem that the Ziebers met the most dynamic

---

[4] Joseph Gaston, *Centennial History of Oregon, 1811-1912* (Chicago, 1912),
II, p. 268.

newspaper man in Oregon at the time, Asahel Bush. He
was the publisher of the *Oregon Statesman* newspaper of
Salem, which still comes off the press every day.[5] He was
a primary force in the Democratic Party and was himself
a political power. And: — It was in the autumn of 1854
that the kindly, gentle, devout young lady, Eugenia Zieber,
and he were married. The official marriage records of
Marion County reveal the following: "BUSH Asahel
BUSH & Eugenia ZIEBER, m 14 Oct 1854; Francis Zieber
S. Hoyt, M. G. Wit: John Zieber & Albert Zieber.[6]

So it was that for the next nine years Eugenia and
Asahel Bush lived their lives together. During that time,
four children were born to them: Estelle, Asahel N., Sally,
and Eugenia. They all grew up to attend colleges in the
East: Estelle attended her mother's alma mater, the Moravian Seminary for Young Ladies.

Eugenia, the mother, did not live a long life; she died
on September 11, 1863, at the age of 30. She was buried
in the Odd Fellows Cemetery underneath a tombstone that
reads, "Eugenia Bush: wife of Asahel Bush, born in Princess Anne, Maryland; Jan. 3, 1833; died at Salem, Oregon,
Sept. 11, 1863." [7]

Today the "Bush House" is part of an historical park,
along with the "Bush Barn" and "Bush Pasture." In the
house are the papers of the Bush and Zieber families, and
that is where we found her journal and, with permission
of the Bush House it is published here. Our special gratitude is due to Jennifer Hagloch, Curator, and to others
on the staff for much assistance in gleaning information
about Eugenia Zieber Bush and her family.

[5] The story of Asahel Bush and the *Statesman* is well told in George Turnbull, *History of Oregon Newspapers* (Portland, Ore., 1939).

[6] Jean Custer and Daraleen Wade, *Marriage Records of Marion County,
Oregon, 1849-1871* (Salem, Ore., 1979), i, p. 8.

[7] Mrs. Edwin A. Jory, comp., *Tombstone Records in the Odd Fellows
Cemetery, Salem, Marion County* (Salem, Ore., 1938).

One final note about Eugenia Zieber: There is an entry in the diary of Judge Matthew Deady on March 29, 1874 (Sunday) that casts an interesting light on how a person's death can be somehow forgotten in the business of life. Deady tells how he went to Salem to the funeral of a friend. It was "Rather a dreary Pagan affair." The burial took place at the Odd Fellows Cemetery. Afterwards Deady walked around the "beautiful burying ground," and he wrote down the following comment: "Saw Mrs Bush[s] grave. Not so well attended as it used to be." [8]

THE JOURNAL OF EUGENIA ZIEBER

April 27, 1851. This is the second Sabbath of our journey. This morning it was windy and unpleasantly cold, but this afternoon the sun is shining brightly, and though the wind still blows ugly, it is warm, and everything seems cheerful, rejoicing in the goodness of its Creator. I often think, as I look up at the bright sky above, around upon the hills, the rocks, woods, and the birds and mighty river, or the sweetly babbling brook that each is giving its ardent adoration to its God not only for creating them but also for his constant care for them. For God does certainly care for them. Does he not each successive Spring renew the verdure of the hills and woods, sprinkle the ground with beautiful flowers, and is he not constantly refreshing by rain, etc., the rivers and brooks. God does indeed constantly watch over everything he has created and man, sinful man is not the last to be cared for, but all this is created for his happiness. We have

[8] Malcolm Clark, Jr., *Pharisee among Philistines* (Portland, Ore., 1975), I, p. 160.

camped for the day in the woods, several miles from
Birmingham, Iowa. It is pleasant thus to be alone
(Mr. Kern's [1] family & our own) separated from all
the world, and yet with all our thoughts are mingled
those of absent friends, of past privileges of hearing
the word of God. But what greater earthly preacher
can be heard than Nature. Continually is she giving
some good instruction, some kind word of encourage-
ment, which none are apt to heed except those who
have learned to love God in sincerity and truth. Oh,
that more were among that number. At noon Mr.
Kern's children and our's including myself, went in
the woods and held a Sabbath school. [2] We sang a
hymn, read the 27th psalm, spoke of it, read a tract,
sang the doxology: "Praise God from whom all bless-
ings flow" then returned to the camp. It was very
pleasant and I trust that good Being of whom we met
to converse, looked upon us approvingly. We had
been a week on our journey yesterday about 11 o'clock.
Last Sabbath we spent at Mr. Gideaon Thomas'. He
and family were very kind to us, refused to receive
any pay for our board, though we were there two
nights & a day. He is an old friend of father's. They
seem to be a fine family. In the evening (Sunday) I
took out my bundle of tracts to distribute them or
rather leave some with the family, and in a humorous

---

[1] J. W. Kern and wife, Ann, traveled from the Peoria, Illinois, area to
Oregon in 1851. They settled on a farm east of Portland to raise fruit.
H. K. Hines, *An Illustrated History of the State of Oregon* (Chicago, 1893),
pp. 955-56.

[2] John Zieber's diary reads for the same Sunday, "This afternoon Eugenia
took the children of our families to the woods and held a Sunday school.
It seemed to please them, and if continued, when the weather and circumstances permit, the custom will be likely to prove beneficial." *Transcations of
the Oregon Pioneer Association*, 1920, p. 304.

way I was told to give one to Jacob Slough,[3] for he
had been heard to say that morning promenade all,
and so of course must have been dancing. I looked
at my tracts and found that the 2nd one in the pack
treated upon dancing. I handed it to him and turned
to offer one to Mr. Andrews,[4] a young man who drives
for Mr. Kerns, but he refused decidedly to accept it.
Polite! Jacob Slough drives for us. Monday night we
camped opposite Mr. Butt's house, also an old friend
of father's slept in one of his rooms. Had quite a time
cooking and eating supper. Tuesday we passed Mr.
Wells'. Father stopped and spoke to him. We rode
on. Mr. W. was very sorry. He wished us to dine.
When we stopped at a Mr. —'s to dine, he (Mr. W.)
came riding after us, bringing father a bag of oats,
a shoulder and a ham. Very kind of him. We camped
out and slept in our tent that and every night since.
We have had very pleasant weather generally, and
are all in good spirits enjoying ourselves. We were
obliged to leave our cooking stove behind at Burling-
ton it being a perfect humbug, and buy cooking utensils for a camping fire.

Monday, 28th. Left our camping place early this
morning. It was rather cool but towards noon became
quite pleasant. We passed through three small towns,
the first was only a mile from our camp ground, its
name Winchester. The second, Birmingham. The children were quite disappointed here. When approaching it they thought they saw a short tower, but it

---

3 Jacob Slough drove wagon for the Ziebers.

4 John Andrews settled in Benton County, Oregon, with his wife, Mary.
According to the land claim records, they were married on September 26,
1852, which meant they got 640 acres instead of 360. *Genealogical Material
in Oregon Donation Land Claims,* II (Portland, 1959), p. 70.

turned out to be a large chimney, used in some manu-
facturing establishment. The third place was Liberty-
ville. The inhabitants ought to be very patriotic, to
suit the name. We camped this evening in the road
opposite to a farm house. It was cool (and refreshing),
but passed the night very comfortably. Father and Mr.
Kern kept watch tonight, Jacob and Mr. Andrews
last night.

Tuesday, 29.   Cloudy morning. Passed through Agency
City and from thence on to Ottumwa. Before we
reached this place it commenced raining & hailing,
then turned into a perfect snow storm. A very unpleasant day. Passed Mr. Noland [5] in that place. He has
ox teams. About noon in crossing a ditch the chain,
connecting the horses, broke, leaving the wagon in
the ditch. It was the four horse team. We were near
a house, in which we went to warm ourselves. Father,
Jacob, Mr. Kern and two gentlemen, who offered to
assist them succeeded in lifting the wagon out. It continued snowing until about four o'clock, the wind
blowing hard. We put up for the night at a Mr. Miller's. The K family were very kind. Everything was
quite comfortable.

Wednesday, 30th.   With a very early start, thought
to have a long drive, but were sadly disappointed. At
Eddyville, four miles from Mr. Miller's we crossed
the Des Moin's river, in a ferry boat. Went on several
miles, until about noon, when we stopped to feed in
a valley, through which a pretty stream of water runs.

---

[5] "Joshua Noland lives in Canyonville [Douglas County]; is a miner;
came to Oregon state in 1851, and to the county in 1858; was born September
11, 1831, in LaFayette county, Mo." A. G. Walling, *History of Southern
Oregon* (Portland, Ore., 1884), pp. 514-15.

We took our dinner here, which consisted of bread, crackers, chip beef, cheese and cold fried meat. This, or what we took of it, we held in our hands and sat on logs, stumps, etc., to partake of it. Many would look upon this as a most awkward way of eating, but I think it really pleasant. The sky above you clearly seen, not kept from your sight by any obstructing roof. The trees looking fresh & happy around you, and flowers peeping up from the bright grass, as though desirous of taking notes of your proceedings. Who would not prefer this to a table profusely covered with dishes filled with dainties of every kind, shut up in a house, the work of art! Give me rather fair Nature's beauties shed abroad to my view, and 'twill lend a charm to everything. – After dinner we took the wrong road, and lost a full hour's time in returning to it. We came to Albia, the county seat of — county, late in the evening. Had great difficulty in procuring accommodations. It being much too late to camp out. We ate in one house and slept in another. The Landlady was a real greahead [grayhead?] body and could scarcely wait for us to pull off our cloaks and shawls before she *ushered* us our supper. We had to sleep in a room, where a man & wife slept in one bed and a man in another. Both men turned toward us and seemed determined to see everything we had to do. Mother and I spread our beds on the floor, put the children to bed and waited until they had gone to sleep before we retired. The wind came in at the cracks in the side of the house and swept over us, as much as though we were out doors.

Thursday May 1st. 1851 – Did not start upon our journey until after 9 o'clock. A very cold windy day.

Wrapped ourselves in blankets, but still were cold. After traveling 3½ miles we came to Clark's Point. Went in to Mr. Clark's and warmed ourselves. How strange to have such cold weather at this season of the year. And from C–'s Point we traveled about 15 or 16 miles to Mr. Prather's, stopping on the way at a big house to warm, and feed, but finding we were only a little distance from Mr. Prather's we did not feed but kept on. The lady of the house we stopped at was very pretty. She was quilting. Had three children. Everything looked clean and nice about her. Mrs. Prather is a very kind, motherly lady, pleasant withal. Gave us a plain but good supper. Some excellent corn cakes. Do not remember whenever I ate a heartier meal. We had one bed in the room, there were three, in which we put Ella, Occa & Zule, and spread one of our beds for Mother, John and myself. Father slept in the wagon, Jacob also. Several men slept in the room, but were more polite than those of last night, turning round and going to sleep immediately –.

Friday May 2nd.   Had more corn cakes for breakfast. They are excellent, wish we could have them all the way. It is snowing again. What a time we have. I am afraid we shall not be able to travel to day. As I expected we could not go to day, but were obliged to remain in the house the whole day. Snow fell to the depth of four or five feet. In the afernoon it rained, washing it all (nearly) away, now there is scarcely any to be seen. Everything is very comfortable here. I cannot but think how much happier these people, who live in log or some house of that kind, than those are who live in the greatest style wealth can afford. They

appear to me at least to be happier. They have not
the thousand and one things to annoy them that the
wealthy have. Their minds are at rest, and frequently
enjoying communion with God. Give me a lowly cottage, where love to God and unity of feeling, among
the members of the household, exist, in preference to
the greatest palace, where these are absent. "Lay not
up for yourselves treasures on earth where moth and
dust doth corrupt, and thieves break through and steel."
But in Heaven our treasure must be, where nothing
injurious will even attempt to touch it. For "where
our treasures are there will our hearts be also." –

Saturday 3rd of May. Cloudy damp morning, but
much warmer than it was yesterday, but it is *dreadfully*
muddy, it (the mud) clings to one's feet, it is almost
impossible to get it off. We think we shall set out
to day. We bade Mr. Prather & family farewell this
morning a little after seven o'clock. I shall ever remember their [kindness] to us during our short stay
with them. The sun shone out a little while this morn-
ig, but it is again cloudy. We crossed a prairy again
this morning, which was filled with gopher or goffer
hills. Strange that animals so small can build or throw
up such mounds of earth. They must labor hard.
Camped on the prairy this evening in front of a log
cabin.

Sunday, May 11, 1851. –

Sunday, June 15th. 1851 More than a month has
slipped me by since I endeavored to write a few lines
in my journal, and now I am many miles –

Sunday June 22nd, 1851. (On) another Sabbath do
I attempt to write a few lines in my journal, which

has been long neglected. There is scarcely time, upon such a journey, for those *who have aught that is essentially necessary* to do, to keep a diary. It must be done by snatches or at any moment, or not at all. That does not suit every one. – We are now many miles from the Missouri river. When I last wrote we had not arrived at Kanesville. We were precisely three weeks in traveling there from Peoria, remained there two weeks waiting there for Mr. Webster,[6] who was detained unexpectedly, and therefore could not meet us at K. – e agreeably to his promise. We had quite a pretty camping ground there, but it rained nearly every day during our stay, which rendered it rather unpleasant. Rev. Mr. Simpson, the Methodist minister of the place, to whom we had a letter of introduction from Bishop Hamlin, proved to be a very intelligent pleasant person. I should like to become well acquainted with him. – Mr. Webster came at last, bringing me a letter from Mrs Stebbins, my Peoria mother. It was like herself, full of pleasantry, yet not devoid of seriousness, but giving many kind instructions (for my benefit), and earnest wishes for *our* future happiness. Mr. Webster was very obliging, and kind at first, but I cannot help but speak of him with an old saying, "a new broom sweeps clean." It was literally the case with him, for he has proved to be one of the most contrary, disobliging persons: *evil* I might truthfully say, ever met with. He purchased two useless Indian ponies at

---

[6] This was George Webster. The *Oregon Spectator* newspaper of Oregon City reported in its September 30, 1851, edition, "FROM THE EMIGRANTS. — Mr. George Webster, of Edgar County, Illinois, arrived here Friday last. He informs us that he belonged to Mr. Zieber's company, of whom we made mention last week, and traveled with him to Fort Boise. Mr. Webster informs us that Mr. Zieber and family were all well. . ."

Kanesville, which he had been trying to work in the wagon with the others, a week or two back, nearly ruining all his other horses, by obliging them to pull the whole load at a great distance from the wagon. Mr. Slough continues pleasant and kind. Until a few days back we have had difficulty traveling through mud and water (since we left the Missouri.) It was very hard upon the horses, now however we have good roads. The first stream of any account they came to, named Papea, had to be bridged. Here we fell in company with a Mr. Palmer,[7] and [sic] elderly gentleman, with three sons and two daughters. Besides several others in company, with whom I am not acquainted. The Elk Horn, a stream about nine miles distant from the other[s], had overflown its banks before we arrived, and we had poor prospects of crossing it at first. Here Mr. Palmer, Mr. Bowman,[8] – Brown,[9] – Grey,[10] a number of others and father formed

---

[7] There was a Palmer family with the wagon train. Mr. Palmer was even captain for a time. There was a Luna Palmer who came to Eugenia's tent on June 23. Where did the Palmers go? They do not appear in any Oregon records. Perhaps they went north or south to a neighboring region in Washington Territory or in California.

[8] Joshua Bowman, according to the land records was a Pennsylvanian who arrived in Oregon in November, 1851. He and his wife, Emeline, settled in Clackamas County. *Donation Land Claims,* II, *op. cit.,* Claim #4635. There is a fascinating reference to this family in the *Oregon Spectator* for September 30, 1851, saying that George Webster brought word that in an exchange of fire with Indians a ball "passed through the bonnet of a little girl of Mr. Bowman's; the ball passed through the front part, barely missing her eyes."

[9] In her diary entry for July 17, she further identifies this man as "Mr. John Brown." John Zieber, in his diary, refers to James Brown as well. (*Op. cit.,* p. 316.) It is interesting to note that there are land records for John and James Brown, both of whom arrived in Oregon during October, 1851. They both settled in Clatsop County near each other and witnessed each other's claims. James was evidently unmarried; John's wife was Elizabeth. They had been married in Tazewell County, Illinois. *Donation Land Claims,* II, *op. cit.,* Claims #3981 and #3155, respectively.

a company bought ferry boats and ferried us across
themselves. Since then we have [all] been traveling
in company together with Mr. Palmer as Capt. except
a few persons who left us. Mr. Bohl,[11] a gentleman
from Peoria, went with us some time, but left us last
week joining a horse company (who crossed the Elk
Horn with us.) Mr. Kern is also in that company.
Mr. Grey has a horse team: the others of our company
have oxen. They have been exceedingly kind, helping
us whenever we were in difficulty, frequently drawing
our wagon out of the snow with their oxen. This last
week they ferried over three creeks in wagon bodies;
very hard work, (and) nearly put some of our number
out of heart. However all are in good spirits now.
Yesterday a great herd of buffalo came in sight, three
passed quite near us. A number put off in pursuit of
them. Mr. Slough one among the number. He helped
to kill one, brought some of the meat home. We breakfasted upon it this morning, tasted very well. To day
we saw a number returning from the river (the Platte,
*between 2 & 3 hundred miles from Mormon Winter
Quarters we are now*) they had been there for water.
We are traveling to day. I regret doing so, but the
company generally are not willing to lie by, and we
of course who would like to, being the smaller number, must comply with the other's wishes. It is very
warm, but little air stirring to day. – This evening
it is cool and rather windy again. I can scarcely make
myself believe that this is Sunday, because we are

---

[10] John Zieber called this man "Newty Gray." Beyond this he is unidentified. Several Gray and/or Grey families arrived in 1851.

[11] The only other reference to "Mr. Bohl" is in John Zieber's diary, *op.
cit.,* p. 509, where he speaks of "Mr. Bohl & family" and adds, "We felt
quite at home."

traveling, it does not seem right. A watch was lost by one of the company to day, a very valuable one I believe. Camped on a small branch of the Platte. We are to remain here tomorrow the women are to wash, the men to search for the watch, and go *hunting*.

Monday 23rd.   Today seems like Sunday, or as though it ought to be. Yet when we commence washing it will not seem thus. We have a most lovely place to wash. Good water for washing close at hand, we are shaded by trees, and there are bushes near by on which we can spread the clothes. There is also quite a pleasant breeze stirring. The water looks tempting. How pleasant it would be to go in wading. – They were not successful in their search for the watch. A great pity. A little after four a heavy cloud was blown up and threatened us with a heavy rain, but we escaped with a few large hail stones. Many such would leave us destitute of wagons and destroy our provisions. Luna Palmer [12] came over this evening and asked me to go over to their tent, they intended having a concert. I went. Several young men played upon flutes, and the rest joined in with singing. Quite a pleasant evening or way of spending it. Bennett, or Mr. B – [13] I should say did most of the singing. He is a merry person. Returned (he) with Ella and me to our tent and bade us good evening. I shall be sorry to leave our pretty wash. house in the morning. How soon one becomes attached to place, and the recollection of it always adds a charm.

Tuesday 24.   Made quite a long drive to day. Crossed Skunk creek. 7½ miles from there came to two springs

---

12 Luna Palmer. See footnote 7, above.

13 There are just too many Bennetts to locate this one who came in 1851.

of nice cold water. We passed the first without noticing it, expecting to find it on the other side of the road. Some who stopped by for their noon halt said it was much prettier than the one we were at, though it was beautiful. The water boiled up from the center and spread out into a sort of basin, a stream flowed from it. Came about 22 or 3 miles to day. Camped on a little stream, but know nothing much of the camp ground as it is raining and we are weather bound in the wagons. The dust has been very disagreeable to day, and the rain will settle it, a favor for us. Besides it is refreshing, for the day was an exceedingly warm one. –

Sunday 29th. A very disagreeable day. The wind is blowing hard, and it is quite cold. Traveling again today, I do wish the company could be prevailed upon to rest on Sundays. It would be better in every respect, both in regard to *duty,* and the welfare of our teams. Pleasanter this evening. We are camped by a spring of excellent water.

Monday. 30th. A lovely day, with one exception, it is rather warm. The road sandy and hard upon our teams. Mother and I walked nearly all the morning. Father and Mr. Slough generally walk the greater part of the time. We passed a place to day, called Ancient Ruins. Father, (*and*) mother & I went to see them, climbed up one of the highest hills or mountains, enjoyed the view from there very much. The only trouble was our time was too limited. We had not leisure to look around and examine anything. The Palmers are offended with us about something or other, cannot tell what. Mr. Webster has been talking, I reckon. Cornelius is the only one though, who shows

any ill feeling, or I should say shows that he has any
hard feelings about us.

Tuesday. July 1. 1851. Camped this evening on the
prairy, a long distance from the river, & opposite to
Chimney Rock, an object of curiosity. It has been in
sight all day. Some few went across to it. We would
have been pleased to have gone, but could not. Musketoes are miserably bad tonight. Strange Captain
Palmer, or Perkins it is now, should be so *unfortunate* in the selection of their camping grounds. Dr.
Perkins,[14] from Indiana was elected Capt. Saturday
evening, but for all, our former Capt. seems to hold
the office still.

Wednesday, July 2nd. 1851. Scott's Bluffs were in
view when we started this morning and although they
appeared near, we were obliged to travel a long dis-
tanc before reaching them. They are objects of greater
interest than the Ancient Ruins or Chimney Rock.
And I think deserve the name of ancient Ruins much
more than those that bear it. It was a grand sight.
When opposite to them (they are on the other [South]
side of the Platte) We saw a storm approaching,
following the course of the river. A dark cloud hung
over the Bluffs, increasing or heightening the grandeur of their appearance to a great degree We gazed
upon it in perfect delight, but suddenly the whole
scene was enveloped in darkness, completely hid from
our view. The wind in a short time changed its course,
blowing towards us. Consequently we had our share

---

14 John N. and Derissa Ann Perkins, according to the land records,
arrived in Oregon November 7, 1851. They settled on a claim in Linn County
on January 31, 1854. They were both from Ohio. *Donation Land Claims,* II,
op. cit., Claim #4643.

of the storm, which was tolerably severe Some hail fell, but not sufficient to do any damage to our wagons. *Only enough to frighten us a little.* We camped in a most dreary looking spot, at a distance from water, and no wood to be seen, and here are only a short distance from Spring creek, 3 miles I believe. How strange such a place is selected, when a better is so near. Father got quite wet holding the horses, who were unruly, during the storm. I fear he will take cold.

July 3rd.   Had a beautiful camping ground this evening. John climbed the mountains or bluffs which were close by, and seemed delighted at being allowed the privilege.

July 4.   The cattle had a stampede to day. The only thing nearly that was done in the way of celebrating the fourth. The stampede was started by dog's jumping out suddenly from under one of the wagons No harm done. I must not forget that the young men marched round the camp this evening after supper, whistling Yank Doodle. Mrs. Bowman, Brown, mother and I caught up some tin pans and sticks and started after, but backed out. Could not go quite so far. We passed an Indian lodge today, and opposite it, on the other side of the river, was an Indian village. It looked well from a distance. This evening an Indian came to our tent begging. We are now among the Sioux tribe, a finer looking race than the Pawnee.

July 5th.   Came to or rather opposite to Ft. Laramie to day. Camped about five miles above it, near the Platte. Found a spring on the shore, of excellent water. A number went across to the Ft. No letters there for us. It would be pleasant to hear from Peoria.

Sunday July 6. – To day a part of the company started ahead, the Palmers, Dr. Perkins and two other families. The remainder of us determined to keep the Sabbath again, & allow our teams rest. The Palmers are bound to rush on, but have promised to wait to-morrow for us. They pretend they wish to find better grass, though there is no prospect of their being successful. They are generally disliked, and they have also little friendly feelings towards some of us. It is supposed they intend leaving us, thinking the most of the company would follow them. By us, I mean, Browns, Bowmans, Grey's and our family. But they were disappointed. The Barnetts [15] are two of them brothers, and a Mr. Bennett is with them, having one team. Mr. Stearns,[16] Vincent [17] and a boy named John —.[18] also owning one team. Mr. Wilhelm [19] and Charlie (Mr. Hammond)[20] one team, all remained with us. These the Palmers wished to have with them, but they refused to go, and their company is so small, they are afraid to go on alone. It is a relief to have them gone, they are so profane and noisy. – How pleasant again to rest upon the Sab-

[15] James Henry Barnett, who settled on a claim in Linn County, Oregon, was another Ohioan. His arrival date was October 4, 1851. No wife is mentioned. *Donation Land Claims,* II, *op. cit.,* Claim # 5240.

[16] Many persons named Stearns traveled the Oregon Trail, most of them in 1853. This man became captain of the wagon train (entry for July 15). The 1851 Stearns family is so far unidentified.

[17] John Zieber, in his writings, refers to R. Vincent. *Op cit.,* p. 331. Nothing more is known of him.

[18] "John" has not been identified.

[19] This was George Wilhelm, another Ohioan, who settled in Benton County. He arrived in Oregon on October 15, 1851, and settled on his claim on December 1, 1853. No wife is mentioned. *Donation Land Claims,* II, *op. cit.,* Claim #2947.

[20] The *Oregon Spectator* advertises letters lying unclaimed in the Oregon City Post Office for Charles F. (or T.) Hammond in several 1853 and 1854 issues. Nothing more seems to be known about "Charlie (Mr. Hammond.)"

bath, to have *time* and *opportuiity* to read and reflect
upon the word of God. Father, I am remiss in this
my duty to thee. Forgive, forgive I am constantly
obliged to cry. Oh! enable me to be more faithful
in discharge of duty.

July 7. Hard traveling to day up and down sandy,
stony hills continually. Caught a view of the government farm belong[ing] to Ft. Laramie. Mr. George
Barnett has loaned us (Ella and I) his grey horse
to ride. Ella rode this morning, I this afternoon. Mr.
Wilhelm rode all the afternoon with me. I was pleased
with him or rather his conversation. He is a fine person. Once, some time back, through mismanagement
of the horses a large wagon was suddenly wheeled
around and every spoke of one of the small wheels
was broken. Mr. Wilhelm, and Mr. Minor,[21] (who
is in company with Mr. Bowman) very kindly mended
the wheel, which was rendering us great service, and
we are much indebted to them. The Palmers did wait
for us. They have spent the day in resetting their tires
to their wagons. A most lovely evening. The moon is
shining brightly, and it is quite calm. One dislikes
to close her eyes upon such an evening. Gladly would
I sit and think over scenes and pleasures past & gone:
but rest is needed.

July 8th. The Palmers started ahead again today,
were to drive only a short distance, we to remain, until
our tires were set and then overtake them. They however drove farther than they intended, so we have not
caught up with them. Another delightful evening.
Camped by a small but excellent spring.

---

[21] The only other reference to this person is in John Zieber's diary, where
he speaks of John Minor. *Op. cit.*, p. 331.

Wednesday July 9. – Have overtaken the Palmers
and are going on in our old way again. The old gentleman seems very desirous that all should keep together, and be friendly. No knowing, however, how
long they will agree.

Sunday 13. 1851. Delightful camping place, as pretty
as we have ever had. We are near the Platte, among
the trees. It is cool and pleasant, and the sweet songs
of birds charm(s) the ear. All Nature is beautiful and
rejoicing, and we can but share its happiness. Another
Sabbath has dawned upon us, another week is begun.
Oh that it may be spent profitably, and in the praise
of our Almighty Parent.

Tuesday July 15th. Came to the Upper Ferry to day,
and then had to make sixteen miles without wood
water or grass. The arrangement about starting upon
this desert stretch was a bad one, having to commence
it at noon. The Captain (Mr. Stearns, elected last Saturday evening) was out hunting. The Palmer company would not wait to see what the Capt. wished,
but rushed ahead, the rest refused to follow at first,
but afterwards concluded to go on, yet refusing to
have anything to do with the other company again.
When evening came we were upon a bluff, at a distance
from water, wood and grass. They (our company)
went a few miles beyond the Palmers, then stopped
to rest their cattle. We being ahead had stopped with
the P – s, but when the moon rose we started on, our
company joined us, and we went on to a small stream
of clear cold water. It was a beautiful, moonlight
evening, but I was too sleepy to enjoy it. We passed
Rock Avenue, but I knew nothing of it, until we were
through it. I regretted it very much. –

Wednesday July 16. Camped upon one side of Grease wood creek, Palmers on the other. They tried to persuade Charlie & Mr. Wilhelm also Mr. Stearns and those with him to leave us and join them, but they refused. –

Thursday 17. Came to Sweet water river to day at noon. This afternoon I was riding with Mr. Wilhelm & George Barnett. We passed Independence Rock. I was rather disappointed in this. It is certainly a fine rock, but being surrounded by hills even higher than itself, it did not appear at all to advantage. Though being disappointed in what I thought it would be like, I may not have considered it in as favorable a light as I should have done. Soon after we came in sight of Devil's Gate. Mr. Barnett, Senior, Wilhelm and I went down on horseback to take a view of it. Mr. John Brown and Bailis,[22] walked down. We went on horseback as far as we could, then dismounted, (Mr. Barnett remained to take charge of the horses.) and proceeded through the whole gate. If it had not been for Mr. Wilhelm's assistance, I could not have gone through very easily, but he very kindly helped me across the stream and down the rocks –

Oct. Sunday 26th. 1851 We are now in Oregon City, were here two weeks yesterday. Yes we are at the end of our journey, and on some accounts I half regret it, on others am heartily glad. Our journey *was* a long one, lasted too long, so that we became uneasy, fearing the rainy season would set in before we would reach the end of it. But now we are here, have been two weeks, and no rain(s) until last night have we had,

---

[22] This is probably her spelling of Bailey, of whom there were many.

(though I must not forget that we were well favored in
that line while at the Cascades of the Columbia river)
this morning it cleared off and the remainder of the
day so far has been pleasant, though no telling how
soon it may cloud up. Right between the hills, a cloud
could come upon us without our knowing it until we
are greeted by it. Oregon City has a strange location.
Among rocks, and right up against a high hill, though
the water power here was no doubt the occasion of a
city's being built here. We are residing across the
river (Willamette) from Oregon City, in what is
called Linn City. Every little place here *assumes* the
title of city. We are but a few yards from the falls,
having a fine view of them from our windows on the
right hand side, on the left we see O. – C. –. Our
situation here taking it altogether is rather a pleasant
one and a *very private* one. Father only intends spending the winter here, may not remain all of that, thinks
of making his claim and settling upon it, but must look
around and endeavor to select one that will please him
well. Not worth while to take the very first ground
we meet, whether it suits or not, after coming so far
for it. Albert is with us again.[23] Came on to where
the road comes to the Columbia river, there he met us.
A happy meeting it was too. Glad, delighted were we
all to see him. Once more we are all together again,
the first time for three years. He has been very kind
in assisting us along. We should not have done so well,
had it not been for him. – I was obliged to give up

---

[23] Albert Zieber was her older brother, who had preceded them to the
West. He met them as they approached the Columbia River above the
Dalles. H. O. Lang, *History of the Willamette Valley* (Portland, Ore., 1885),
p. 750.

keeping a journal, there was not sufficient idle time
for me to write every day, so that I would get behind
hand, then could not fill up the space, so concluded
to let it go altogether. I regret that I had to do so.
When I last wrote I was speaking of Devil's Gate.
Never before was I so delighted with a view of any
kind. It was a splendid sight. The walls on each side
three hundred feet almost perpendicular, the water
rushing through over the rocks, the sweet songs of
birds mingling with its roar and the last rays of the
sun reflected from rock to rock illuminating the whole
scene then dying away as it were upon the many beautiful flowers around us, all burst upon our astonished
sight at once. Every. . .

By Windjammer and Prairie Schooner
London to Salt Lake City
⸎ Jean Rio Baker

INTRODUCTION

The diary of Jean Rio Baker is an exceedingly fascinating document out of the American past — and here is how we found it:

We were in Salem, Oregon's capital city, one day, and a young woman stepped up with the question, "Are you Doctor Holmes?"

"Yes," I replied.

"You're the Doctor Holmes who is collecting women's diaries?"

"Yes."

"Well, I'm Nancy Richings, and I have a neighbor who has a diary that will interest you."

The upshot of this episode is that we made the acquaintance of Mrs. Margaret Clift, and she has graciously made available the diary of Jean Rio Baker, an ancestor on her late husband's side of the family. It is a typescript, the original being lost.[1]

The opening lines of the English Mormon widow give a hint of what is to come. She wrote on January 4, 1851, "I this day took leave of every Acquaintance I could collect together, in all human probability, never to see them

---

[1] Typescripts of the diary are in the hands of family members, and several have been given to Utah depositories. One of the latter was used by Leonard J. Arrington and Davis Bitton in their book, *Saints Without Halos* (Salt Lake City, 1981). Jean Rio Baker's charm is not lost in their chapter on her, "Jean Baker: Gathering to Zion," pp. 39-48.

again on Earth; I am now (with my children) about to leave for ever my Native land. . ."

The rest of the diary is her day-by-day record of a journey from England by sailing ship in mid-winter to New Orleans; then by river steamer up the Mississippi to eastern Iowa; then by prairie schooner across Iowa and over the Plains to Salt Lake City, where they arrived on September 29, 1851.

Jean Rio Griffiths was a Scottish woman, having been born in that country on May 8, 1810. She wrote in her journal on May 8, 1880, "I am seventy years old this day." She and Henry Baker, one year her senior, had been married on September 24, 1832, in London. He had died on September 3, 1849, leaving her with seven children: six boys and a girl. Their names and ages (as of January, 1851) follow: [2]

Henry Walter Baker, born July 4, 1833, who was seventeen-year-old at sailing time. She called him Walter in her diary. With him was his wife, 21-year-old Eliza Ann.

William George Baker, fifteen, born June 10, 1835.

Charles Edwin, called Edwin, eleven-years-old.

Elizabeth Ann Baker (not to be confused with Eliza Ann, Henry's wife) nine-years-old, born April 20, 1841.

John Edye Baker, seven, born March 31, 1843; referred to by his mother as, "John the dear child."

Charles West Baker, born October 21, 1844, called by

---

[2] Information about the Baker family has come from several sources. Most important of all, of course, is Jean Baker's own diary and the notes she appended to it in later years. Especially helpful has been the passenger list of the ship on which they crossed the Atlantic, the *George W. Bourne*. The list is the entry for January 9, 1851, and is on page 2 of the British Mission Manuscript History, in the L.D.S. Archives in Salt Lake City. Dr. Leonard J. Arrington, Director of the Joseph Fielding Smith Institute for Church History, kindly looked up the information, copied it out, and sent it to us. In addition we have used census records, and various family papers supplied us by Mrs. Clift. These include pedigree charts, and one which was especially helpful — "Program for the Baker Family Reunion, August 16-17, 1951," printed for a family gathering in Salt Lake City.

his mother, "My poor little Charles," and described by
her on October 6 in Salt Lake City as "our dear little Babe"
who "begins to grow a little, and I hope will be given to
our many prayers, but he is very small and very delicate."
He died in Ogden at age nine.

Josiah, age four, who was ill at sailing time, died on
February 22 on board ship and was buried at sea. This was
the great tragedy of the overseas voyage. The little boy
died on Sunday, February 23, at "½ past 5 P.M."

There was one other Baker taking the journey: That
was Benjamin, who's name appears on the *George W.
Bourne's* passenger list. She describes him as "my late
Husband's Brother."

The first part of the long journey was the sea voyage
on the sailing ship, *George W. Bourne.* They boarded the
ship at Liverpool on January 7, sailed away on January
23rd, and reached New Orleans two months later on March
20 after a rough winter voyage during which few were
not seasick. Jean Baker seems to have suffered less than
most.

After the March 20 arrival in New Orleans the family
stayed on board ship until the 23rd, when the *Concordia,*
a Mississippi River steamboat, "came along side and received us and our luggage, and we started for St. Louis."
Her description of the steamer is a classic one, equal to
anything written by Mark Twain on the subject.

They arrived in St. Louis on March 29, and Jean Baker
"took a house for a month" while awaiting passage up
river. She and her family were greatly aided by a "Brother
Howard" and his wife, who were there to help Mormons
on their westward way.

In St. Louis she purchased wagons and supplies for the
overland journey. She wrote on April 4 as follows:

I have purchased four wagons and eight yoke of oxen, each
wagon to hold a fourth part of our luggage, and provisions for

our journey, our four wagons are to leave here in company with sixteen others, on April the 19th [should it be 9th?] for Alexandria Missouri, at the juncture of the Mississippi and the Des Moines Rivers by Steamboat, and then to travel overland to Council Bluffs, to joine the company, who intend to go on to the Valley this year.

The question arises, Why did they sail up the Mississippi from St. Louis, when it would have been much shorter to go up the Missouri to the Council Bluffs crossing in a more direct route that would make it unnecessary to travel by wagon all the way across Iowa?

The answer is found in the newspapers of the day:[3] On April 19 the St. Louis *Daily Intelligencer* reported, "The *Kansas* returned yesterday . . . Her officers report the navigation of the Missouri extremely difficult, even more so than they ever saw it at this season."

Again on May 9 the captain of the *Kansas* reported that he had never seen the Missouri "as difficult and hazardous of navigation as it is at present." The "*St. Paul* and *Mary Blane* were 'laid up,' and had paid off their crews."

So on April 9 at five p.m. they went aboard the steamboat, *Financier,* for another boat journey on the Mississippi. They slept in their wagons on board the steamer. They arrived at "Alexandria in the State of Missouri, immediately opposite to Warsaw, in the State of Illinois" on April 18, and on the 22nd began the wagon journey west. The first part of the journey was across Iowa, stopping at farms and small towns, an agonizing 71-day trip covering some 270 miles.

On July 2 they arrived at Kanesville, the Mormon community of that day ("or what is known as Council Bluffs"). They crossed the Missouri on July 5th. The next 86 days were spent crossing the Plains to Salt Lake City, where

---

[3] The newspaper quotes are from Louise Barry, *The Beginning of the West* (Topeka, Kan., 1972), pp. 995-96.

they arrived on September 29, 1851. On October 6 she wrote, "I have purchased a small house; with an acre of garden attached to it." It fronted on the public square. However, Salt Lake City was not to be her eventual landing place. On March 22, 1852, she wrote, "Removed to Ogden . . . and now I suppose I have finished my ramblings for my whole life."

Many years later she appended a note to her cross-country diary summing up her life since arrival in Ogden. She wrote,

> September 29th, 1869 — I have been 18 years this day, an inhabitant of Utah Territory, and I may say 18 years of hard toil, and almost continual disappointment. My 20 acre farm tuned out to be a mere salaratus patch, killing the seed which was sown, instead of producing a crop; and I am now in Ogden City, living in a small log house, and working at my trade, as a dressmaker . . . I came here in obedience to what I believed to be a revelation of the most High God; trusting in the assurance of the Missionaries, whom I believe to have been the spirit of truth, I left my home, sacrificed my property, broke up every dear association, and what was, and is yet, dearer than all, left my beloved native land, and for what? *A Bubble that has burst in my grasp.* . . In 1864 I married Mr. Edward Pearce, I had been a widow 15 years, my children all married, and I felt I had the right to decide for myself, in a matter than only concerned myself. I hoped that my old age would be cheered by his companionsip that I should no longer be *alone*. But it was not to be; he only lived six months. . .

In November, 1869, she traveled to San Francisco, where she visited her two sons and their families, John and Charles.. She stayed on and spent the rest of her life in California, with an occasional visit to Utah.

It was on July 21, 1883, that Jean Rio Baker Pearce died in Los Gatos, California. The body was buried in Antioch.[4]

---

[4] Pedigree Chart of the Baker Family.

DRAMATIS PERSONAE

Isaac Allred was a Tennesseean, had been a Mormon since 1832. He and his family, two wives, Julia and Mary, traveled across the Plains to Utah in 1851. He was captain of a company. The Allreds settled in Kaysville, Davis County, Utah. Andrew Jenson, *Latter Day Saint Biographical Encyclopedia* (Salt Lake City, 1920), III, p. 3. (Hereafter designated as *Biogaphical Encyclopedia*.)

Thomas and Joseph Bateman, brothers, and their respective wives, Margaret and Elizabeth, were elders of a large clan of Batemans from the Manchester area of England. They were farmers.

John Milton Bernhisel, whose surname Jean Baker spells "Bernhill," was Utah's first delegate to Congress. He had been elected to his new position in Utah Territory's first general election and was on his way to Washington, D.C. *Biographical Encyclopedia,* I, pp. 723-24.

William Booth had come from Staffordshire in England, his birth date October 7, 1814. On March 9 on shipboard Jean Baker wrote that he had been "suspended from fellowship for inconsistant conduct." This was the "Elder Booth" who had conducted the burial-at-sea service for little Josiah Baker. Booth continued on to Salt Lake City and on January 27, 1852, he received the blessing of the Church. He, too, kept a diary of the overland crossing from the Missouri to Salt Lake City. It was published in Betsy R. H. Greenwell, comp., *Early Utah Pioneers: Levi Hammon and Polly Chapman Bybee* (Kaysville, Utah, 1963), pp. 30-50. Booth's unit traveled at times a day or two behind the one to which Jean Baker belonged, at other times right even.

"Sister Boss" was Dorothy Boss, who with her husband, Willis, is listed in the 1860 Utah census for Box Elder County. She would have been 19-years-old in 1851, and Willis would have been 24. She was born in Maine and he in South Carolina. By 1860 they had four children, all born in Utah.

John Brown was a major Mormon figure, a Tennesseean who had been baptised in 1841. He had been a captain in the first Pioneer party that reached Salt Lake City in 1847, also a hunter for that party. Now he was a captain in the 1851 emigration. *Biographical Encyclopedia,* I, p. 512.

John Chatterly was with the same 1851 party from England to Salt Lake City as Jean Baker. A typewritten autobiography written by him in 1918 about his long journey is in the Utah Historical Society collection.

Alfred and Emma Cordon were emigrants from Staffordshire, England. They became Ogden settlers. Cordon was chosen captain of a company.

Zacharias A. and Mary (Shepherd) Derrick were close friends of the Baker family. Mary had been born in August, 1812, in Yorkshire; Zacharias had been born on March 1, 1814, in Somersetshire.

Crandall Dunn had been a Mormon since 1840. It was partly through his missionary efforts in England since 1845 until the 1851 voyage that so many English Mormons migrated to the new Zion. The Dunns became pioneers of the new city of Ogden.

Elder William Gibson, "our president," was a Scot who had been a vigorous advocate of the Mormon cause in Britain ever since his conversion in 1840. There is in the Oregon State University Library in Corvallis a copy of a rare item published in Liverpool in 1851: Orson Pratt, *A Series of Pamphlets . . . to Which is Appended a Discussion Held in Bolton, Between Elder William Gibson, President of the Saints in Manchester Conference, and Rev. Mr. Woodman.*

"Hawkins" was probably Hawkes. On August 7 there is a reference to the death marker of "Hanna Hawks." This would have been the wife of Joshua Hawkes, who went on to become a pioneer settler of Ogden in late 1851.

"Sister Henderson," who gave birth to a baby daughter and later died, is unidentified. There were a number of Hendersons with the 1851 emigration from Britain. They were Scots.

"Brother Howard" and his wife, who gave the English emigrants so much help in St. Louis, were evidently sent there to give such aid. No first names have so far been discovered. Leonard J. Arrington and Davis Bitton, *Saints Without Halos* (Salt Lake City, 1981), p. 42. There were many Howards among the early Mormons.

Orson Hyde was a longtime Mormon leader. He had been a member of the mission to England as aerly as 1837. In 1851 he was making his second journey to Salt Lake City. *Biographical Encyclopedia,* I, pp. 80-82. See also Hubert H. Bancroft, *Utah* (San Francisco, 1890), p. 773.

Captain Dan Jones spent several seasons as a guide for Mormon emigrants from the British Isles. Bancroft, *Utah,* p. 297, fn, 27.

Kay was a common surname among the pioneer Mormons. The 1860 census of Utah lists 35 of them. With no more information than Jean Baker provides it is imposible to tell which one she refers to.

There were several Kemptons among the early Mormon overlanders. It is not possible to sort out this "Sister Kemton" referred to by Jean Baker.

"Sister Kingeby" is mentioned on August 30 as having been killed in a cattle stampede. She is so far unidentified.

Thomas and Alice Margetts had been living in London, where he had practiced his trade as a coach builder and wheelwright. The Margetts family was a large one among the English Mormons. The Brigham Young University Library has the family papers.

"Brother Norton" mentioned on September 10 was probably John W. Norton, born May 13, 1810, in Franklin County, Tennessee. John and Doriatha Norton traveled the trail to Salt Lake City in 1851.

Mrs. Joseph Pearce is mentioned on July 8 as helping to care for an injured man. There were several Pearces in the Mormon exodus from Great Britain in 1851. Later, in 1864, Jean Baker, herself would marry Edward Pearce. He lived only six months after the wedding.

Morris Phelps was a widower in 1851, who was already a longtime Mormon in that year. He and his family became settlers in Alpine, Utah. *Biographical Encyclopedia,* I, pp. 373-4.

Orson Pratt was a major figure in Mormon history, especially in stimulating emigration from the British Isles. He was adept at bargaining with the shipping companies by guaranteeing a community of passengers. The 1851 migration was the result of his inspiration and planning. Reva Stanley, *The Archer of Paradise* (Caldwell, Idaho, 1937). See also article, "Orson Pratt," by Kimball Young, in *Dictionary of American Biography,* XXI Supplement 1 (New York, 1944), pp. 607-08, for Pratt's British activities.

John and Agnes Richards were Britishers who had settled in Canada. They became Mormons in the early 1840's and moved south to Nauvoo in 1842. They were now on their way to Salt Lake City.

They later became pioneer settlers of Cache Valley, Idaho. See article on Joseph Hill Richards in *Biographical Encyclopedia,* II, pp. 213-14.

Alexander and Ann Robins were New Englanders, natives of Massachusetts, who traveled over the Plains in 1851 to Salt Lake City. They were baptised there immediately after their arrival with the wagon train.

Robert and Emma Sharkey were British Mormons who migrated to the new Zion in Utah in 1851. She had been born in Warwickshire on November 11, 1832, he in northern Ireland on December 28, 1831.

Hayward Thomas was a well-known missionary preacher. He had served with the Mormon Battalion, had been to Salt Lake City in 1847. After a year in Council Bluffs, he was once more on his way to the new Zion. Davis Bitton, *Guide to Mormon Diaries & Autobiographies* (Provo, Utah, 1977), p. 357.

William Thorn's wife was having some kind of an affair aboard ship, as described by Jean Baker on March 12, 1851. She left Thorn. He went on to Salt Lake City, where he married Maria Susanna Merrick in 1852. The Thorn family was from Oxfordshire. *Biographical Encyclopedia,* I, pp. 610-11.

Hanna Wallace, whom Jean Baker visited soon after arriving in Salt Lake City, was the wife of George Benjamin Wallace. He had met the Bakers in England and was still there on a mission. *Biographical Encyclopedia,* I, p. 291.

George D. and Elizabeth Golightly Watt were English Mormons on their way to Salt Lake City in 1851. See article on "Golightly Watt," in *Biographical Encyclopedia,* III, p. 278. George Watt preached a sermon to the emigrants on "The New Birth" on Sunday, August 31.

"Sister Whitaker" could have been one of two who traveled the trail of 1851. There was an Isaac Whitaker and his young wife, Betsey, born May 4, 1833, from Cheshire. There was also an older couple, George and Sarah Whitaker from Staffordshire. They traveled with an eleven-year-old daughter, Mary Ann.

John Willis was born in Bedfordshire, England. He would be baptised on September 29, 1851, upon arrival in Salt Lake City, on his 43rd birthday.

THE DIARY OF JEAN RIO BAKER

January 4, 1851

I this day took leave of every Acquaintance I could collect together, in all human probability, never to see them again on Earth; I am now (with my children) about to leave for ever my Native land, in order to gather with the Church of Christ, in the Valley of the Great Salt Lake, in North America.

Jany. 5 – Left London for Liverpool, on arriving at Euston, S.W. found that the train had gone two hours, took lodgings for the night.

–6– Arrived in Liverpool at ½ past 8 P.M.

–7– Passed our Medical Examination, and went on board the ship, George W. Bourne in which our passage is taken. Myself 6 sons,[1] 1 Daughter, 1 Daughter-in-law, and my late Husband's Brother and Uncle and Aunt, also Mr. and Mrs. Derrick and their 4 children.

–8– Myself and Eldest Son paid a farewell visit to Mrs. Naisby, at Oxton in Cheshire. I have now as I suppose seen the last of all my Friends, in this Country.

–11– The Ship towed into the river, to be ready for a fair wind.

–12– Sunday-Meeting on Deck in the afternoon, spent the evening singing.

–13– Provisions served out for a week, laughed heartily at our supply of Oatmeal. *70 pounds.*[2]

---

1 The passenger list of the *George W. Bourne* in the L.D.S. Archives in Salt Lake City justifies her mention of "6 sons, 1 Daughter" in her entry for January 7, 1851. Others have suggested that there were only five sons, and one reference says there were four.

–15– The Ship has just got part of the mooring chains of a Government Hulk, and lost her largest Anchor and Cable, the wind has been very high the last four days, but against us, the ship rolls as badly as if she were off the North Foieland in a Gale, and that is no joke as I well knew.

–17– The anchor has just been fished up.

–19– Sunday-Meeting between decks, wind still contrary.

–23– Shift of wind in our favor, at 10 AM the tug hauled us out of the river, into the Irish Sea, at 6 PM the wind turned dead against us, more than half of the passengers sick, and us who have hitherto escaped, are obliged to hold on to anything that comes in our way, in order to keep our feet.

–24– The wind blowing tremendously, only 10 out of our company of 181 but are Sea-sick. Myself I am happy to say, with Eliza, are in the *minority*.

–25– We have had a dreadful night, the ship has seemed as if she really must turn over, several times, some of the passengers much frightened, but as to myself the sea has never had any terrors, at any time; One of the Sisters delivered of a fine healthy Boy this morning.

–26– Sunday-Meeting between decks, the Sacrament

---

2 The price of passage included measured amounts of food to be cooked by the passengers themselves, such as bread, flour, oatmeal, rice, sugar, tea. During the next year Parliament passed the "Passengers' Act" of June, 1851, which spelled out strict rules for providing food for the long voyage. Frederick Piercy, *Route from Liverpool to Great Salt Lake Valley* (Liverpool, 1855), pp. 54-57. Piercy's classic has been reprinted by the Belknap Press of Harvard University Press (Cambridge, Mass., 1962), edited by Fawn M. Brodie.

administered, after which a couple were married, by Elder Gibson our President.

–30– I went on deck to-day, the first time for a week, and a bad week it has been, all my children have been sick, but Eliza, contrary winds all the time. the Ship has not advanced 20 miles for the last 6 days.

–31– A Clear view of the Irish coast, it appears very mountainous at this distance, quite as much so as the Welsh coast saw many fishing Boats in Dublin Bay, also 5 ships, the wind has changed in our favor, and if it continues we hope soon to be out of this terrible Irish Sea. my dear little Josiah continues very weak but is not I think any worse, than when we left home. Oh how I do pray that the sea air may restore his health.

Feb. 1– We are going at the rate of 11 miles an hour, Mr and Mrs. Derrick still poorly, also Aunt and John, the dear child has suffered more from the sickness than any of us, Josiah has escaped it, and I hope is recovering.

–2– Sunday We are now on the broad Atlantic, the wind still favorable, Meeting as usual, cooked our last piece of fresh meat to-day.

–3– Plenty of wind, going at 12 miles an hour. 7 or 8 Porpoises playing round the Vessel, passed a Dutch Ship which saluted us.

–4– Spoke an English Schooner. Wind not so good.

–6– Almost a dead calm the last two days, the folks at home are I suppose sitting by a good fire, while we are on deck enjoying the view of a smooth sea, in warm sunshine.

–9– Sunday Meeting on deck, a fresh breeze has just sprung up.

–14– Still favorable wind. we have averaged 8 miles an hour since Sunday last, preaching on deck this evening by Elder Thomas Margets. I can hardly describe the beauty of this night, the Moon nearly at full with a deep blue Sky, studded with stars the reflection of which makes the sea appear like an immense sheet of diamonds, and here are we walking the deck at 9 o'clock in the evening without bonnet or shawl; what a contrast to this day three weeks, when we were shivering between decks, and not able to keep our feet, without holding fast to something or other, and if we managed to get on the upper deck, the first salute was a great lump of water in the face; Well I have seen the mighty deep in its anger with our ship nearly on her beam-ends, and I have seen it, (as now) under a cloudless sky, and scarcely a ripple on its surface, and I know not which to admire most. I can not describe it as it ought to be described, but I feel most powerfully the force of those words, "the Mighty God" which Handel has so beautifully expressed in one of his Chronicles.

–15– Still a fine wind, 3 Sail in sight. My dear little fellow not so well to-day, signs of squally weather this evening.

–16– We have had a heavy gale all night, scarcely one of ten of us can keep our footing on the deck. The sea looks like a number of hills, rolling over one another. We are obliged to sit on the deck to our meals, and hold our plates pretty firmly to prevent their running away from us. My Charles fell down the hatch-

way this afternoon. It seems almost miraculous that
he is alive, having fallen on his head. Josiah very
poorly.

–17– The wind has moderated a little but still squally.

–18– The weather very rough all night, saw shoals
of flying fish this morning, Josiah neither worse tho
no better I am afraid

–19– A good breeze in our favor.

–22– At ½ past 5 P.M. my dear little Josiah breathed
his last. He had sunk rapidly since Tuesday, when he
partially lost his speech. I did not think his death was
so near, though when witnessing his sufferings; I have
prayed that the Lord would shorten them. He has done
so and my much loved Child is now in the world of
Spirits, awaiting the morning of the Resurrection, to
again take possession of a Tabernacle purified and
fitted to enter the presence of the Great Eternal, in
the Celestial Kingdom. The Captain [3] has given me
permission to retain his little body till to-morrow,
when it will be committed to the deep, nearly a thousand miles from land, there to remain till the word
goes forth for the sea to give up its dead, then shall
I have my child again, with those others who have
gone before him, to present before the Lord, never
again to be separated. I do feel this trial to be a severe
one. I had hoped to have been allowed to take my family safely through to the city, *in the tops* of the mountains. My poor little Charles is suffering too, with
inflamation of his eyes, he has been quite blind for
two days. Spoke a French War Brig.

–23– Sunday – A beautiful morning, the body of my

---
[3] This was Captain Williams. Piercy, p. 43.

dear Boy is removed to a snug little cabin under the forecastle where the male adults of my family have watched it all night, the second mate, with the assistance of Uncle Bateman, have just sewn up the body of our dear little fellow, ready for burial. At 11 o'clock the tolling of the ship bell informed us that the time had come, that the mortal part of my dear Child was to be committed to the deep. Elder Booth conducted the service in the long. 44'/14 West. Lat. 25'/13 North. this is my first severe trial after leaving my native land, but the Lord has answered my prayer in this one thing. That if it was not his will to spare my Boy to reach his destined home with us that he would take him while we were on the Sea for I would much rather leave his body in the Ocean than bury him in a strange land, and leave him there. Charles' eyes are better to-day. he can open them a little; the rest of us are in good health.

–24– A most tremendous Squall this morning, with such a storm of rain as I ever saw before. It has the appearance of a dense fog, the deck was covered with water to the depth of 3 or four inches, in less than 5 minutes, rushing through the scuppers in a torrent, the passengers were all ordered below, so that I was unable to watch the effect of the storm. but our ship was in a greater bustle for a short time than we had ever seen it. Every sail was taken in and in a minute or two, the Vessel began to roll and pitch, as if she would turn us all into foot-balls, keeping your footing was impossible so that our only alternative was to sit on the deck and hold on how we could. This lasted about an hour when we could go up on the deck again, we found that the storm had passed away, but we had the effect of it in a heavy swelling sea, during the remainder of the day. Charlie's eyes are much better.

–25– Fine morning, numerous shoals of Porpoises, just ahead of us, one of the Brethren struck one, and hauled it on board, it measured five feet in length. it was soon skinned and cut up into pieces, a part was presented to me. I did not admire it, it was like very coarse beef and in color nearly black.

–26– Squally weather and the heat almost unbearable; Charles' eyes nearly well, the rest of us in pretty good health, the Sea is covered with foam and Gulf-weed with a flying fish here and there springing out of the water and a few porpoises tumbling over and over, as if enoying the warm sun. Our ship the center of an immense circle, bounded only by the clouds, all is grand and beautiful, and fully repays me for the inconveniences of a Sea Voyage. By the buy I have said nothing as yet about our every day life.

A bugle sounds every morning to let us know it is six oclock, when all who think proper, arise; at one half past seven it sounds again, for morning prayer, after which, Breakfast; we then make beds so we employ ourselves during the day, according to our inclinations. Sometimes a few musical ones got together and had a few tunes, sometimes sit down and gossip, and so the days pass along. When we have rough weather, we have enough to do to keep on our feet, and laugh at those, who are not so clever as ourselves, but we are most of us getting what the sailors call, our Sea legs; for my part I can now walk about the ship when she is rolling or pitching, with the tolerable ease; I have only had two tumbles, from the first; sometimes a lurch will come on a sudden, when we are at our meals, and capsise our Tea-pot, and send us, one over the other, but we are gettin accustomed to it, so we can be on our guard. Our general custom is to sit on the deck and take our meals on our lap; each family have their own department, in front of their berths, and can have their meals, without being intruded on by others. We can cook our food, in any way we please and can amuse ourselves in any way we like, (without the bounds of decorum) go to bed and get up when we choose, indeed we are under no restraint whatever. Our President is I believe a really Sincere Servant of God; his name is William Gibson, a native of bony Scotland, his office is to watch over us as a pastor, to counsel, exort, reprove if necessary, in short to see that all our doings, are in accordance with our profession as Saints of the most high God. I much regret that we shall not have his company to the Valley, but he will leave us at St. Louis.

March 2 – Sunday – Meeting as usual. The last three days have been a succession of exceedingly heavy squalls to the terror of many of our company, who have been again attached with sea-sickness. I have much course for gratitude, that neither myself or family have suffered; I have gone on deck, as often as I could, but the motion of the vessel was so violent that I could not do so without difficulty; it was awful, yet grand to look upon the sea, I could only compare it to the boiling of an immense Cauldron, covered with white foam, while the roaring of the winds and waves, was like the bellowing of a thousand wild Bulls; conversations on deck was out of the question. I could only look and wonder and admire, for through all our lit-

eral ups and downs, I have felt no fear, and were it
not that my bones ache, with the incessant motion, I
should feel no inconvenience. I was on deck this morning just about six o'clock in order to see the sun rise,
but was disappointed, the weather being very cloudy
but not so boisterous as it was yesterday, we have now
a fair wind, and are progessing at the rate of nine
miles an hour. I hope it may continue for the last few
days have driven us back some hundreds of miles.

–9– Sunday – Fair wind and plenty of it for the
whole of last week, we have passed the Bahama Islands,
and are happy in the expectation of seeing land of the
America very soon. We had a sad meeting this afternoon. Elder William Booth was suspended from fellowship for inconsistant conduct

–10– I came on deck this morning before five o'clock,
to enjoy the cool breeze, and see the sun rise, the heat
is intense during the day and it is dangerous to be on
deck with the head uncovered. Nearly half of our company are effected, more or less, with the prickly heat;
the Captain has supplied us with a large tub for the
purpose of bathing the children, and the little ones
are (many of them) dipped in it every morning the
men amuse themselves after another fashion; they put
on a thin pair of drawers and pour buckets of water
over each other, proving the benefit they receive, by
the increased healthiness of their appearance. This evening we came in sight of the island of Abercoa; it has
a stationary light.

–11– Passed the Island of Great and little Isaacs,
Green Turtle-Island; the last we were within three
miles of and could distinctly see the houses upon it,

with a number of small schooners lying by anchor. About the middle, on a rising ground stands a revolving light, which made a brilliant appearance; the island is 40 miles in length.

—12— Passed Bush Island, also double-headed-Shot; this last is not exactly an island, but a long chain of rocks. At the distance we were, it had the appearance of detached buildings; on one stands a tall lighthouse, bearing a stationary light.

We are now in the gulf of Florida; held a meeting this afternoon at which three of the sisters were cut off the church for levity of behavior (with some of the Officers of the Ship) and continued disregard to the Counsels of the President; also Elder Booth and Sister Thorn; the conduct of these two has been most shameful ever since we came on board the Ship and since they were placed under suspension, it has been worse than before. Brother Thorn is deeply grieved at the conduct of his wife. He is an excellent man and a pattern for every man in the church; we all hope he will soon be able to forget her entirely; such a woman deserves no place in the remembrance of a Man of God.

—14— Fine weather, but intensely hot. Passed 17 sail of various sizes, upon measuring the water, it was found that we have sufficient for 23 days supply. Our allowance has always been ample. I was on deck this morning to see the sun rise; there was not an atom of cloud to be seen in any direction. I have often read of the beauty of Italian skies but I am sure they cannot exceed in splendour, that which at this moment, arches over the gulf of Florida, or Mexico, as it is mostly termed.

–16–   Sunday – Meeting as usual, saw a Water-spout at 11 A.M. At seven in the evening a Violent Squall came on, driving most of the passengers below, myself with a few others remained on deck, bidding defiance to the rain, for the sake of enjoying the night of the lightening, which was very beautiful, seeming to illuminate one half of the horizon at once. We heard no thunder.

–17–   We have had a very tough night, and have been rolled about nearly as bad as we were when skirting the Bay of Biscay. Aunt and Mrs. Derrick as sick as they were in the channel. Foul winds all day. When I came on deck this morning, it was as much as I could stand, and to my astonishment the sun was rising on our starboard bow, instead of astern of us. It is now 8 P.M. and the wind has veered a little in our favor.

–18–   A fine boy has been born in the night. At 10 A.M. a boat brought a Pilot, a horrid looking fellow; the very fac-simile of a Pirate. We can now see land plainly – at 12 o'clock a steamer came and took hold of us and at 2 o'clock we were at anchor, off Belize, a pretty looking little village. A boat has come alongside, loaded with oysters, which have found a ready market.

–19–   Coming on deck this morning I was struck with the appearance of the water; it is a perfect mirror, the reflection of the houses on shore is seen as clearly in the water as they are above it. There is a small schooner lying at anchor just by the landing place, and every rope and block in her rigging is seen reversed, exactly as if standing on an immense looking glass. The water seems quite still. as much so as in one of our cisterns at home; at 9 A.M. a steamer took us in tow and we are now going up the river. The Mississippi.

–20– Our ship is at anchor at New Orleans; 170 miles from the mouth of the river. We arrived here at 5 P.M. to-day.

To describe the scenery on each [bank] of this mighty stream needs a better pen than mine; no description that I ever read has done it any thing like justice. sugar and cotton plantations abound, the houses of the planters are built in the cottage style, but large with verandahs on every side, and beautiful gardens; at a little distance are the Negro huts, from 30 to 50 on each plantation; they are built of wood, with a verandah along the front, painted white, and mostly have either Jessamine or Honeysuckle growing over them. Each cottage have a large piece of garden ground attached to it, in general appearance they are certainly very far superior to the cottages inhabited by the poor in England. Groves of Orange trees are very numerous, the perfume from which is very delightful, as the breeze wafts it towards us; thousands of peach and plum trees are here growin wild and are now in full blossom. We saw plenty of wild geese, also foxes and a raccoon or two; storks fly here in numbers, over our heads, and settle down on the river side and stretching out their long necks, look at us as if in astonishment; there is an endless variety of Landscape; the only thing which deteriorates from its beauty is the sight of hundreds of Negroes at work in the sun. Oh, slavery how I hate thee.

–21– I and Walter went on shore; I had a letter of introduction from Miss Longhurst of Gower Street, Bedford Square, to her sister, the wife of a French Gentleman, residing here, so we started at once for her residence. She received us with a truly English welcome, and actually burst into tears, at meeting with a countrywoman; she had been here 13 years; I stayed with her two days, and would have liked to stay longer; I had a good drive through the principal streets, which are very wide and handsome, visited the Markets. They are just like Covent-Garden. The houses are from 3 to 6 stories, some of them as noble in appearancce as any in Regent Street. I was showen the house in which Jenny Lind lived during her late visit, but it is more like a palace than a hotel; the Custom House, Churches, and Theatres, are splendid buildings, of course I can only speak of the exterior; the roads themselves are not kept in order as they are in London, they are not paved; Just now the weather is hot and dry, so in crossin them you sink in dust up to the ancles, in wet seasons I am told, they are one continued canal, and great lumps of stone are placed across the ends of the streets, about two feet asunder to enable foot passengers to go from one side to the other, the side walks are from 16 to 20 feet wide, and very nicely paved with flagstones; they are raised 18 inches above the carriage road, so that they are always clean and dry. The streets are laid out in exact squares, crossing each other at right angles; The spaces between the streets are called blocks, thus on enquiring for St. Peter Street, I was told it was 5 blocks further. The city stretches on one side of the river for about five miles as near as I could judge, the whole of which

length is one continuous Wharf or Levee, as the French
have named it, the ships and steamers, lie 3 or 4
deep, the whole length, and as close as they can be
stowed, the river is about as wide as the Thames at
Blackwall; the Levee is not level like the Brunswick
wharf, but of a gradual decent, from the houses to
the river, and completely covered with Bales of Cotton, and other articles of Merchandise, leaving sufficient room for the drays, which are used for the con-
veying the cargoes from the ships to the warehouses;
New Orleans was originally a French Colony, and
a large proportion of its present inhabitants are French-
men, mostly married to English women. They seem to
live in very luxurious style, during the two days, I
stayed with Mrs. Blime. I was amazed at their manner
of living; for Breakfast they take Coffee (boiled in
milk) with Eggs, Ham, Hung-beef, dryed Fish, Sal-
ads, hot Soda Cakes, Bread and Butter. for Dinner
we had Red-fish, boiled, stewed pigs feet, Rumsteaks,
Wild Goose, (Rabbits, and Squirrels too are commonly eaten) with Vegetables, Pickles, and Salad.
Two tumblers are put to each plate, and wine, and
Brandy are placed on the table, and each takes which
they please; the idea of pouring either, in *wine glasses,*
they will laugh, even Ladies will drink off a tumbler
of Port, as if it was water; Pies, tarts, cheesecakes,
confectionary, fruit, ice-cream, are brought on table,
after the meals are removed, and french brandy, poured
into a glass and most beautifully sweetened with pul-
verised sugar, furnishes the meal. Tea, as a meal they
know nothing about, but at 7 o'clock, they take supper,
which is quite as luxurious an affair as the dinner. By
10 o'clock every one is in bed and the streets are de-

serted. Now for the dress part of the affair the higher
class of Citizens (there is no nobility in America,
though never was there a people, fonder of titles, Colo-
nels, Majors, Captains, Judges, and squires, being as
plentiful as blackberries) the Upper-Ten, dress very
handsomely in European style, the Ladies especially
and they dress their slaves even more expensively. I
saw slave girls following their Mistresses in the streets,
clad in frocks of embroidered silk, or satin, and ele-
gantly worked, muslin trowsers, either blue or scarlet.
Morocco walking shoes, and white silk stockings, with
a French head-dress, similar to that worn by the Sa-
voyards, composed of silk, with all the colors of the
rainbow comingled; Jewellery glitters on their dusky
fingers, (which are plainly seen through their lace
gloves) and in their ears. Their only business in the
streets seems to be to follow the ladies, who *own them,*
and carry their reticule. Bonnets are not known to
be worn, but a queer looking thing made of muslin,
something like the Quakers bonnets, except that the
front is not rounded off, they are stiffened with cane,
or strips of pasteboard. The front is 12 inches deep,
with a horseshoe crown, and curtain half a yard in
depth, and when on the head answers the purpose of
bonnet and shawl. I thought them the most odd looking things, I had seen, but was soon glad to avail
myself of the comfort of one, in this blazing sun; I
also visited the Female Slave-Market, (no Lady enters
that for Males). It is a large Hall, well lighted, with
seats all around, on which were girls of every shade
of colour, from 10 to 30 years of age, and to my utter
astonishment they were singing as merrily as larks;
I expressed my surprise to Mrs. Blime, as she said,

"though I as an Englishwoman, detested the very idea of slavery, yet I do believe that many of the slaves here have ten times the comforts of the labourers in our own country, with not half the labor; I have been 13 years in this country and although I have never owned a slave, or ever intend to do so, still I do not look upon slavery with the horror that I once did, there are hundreds of slaves here, who would not except their freedom, if it was offered to them, for this reason; they would then have no protection, as the laws afford little or none to people of colour." I could not help thinking that my friends feelings had become somewhat blunted, if not hardened, by long residence in a slave state. From further conversation I found that if a free man married a slave, all the children of that marriage are the property of the owner of the Mother, but if a free woman marries a slave the children are free. I was shown a Gent of Colour, who is what we should call, Managing Clerk in one of the largest stores in this city; he is the property of a rich proprietor in the neighborhood; he pays his master 500 Dollars annually, his salary is $1000. He is married to a free woman, quite a light Mulatto, by whom he has a family. They live in a very handsome house which is the property of the wife, as a slave is not allowed to posses real estate; they keep a carriage and four servants, and this is by no means a singular case; it is a common occurance for master to hire out their slaves in this manner, at a salary of from 50 to $70 per month, out of which they pay their masters an agreed upon sum, the rest is their own, but spite of this all, the system is a horrible one, to English minds. Well might Sterne say, "Oh Slavery, disguise thyself as thou wilt, thou are a bitter drought."

–22– I returned to the ship this evening, with much regret; I should greatly have preferred spending a few more days with this truly amiable and generous lady and her family. She loaded us with presents, consisting of the delicacies of the climate, accompanied with several bottles of French Brandy and Claret; We agreed on a   and separated with, I believe, a mutual feeling, that we should meet no more on Earth.

–23– The steamer Concordia came along side and received us and our luggage, and we started for St. Louis.

–29– Arrived at St. Louis, our passage up the river has been delightful; yet you must know that an American steamboat is nothing like an English one; if I describe the Concordia it may serve for a general description though some are larger and some smaller. Its length is 300 feet and its width 60 feet, it is flat-bottomed, and when heavily laden, draws 7 feet water; she is built of fir, and is consequently very light; the engines and boilers are on the deck, the stoke-hole quite open on each side and the firemen have an uninterupted view of the country; the head of the vessel is pointed, the stern circular; there is a clear passage of 8 feet in width all round the boat, except where it is stoped by the paddle boxes, and those have good steps both up and down; from this which is called the lower deck you ascend by a handsome flight of steps to what is called the Hurricane deck, which is an open gallery 5 feet wide, entirely round the vessel with a low railing next the water and roofed overhead, there are chairs here, for the accomodation of the passengers. On the inner side of this gallery is a row of cabins with 2 doors each, one opening on to the gallery, the other into the Saloon, which is 150 feet in length by 30 feet in width; here the cabin passengers dine, etc., the ladies cabin is placed astern, its size is 50 feet by 30, and is splendidly furnished with sofa's, rocking chairs, work tables and a piano; the floor (as well as the saloon) is covered with Brussels carpeting; there is also a smoking room for the gentlemen, opening out of the saloon, forward in which are card-tables, etc., and in front of this there is a large open space, the whole width of the ship roofed over like the gallery and furnished with seats; from this is another staircase, ascending to the upper deck, on which are built several neat cabins, for the officers, the one forward encloses the steering wheel; here stands the pilot; completely secured from wind and weather; to the wheel two ropes are attached which are conveyed downward to the lower deck, each rope is then fixed to a lever, which works the rudder, the whole arrangement is very simple, and the elevated position of the pilot, (40 feet above the lower deck) enables him to see and avoid any collision with snags, which are pretty plentiful still, though Government has done much toward clearing them away, by sending out what they call snag-boats, with men in them, to either drag away the snags by force, or let them float off, or by sending down divers, to cut them off close to the mud. I do not know whether you know what I mean by snags and sawyers. A snag is a large tree, which has either been uprooted by a hurricane, or loosened by an inundation, and at last has been blown into the river, the heaviest part of course sinks to the bottom, and it becomes fixed in the mud, generally

in a nearly upright position, and as the foliage decays
the naked trunk remains above the surface of the water;
a sawyer is the same thing, with the exception that the
top of the tree is below the surface, and of course more
dangerous, and steamboats coming in contact with
them, are likely to have a hole knocked in the bottom
in a moment, they then generally sink at once. Scores
of steamboats have been lost in this manner, however
I have ran away from the upper deck, which is not
a very pleasant place, except in cloudy weather, and
you are seated at an elevation of 40 feet from the
river, although on a moonlight night, the view is delightful, at least to such an admirer of wild scenery
as I am; the tops of the two funnels are 10 feet higher,
they are placed forward and when there is a head
wind, the upper deck is covered with hot cinders; they
burn wood, (not coal) and when the steam gets low,
or they want to pass a steamer in advance of them,
the firemen throw on rosin by shovelfuls; the Concordia carries the mail and is as may be supposed,
one of the fastest boats on the river; the Captain be-
haved to us as a company in the most respectful manner; he conversed with me a good deal about England,
and English manners, and to him I am indebted for
most of the information I have given you.

St. Louis is 1250 miles from New Orleans, in the
State of Missouri, it is a large and fine city, extending
5 miles along the river side, and about half as far
inland, the plan of new orleans will apply to this city,
so that no other description is necessary. I took a house
for a month, into which we had our luggage brought,
and once more found ourselves in a home, though but
a temporary one; it contains two parlours, two bed-

rooms, an outhouse answering all the purposes of
kitchen and washhouse, a large yard. with back entrance and a cellar, in which I found coals enough
to last me three months, left by the last tenant, I suppose the reason of this apparent waste, is to be attrib-
uted to the cheapness of the article as the mines are
but seven miles from the city. The next discovery I
made was that I wanted a cooking stove which I purchased with all the utensils belong for $14. Early in the
evening a gentleman by the name of Howard came to
the door, and introduced himself as a member of our
church, appointed by his branch to visit all new comers, enquire of them if they are in want of any thing,
and see their need supplied, and here I would say,
that I feel under much obligations to Brother Howard
for his untiring kindness, and advice to us all during
our stay in St. Louis; his wife also greatly attached
herself to me, she introduced me to the best stores of
all kinds, and was the means of saving me many a
dollar; their house is exactly opposite to mine. They
have a family and their children and mine soon became acquainted and enjoyed themselves finely in their
rambles about the town, and the open country beyond;
the Markets are extremely good, they open at four
o'clock every morning except sunday, all kinds of
meat, poultry and fish, is very cheap, the flesh meat
is good, but not so large and fat as in the English
Markets. Vegatables and fruits are abundant, and of
great variety; Groceries, wines, and spirits, are very
cheap, I have omitted to say that we have found the
weather gradually cooler, coming up the river.

April 4– We had a heavy fall of snow, and were glad
to sit by a good fire, on the next day to our astonish-

ment, we were glad to throw open the windows, and
this, I am told is the general character of American
springtime, but the summers are entensely hot; We
had one days heavy rain with thunder, on the following morning I looked in vain of the road, but saw a
perfect river in place of it, and Mrs. Howard at her
parlour window, laughing at my evident astonishment; the side walks are all right, being raised so
much above the road, and the lumps of stone, I have
before mentioned, in describing New Orleans, enable
the pedestrians to get on pretty well, as to the horses
and oxen, (which last are more commonly used, except
in private carriages) they dash through it without
ceremony, sending the watery mud in all directions,
which to those like us, do not believe in sprinkling,
is not very agreeable; the town however being built
on a raising ground from the river, is soon dry again;
the churches are magnificent buildings, by the buy
any place of worship, let it belong to what denomi-
nation it may, has a steeple and is called a church,
the catholics have three churches, each surmounted
with a large gilded cross, the presbyterians three, (two
of them splits from the first) the Baptists four, the
Episcopalians and Independents, several each, then
there are the Methodists and Luthern and Swedish
churches, so that religions are as plentyful as can be
wished; the poor despised sons of Africa too have a
little church to pray and praise the Lord in, but it is
only lately that their Masters have allowed them this
priviledge; the Mormons have six Meeting rooms,
they have also the use of the Concert Hall in Market
Street, on Sundays, which holds three thousand persons, and I could but feel amazed to see that spacious

room filled to overflowing, and the staircase and lobby
crowded with those who could not get inside; they
have an orchestral Band, and a good choir, ten of
whom are trebbles; I went on Palm Sunday to one of
the Catholic Churches, I had as good a squeeze as
ever I had, when endeavoring to gain admission to
one of Julian's Concerts, when I did get inside, the
lay-brothers in attendance, put me in a seat where I
could both see and hear to advantage, the Mass was
splendid, they have a powerful Organ, and a fine set
of singers; the solos and duetts were beautiful performed, the Organ began, which gave to the Choruses
a much finer effect, after the service was ended I was
allowed to look around the interior of the building,
at the upper end, are three alters, the high alter of
course in the center; the alter cloth is of white satin,
richly embroidered, edged with rich lace, half a yard
in depth, the coverings for the cushions are of purple
velvet; the alter rails are of black walnut handsomely
carved and polished; on each side are seats for the
scholars and Nuns of the adjoining Convents, strange
looking beings these last, they wear black wollen shawls
reaching down to the hem of their coarse black camlet
gowns, a close bonnet made of black glazed cambric,
and black crape veils, reaching to the knees, well may
they be called the *black-nuns;* the attendant priests
wear long gowns, also black, with a hempen cord round
the waist, to which hangs a rosary and crucifix; on
each side of the building are Confessionals, with dark
green curtains, the walls are ornamented with a number of finely executed oil paintings, but horrible to
look at, being all of them representations of the Marty-
dom of different Saints, in the upper part of the church,

(above the Gallery) are several little chapples, dedicated to various saints, and gloomy looking places they
are but the alter in each of them is much ornamented;
adjoining the church is a College similar I am told to
that at Maynooth, so much for public places. I have
purchased four wagons and eight yoke of oxen, each
wagon to hold a fourth part of our luggage, and provisions for our journey, our four wagons are to leave
here in company with sixteen others, on April the 19th
[probably the 9th?] for Alexandria, by Steamboat, and
then to travel overland to Council Bluffs,[4] to join the
company, who intend to go on to the Valley this year.

–19–[9?]   At 5 P.M. went on board the Financier
Steamboat; on each [side] of the vessel was lashed a
barge, one of which received our waggons, the other
our cattle; seeing this, we thought it better to wave
our right to berths in the steamer, and betook ourselves
to our waggons, here we made our beds, and slept in
comfort, without the constant jerking, which is always
caused by the action, of machinery. In the morning
when I drew aside the curtains at the end of our
wagon, I was almost startled at finding myself close to
what I took to be a high stone wall, but on looking
upwards I found it to be a pile of rocks, some hundreds
of feet in height, the top of which was covered with
verdure; I cannot describe the grandeur of the scenery, it was almost appalling, in some places it seemed
as if the pressure of a finger would have sent it top-
pling down; their rocky shores are so perpendicular,
that our boat could in safety run in close enough for

---

[4] The question arises as to why they sailed up the Mississippi and not the
Missouri to Council Bluffs. For an answer to the problem see our introduction
to Jean Rio Baker's diary.

us to pluck the blossoms off the trees which grew at their base, and in the cravasses within our reach here and there. masses of the rock had fallen and trees and shrubs had grown in their places; every few miles we came to a town, built near the river side, the hills behind, rising above the tops of the houses; leaving the towns, we every now and then saw the cottage of the solitary settler, with its enclosure of perhaps 40 or 60 acres of land, the cattle and sheep grazing, and pigs and poultry running at liberty, the man and his elder children would in most cases look at us as we passed, sometimes waving their hands to us by way of a salute, while the wife would stand at the door, mostly with a child in her arms; we passed hundreds of these farms, besides seeing tens of thousands of acres without an inhabitant. While gazing on these scenes, a gentleman passed me on the edge of the barge, and looking up I saw that he was intoxicated. I had scarcely turned my eyes from him, when I heard the shouts of the passengers, that somebody had fallen into the river; going around to the other side I saw the same Gent, who had just passed me struggling for his life, the boat was stopped instantly, and every effort made to save him, but to no purpose, as he sunk he threw out his pocketbook, which was picked up by one of the men, and given into the hands of the clerk, in order to be restored to the relatives of the deceased; it contained his address, and 275 dollars; it appeared that he was a citizen of the town of Hannibal, in the state of Illinois; he was the owner of what is here called a flat, which is a sort of a barge very wide and long and made square a both ends, these are filled with produce, of various kinds, and then roofed in, and

the sides closed; at one end a cabin is built for sleeping
and cooking in, these flats are taken down to New
Orleans, the freight is taken out, and sold, and the
vessel is then taken to pieces, and the timber sold also,
the owner taking his passage in a returning steamboat,
to his home and when arrived there set to and build
another, load it, and away again; those flats are built
entirely of fir planks, and are very light, they seem
to just lie on the surface of the water, and when laden,
will carry from 60 to 80 tons. Our unfortunate fellow
passenger had been down to New Orleans and was returning with the profits of his journey, when he met
with his death in the way I have described, not more
than 50 miles short of his home; our vessel remained
some time stationary but we saw him no more, the probability is that he had been sucked into one of the holes
with which the bottom of this river abounds, or his
clothing caught by a sawyer, and he was unable to
extricate himself, this occurence cast a gloom over us
for the remainder of the passage, and I was glad when
we landed on the 18th [of April] in the evening, and
a bad landing is was for our poor cattle, for the brutality of the men belonging to the boat, was most
shameful, and many of the poor beasts suffered much
in consequence; however we all go ashore at last, and
without losing any of our luggage, which was more
than I expected. We drew up our wagons, on an open
space of ground, by the side of the river, close to the
town of Alexandria in the State of Missouri, immediately opposite to Warsaw, in the State of Illinois,
and here we made our first encampment, we then had
a fire, there being plenty of wood lying about, in all
directions and soon had our kettles boiling, and we

sat down to a comfortable cup of tea, afterwards the
men took our cattle to water, and then placed them
in a large yard near at hand, having procured some
hay for their food for the night; during this time we
got our beds made in our wagons, and on the return
of the Brethern, we unitedly offered up our thanks-
givings to the God of Heaven, for bringing us here
in safety, through unseen, and unknown danger, and
then retired to rest, feeling sure of his protection during the night.

I should like here to say a little about this mighty
river, which I have seen in all probability for the
last time; Mississippi is the name given to it by the
Indians, signifying the *Father of Waters*. It has been
explored, I am told for 4800 miles without coming
to its source, and is supposed by some, to at last lose
itself in the Pacific Ocean, it has tributary streams,
more than any other river known in the world, it is
of various widths and on its surface are many small
Islands, inhabited only by birds and otters, the water
is very muddy, but perfectly sweet, and as soft as rain
water, the instant you leave the Gulf of Mexico, the
water is entirely free from salt, the current running
only one way, that is toward the sea, the distance from
St. Louis to this place is 230 miles, so that I have travelled on this river 1630 miles, and I will say that such
splendid scenery, both wild and beautiful, I never expected to have looked upon, it has seemed to repay us
for all our inconveniences, and here we are all in good
health, I do not anticipate as much pleasure in our
overland journey, as we must expect a life of toil,
fatigue, and many privations, to which we are un-
accustomed, still when I recall to mind the various

scenes through which we have passed, and the thousands of miles we have travelled, during the last three weeks or I would say the last three months, and the manifold instances of preserving mercy we have received at the hands of our Heavenly Father, I doubt not I shall still, (If I remain faithful) enjoy the same protection, upon the land, as I have done upon the waters, I have told you as well as I could the major part of what I have come in contact with, and the future will most likely be an account of the trials, difficulties, and privations, such as at present I have no idea of, so as to be able to provide against them, but as you are aware I am not one to go though the world with my eyes shut, I expect to be able to send you some little description of my travels by land, to amuse you in a winter's evening. In the mean time may the God of Heaven bless you eternally.

JEAN RIO BAKER

May 21 – 1851 [Should be April 21] We have been at Alexandria three days, it is a newly settled town, containing about a thousand inhabitants, and boasting of its Mayor, Corporation, Court-house, and school-house, which last does duty for Chapel on Sundays, there are some very good stores here with a public bakery, post-office, 2 doctors shops, 2 public houses, a saddlers, a furniture store, a small levee, near which a wornout steamboat is moored, and styled the *Hotel,* and is a place of resort for the Gents of the town, who are fond of gambling and drinking, the lower part is fitted up as a general provision store and is very convenient for passing steamers, which generally stay a short time for passingers to make purchases.

–22– We left Alexandria this evening a 5 o'clock, intending to go to a mile out of the town and then turn out our teams to graze, I can just fancy how you would laugh, could you see us, taking our first lesson in Ox-driving, and our cattle taking every direction, except a straight forward one, I regret to say that two of my oxen have been so much injured by the brutality of the boat-men, that I have been obliged to buy two more in their place, thus losing at once 46 dollars to begin with, on encamping and examining our animals we discovered that another had been so badly strained, as to make it doubtful whether it will recover or not.

–23– After breakfast, we moved on 4 miles, and encamped on a very pretty spot, with plenty of grass, we are close to a wood through which runs a branch of the Des-Moine river, here we intend to stay for a week in order that the cattle may recruit, as they are in a far worse condition than they were when we left St. Louis thanks to the steamboat men.

–28– We have had a very pleasant week, lovely wether and I have been reminded of the days we used to spend in Epping, Forest lang syne, the only drawback has been, that my sick Ox has died and I have had to pay 26 dollars for another. There is a very comfortable farmhouse near our encampment, where we have procured a plentiful supply of butter at 10 cents the pound, and milk at 10 cents the bucketful; Our boys also have been several times to the wood, shooting, so we have been able to add a little game to our table, when they started, I charged them to respect the Hay-stacks, but to my astonishment they came back, bringing with them a squirrel, and a bird

about the size of a pigeon, both of them very nice
eating, we have been visited by some of the country
people who behave in a friendly manner, and seem
ready to give us any information that may be useful
to us in our travels, some of them appear to be intelligent, and some exceedingly uncultivated, one man
congratulated me on having been able to escape, from
such a land of slavery, and oppression, as he said he
understood England to be, I felt all my British blood
rising, at his insulting speech but the poor mortal
evidently knew no better, so I only smiled in reply;
he had just caught a very fine catfish, weighing 25
pounds which I purchased of him for a quarter of
a dollar, he enquired if we had any such food in the
old country I acknowledged we had no catfish, but
said I, we have spouts and shrimps, I thought of our
Hallibut suppers in Bow-Lane, when partaking of
our purchase to which in flavor and richness it bears
a striking resemblance.

May 2– We have travelled some few miles every
day, and are now stopped by a snow storm, and the
cold is go great, we are glad to take refuge in our
wagons; do not expect me to describe our road, as
they call it, it is a perfect succession of hills, vallies,
bogs, mudholes, log bridges quagmires, with stumps
of trees, a foot above the surface of the watery mud,
so that without the utmost care, the wagons would be
overurned, 10 times a day, Oh for the Town-roads,
of Old England, we each day hope, that we shall have
better traveling on the next, but as yet our changes,
have only been from bad to worse.

–3– The sun shone brightly this morning, and the
snow which fell yesterday is fast melting away, we

have stayed here the whole day; a middle aged man from whose farm is close by, joined us in the evening by our camp fire, and chatted with us for two hours, giving us a deal of information, interesting in itself, and very useful to us.

–4– Sunday we started this morning, much to my regret, for I do not like Sunday travelling, but our Captain gave us a reson for doing so, the fear of not being in time to meet the company at the Bluffs: At first starting one of my teams turned sulky, and would not move in any direction, when all at once they gave a sudden start, and running round broke the tongue of the wagon, I felt my heart sick at this beginning supposing in my ignorrance that we should have to remain until a wagon maker could be procured from the nearest town, however Uncle Bateman, without asking any questions, proceeded at once to lash a piece of cord and then affixed a chain to the wagon, one end of which he fastened to the Oxen's yoke, and so enabled us to move onward, we found the road very heavy, and the water still lying in the hollows, we managed to get along until noon, when we halted for an hour, to feed the cattle and ourselves; on looking among our company I found that there was scarcely one wagon but had received some injury, or met with some disaster or other; after dinner, we set off again; our travelling to day, is over Prairie land, it is 15 miles from one wood to the other, covered with grass, but not the smallest shrub to be seen; in the hollows the mud is so deep that the wagons sink to the axles, we have had to double teams, and so help each other out of our muddy difficulties, we got along pretty well, until we came to the top of a higher hill than those

we had passed, and on looking down we saw Elder
Margett's wagon, sunk to the axles, and himself with
some others unloading it, the prospect was a gloomy
one, as each of us might expect the like disaster, however we got *him* out, and by going up a little higher,
we got ourselves over, after getting to the top of the
next hill, we saw before us as bad a gully, as the last,
we at once doubled our teams, in order to take over
half the wagons, and then returned for the remainder,
this time one of my wagons struck breaking the tongue-
pin, with the jerk, fortunately it was the last vehicle in
company so we at once made up our minds to hault
for the night, we soon had a fire, and the kettle on,
while we were preparing our supper, a Farmer-look-
ing man, accompanied by a tall well looking negro,
came up and offered to assist us in repairing our
wagon, and setting at once to work, in about two
hours, all was right again, the farmer then bade us
good night, refusing all recompence, and taking two
of the lads in order that they might bring back a
supply of corn for our cattle, our black visiter remained with us and shared our supper, which consisted of coffee, bread and butter and remains of two
fine geese, which I purchased yesterday for 25 cents
each, our new acquaintance proved himself a very
intelligent man, and amused us very much, by his
description of some Indian wars, and their term-
ination, in which he had been engaged, told us of the
manner in which the great Chief Keokuk, was by
strategem taken prisoner with one of his warriors,
and how he was taken to St. Louis receiving there
the visits of almost all the city, spoke of the dignity
of his whole bearing, and the splendid blanket and

leggings he wore, this is 12 years since, and the town is now built near the spot where the last fight took place, which is named Keokuk. He was afterwards taken to visit several of the large cities, and was presented with a valuable rifle, plenty of ammunition, a horse and trappings of the most expensive kind, and liberty to return to his own nation, and tribe when a peace was concluded between him and the Whites, which has never been broken, we sat conversing until 12 o'clock, when our friend bade us good night, and left us to go to his own home, a bout ¼ mile off, after he was gone we expressed to each other our surprise, at finding so much intelligence, and I may add refinement, in the language and manners of our late visitor, when Walter told us, that he learned from the farmer who had supplied us with food for our travel, that John, was a slave, and had been from his birth, but that he was free in every thing by the name, that he had the sole management of a large farm, out here on the Prairie, that he bought and sold how he pleased, and went out, and came home when he thought proper, by this time all our company had gone to bed, excepting Uncle, Mr. Derrick and myself. I thought of you all, and what you would say, could you see us, sitting in the open air, with nothing to tell us of a living world, but the croaking of the frogs, in the spring time near us, the stars glittering in the heavens, and the moon shining brightly, enabling us to see for miles around us, I felt at the moment a sense of security, and freedom, I cannot describe, and retired to rest, with a thankful heart, that we are brought thus far, in safety.

–5– We started this morning early, and travelled

on, (allowing time for dinner) till the evening, when
we saw before us a tremendous hill, or rather a con-
tinuance of them, for as we got to the top of one, we
discovered three others, each towering above the rest,
one of them Bretheren called it going up a flash of
lightening edgeways, however we arrived at the top
at last, and encamped for the night, we then sat down
by the camp fire, enjoyed our warm coffee and toast,
and went to bed.

–6– Started at 8, this morning, and went on pros-
perously it being level prairie, about the middle of
the day, we came in sight of a log house, surrounded
by a very neat garden, near the roadside, when out
ran a tidy looking woman, and enquired if we wanted
any groceries. I and Eliza went into the house, and
found that it was kept by an English woman. she
had been in America 7 years, and was a native of
White Chapel, when she found that we came from
that neighborhood, she seemed as rejoiced as though
she had found some of her family, we stayed about
half of an hour, bringing with us a plentiful supply
of various kinds of eatables, we then traveled on again,
and came to dogtown, a little village containing about
30 houses possessing however, a postoffice, and a
doctors shop, about from this we entered the state
of Iowa.

–7– This day one of my Oxen took sick, so at night
we encamped by the side of the wood, through which
ran the Sac-and-Fox river, intending to remain the
next day, in order to doctor it up a little, the weather
is beautifully fine, and a ramble in the forest very
agreeable. Eliza and I, with some of the children,
visited a little town at a short distance, and were

invited into one of the houses to rest, and refresh
ourselves, we found the Lady a kind motherly woman,
and her husband as friendly and sociable, as could
be wished, we stayed 3 hours, and left, promising to
visit them again the next day if we had time.

–9– Paid our promised visit to Mr. and Mrs. Big-
gins they much wished the camp would stay a few
days, to recruit the cattle, this little town does not
contain more than 40 houses, among them is the post-
office, Merchant store, for the sale of linen drapery,
Ironmongery, stationary glass, earthware, saddlery,
grocery, boots and shoes, powder and lead, & & &,
the bar-room, or whiskey shop and the school house,
which last does duty for Church on Sundays, and
a little out of town, on a bend of the river is the mill,
the name of the place is Stringtown, we remained
with our kind hosts, till the train came up, and I
left them with regret. I would just remark here, that
nothing can exceed the kindness of the people as we
pass along, many a time, when our wagons have been
in a mudhole that the men working in the fields, have
left their ploughs to come and help us out, men too
who in our country, would be called Gentlemen, owning 500 to 1000 acres of land, but it seems to be rule
among them to help every one who is in need, and
they are ready at all times to impart any information
which they think will be useful to us, their wives are
just the same, and we in general, encamp near a farmhouse for the convenience of supplying ourselves with
butter, eggs, milk and we sure are to be invited to
their houses, in order to partake of their hospitality,
I often think that there is no person so thoroughly
independent as an American Farmer, his land is his

own, beef, mutton, pork, and poultry, shears his own sheep, and his wife spins the wool, dyes it of various colours, and in many cases weaves it into cloth for dresses, and other articles of clothing, Blankets, flannels. I have been in many a farmhouse, and never could discover, any thing like scarcity of the comforts of life, their furniture is plain, but good of its kind, and in most cases, their houses are very clean.

–9– We left Stringtown to-day, and encamped at night in a spot, to which I gave the name of Devil's Glen from its horrible entrance, having to pass through a bog, in which the wagons stuck to the axles, however we got through without accident, made our coffee had our supper, and went to bed.

–10– Purchased three yoke of Oxen this morning, and started forward on our journey, passing through a town called Drakesville, (Jonathon [5] is very fond of French terminations) we encamped at night on a hill a mile from town, here I bought a pig, (which when killed and cleaned weighed 70 pounds) for a Doller, also three fowls for 25 cents.

–13– We have been detained, by incessant rain for two days, we set off this morning, and by two o'clock arrived at Wap-creek, and now I want you all by my side, for I cannot by any description of my own do justice to the scenery around us, imagine yourself standing upon a hill at least 3 times the height of that in Greenwich park, and looking down into a complete basin, across the bottom of which runs a wide stream of water, which we have to ford, the

---

5 "Jonathan" or "Brother Jonathan" was a nickname given by Britishers to Americans.

drivers wading up to their waists one on each side of the cattle, in order to keep them in the right track, I confess I trembled as I looked, for I expected no less than to see the waggons run over and crush the cattle, during the descent, as soon as we got over, we made a good fire and concluded to turn our animals out to graze, as they were much exhausted.

–14– Our route to-day has led us through a complete quagmire through which the cattle are floundering, for nearly 4 hours, at the end of which we had progressed about 3 miles, we came out on a rising ground, and encamped for the night.

–15– Rest all day.

–16– Started at eight o'clock, and in an hour came to a worse bog, than the last if possible, it took 16 oxen to a wagon so we could proceed but slowly, we were obliged to leave one wagon, our animals being worn out, after going through a small wood, we came out on the top of a hill, and encamped.

–17– some of the company set out to fetch the wagon we were obliged to leave behind yesterday, and which they were between 3 and 4 hours accomplishing, this night we had an awful thunder storm, with the rain literally pouring in England we knew little about thunder, but here among the hills the echo's are so numerous, that we frequently hear the second clap begin to rattle before the first has finished, we were confined to our wagons the whole of the next day.

–19– This day one of our company lost a dear little babe by death, we started this afternoon, but found the roads quite impassible, we managed to proceed for about 2 miles and came to a nice dry hill, at the

bottom of which runs a clear stream, with a pretty
waterfall, the weather is now fine, and the flowers are
lifting their heads, and looking more beautiful than
ever, there are a great variety of flowers growing on
the prairie, such as are cultivated in our gardens at
home, we are constantly walking over violets, prim-
roses, daisy's, bluebells, the lily of the valley, col-
umbines, of every shade, from white to the deepest
purple, virginia stocks in large patches, the wild rose
too is very plentiful, perfuming the air, for miles,
with a numerous variety of beautiful plants, whose
names are unknown to me. Onions also grow wild,
by the sides of several streams, while in the forests,
hundreds of trees have their trunks covered with the
hop, or the grapevine.

–20– Started at 7 this morning, and by 12 o'clock,
came to Dodge's Point, halted for dinner in a delightful grove of cottonwood trees, afterwards started and
came out on the open prairie, travelled on till dusk,
without seeing a human habitation, or a single tree,
encamped, had our supper, and then to bed.

–21– We have a most awful thunderstorm, during
the night, surely this is a stormey land, this morning
a large wolf ran across the prairie in front of the
camp, we passed yesterday a great many of their dens,
there are simply mounds of earth, which the animals
throw up, and made their nests in the hollow underneath, leaving an entrance hole on one side, they do
not attack the human race, or any large animals, living chiefly on deer, rabbits, squirrels, and which are
very numerous, at 10 o'clock we had another storm
begin, which has continued the whole of the day;
while I am now writing the claps of thunder are

awful, they seem to be all round us at once, our vehicles shake violently at every clap, the little gully
at the bottom of the hill across which I could have
stepped with ease yesterday evening, is now a rapid
stream, at least 20 feet in depth, I mean width, and
is rushing down the hollow in a perfect torrent, we
are quite snug in our castles. this evening after the
rain cleared we saw myriads of fire-flies the first we
had ever seen, and I thought them the most beautiful
natural phenomena, I had ever beheld.

–22–   Thunder again during the night, with the wolves
howling in concert, we set off this afternoon, at 3 o'clock
intending to go 8 or 10 miles, when at the first start
our Captain's oxen ran round, and before they could
be stoped broke the wagon tongue, so we have to stop
here to-day to repair it, tedious travelling this, 32
days since we left Alexandria, and only advanced
116 miles.

–23–   Started after breakfast, and traveled on till
four o'clock, when we came to what they call a Slue,
that is a hollow part of the prairie, where the rain
has settled, and created a perfect bog, sometimes es-
tending for miles, when we have to double teams, and
perhaps triple them, in order to get the wagons over,
well we came to the slue and had succeeded in getting
all the vehicles to the opposite side, except Elder Mar-
get's, and two of mine, I and Eliza were sitting in one
of them, when Margett's cattle started round. Mrs.
Margett and her sister-in-law, Mrs. Bond, each with
an infant in her arms, were standing near, and in trying to stop the oxen, were thrown down by them,
how I got out of my wagon I know not, but on coming up with them, I found that the wheels had gone

over Mrs. Bonds waist, and Mrs. Margett's legs just above the ancles, the children were unhurt, William snatched up the two babies and ran off with them to Eliza, he then came back and assisted me to raise the poor women, the weight of the wagon had completely forced them down into the soft mud, and providentially they had no bones broken, had it been on the hard ground, nothing could have saved them from being crushed, we laid they on my bed, and in this way we got them over the bog, as soon as we got on the solid ground we halted for the night.

–24– Started this morning at 9 o'clock, Mrs. Margetts has had a good night and is able to walk with assistance, Mrs. Bond has slept part of the night, but suffers much pain, and is not able to move, but as she is lifted; we got through to-day, without any disaster; encamped and had our supper, and afterwards sat down around the camp fire, and enjoyed ourselves in singing for an hour and then to rest.

–25– Sunday– Our leaders had agreed upon travelling to-day, in consideration of having had to wait so long, for favorable weather; and the fear of not being able to reach the Bluffs, in time to join the principal camp, else it is the rule, never to travel on the Lords-day. We started at six and one half and travelled on very comfortably for a couple of miles, when we came to a little town, composed of log and plank houses; the first of which was raised, last June. I went into one of the houses, to get a draught of milk and have a few minutes chat. About 11 we came to the head of Sheridan [Chariton] river, which we had to ford, and ascend a dreadful hill on the other side; however we got along without accident, and then halted for dinner, we then travelled on till 3 and then encamped for the night.

–26– A violent thunderstorm, with rain from midnight till 8 in the morning; started about noon, the roads very heavy, went 6 miles, when the Captain's wagon tongue and axle broke, so we are obliged to wait.

–27– All day repairing the Captain's wagon.

–28– Got 4 miles, when Jones run on a bank and smashed one of his wagon wheels– and awful thunderstorm this evening.

–29– and 30– Thunder and rain all the time, started at 11 A.M. and by doubling teams, managed to get about 8 miles. Arrived at little White-breast creek found it a roaring torrent; encamped for the night, on the side of a hill; plenty of wood, and the water cool, and sweet; plenty of gooseberry bushes also plum and peach trees loaded with fruit.

–31– Our men rose at 4 this morning, in order to make a bridge, when one of the storms we are so used to, came on and in a few minutes they were drenched through; finished the bridge at 8, had breakfast, began to get the wagon over; the creek rising fast, 3 feet in 3 hours; got 4 wagons over, when the bridge washed away, all but the sleepers waited till the waters subsided, rebuilt the bridge, and got the rest over by 6 o'clock; a right hard days work– mosquitoes plentiful.

June 1– Travelled 12 miles, to a creek which we had to ford, encamped among some gooseberry bushes, and picked fruit enough for a pudding for supper.

–2– Started at eight, came to a creek with a sandy
bottom which we forded, wagon turned over on its
side, but was lifted up uninjured, halted for dinner,
crossed crooked creek stopped for the night at 6,
found muscles 4 inches long– heard the whippur-
will, thunder and rain at night as usual.

–3– Started at 8, came to a deep creek at 11, no place
to ford, so encamped while the men built a bridge,
very pleasant spot, being a perfect grove.

–4– Started at 8, made one mile, and stopped by
another creek, were 6 hours getting over it thus encamped.

–5–6– The road impassible. I went to a farmhouse
one half mile off in hopes of being able to purchase
some butter, heavy rains came on so that I could not
return to the camp, the water being in the hollows,
higher than my knees. I have stayed all night at the
farmhouse, the thunder has been fearful, it seemed
even to have frightened the wolves, who have been
howling and yelping round the house all night, we
have had thunderstorms every day for 4 weeks–
arrived at [Mt.] Pisgah, found the river was swollen,
we could not cross it, the low lands being under water;
encamped on the high prairie one half mile from
[Mt.] Pisgah, wild stawberries in abundance.

–7– The men all day making a bridge over a part
of the bottom, which had been broken up by the overflowing of the river just in our road; the river is falling slowly. only five families left in [Mt.] Pisgah,
I visited the graveyard, it tells a sad tale of the sufferings of the Church in the driving from Nauvoo.

–8– Crossed Grand river on a dug out, dined with

a womans family who had been washed out of their habitation, travelled 3 miles, crossed another creek. and stopped for the night.

—9— Started at 10. Crossed a sand-hill at noon, got to 12 mile creek at 6, forded it without accident, and encamped on the edge of 20 mile prairie.

—10— A miserable day altogether   got 16 miles, crossed five ravines, and four creeks, upset three wagons, got my own bedding wet through, and encamped by ourselves, surely this is anything but pleasant.

—11— Started at 7, overtook the camp, breakfast with them, and started at nine and one half, Margetts and Taylor, took themselves off, much to the satisfaction of us all, they being not very agreable travelling companions, we stopped at night in a wood by a river; a pretty spot, but mosquitoes plentiful.

—12— The river being deep, we had to unload the wagons previous to fording it; the men laid two logs across the stream, in order to carry over our luggage, all was accomplished in safety; we made 3 mile and were stopped by a storm, which has every apearance of continuing; enjoyed a hearty supper of fried ham, pancakes, and cocoa.

—13— The storm increased during the night; about midnight it seemed as if the thunder was close to the earth. About 5 it cleared off; some of the men got up, and made us a good fire, and the Captain rode forward to examine the road; found a creek one mile off, but so swollen, as not to be fordable. Our camp is on a hill, with a small wood on one side of us. This afternoon it has dried up a good deal, and I took a walk back of our last camping place, which was in a bottom, but found it completely under water. We are reduced to 6 wagons. (division having entered among us, the rest have left us at different times) the Captains Jones and my 4, there is every prospect of another storm tonight, but roses are in full bloom all around us, with various other flowers; their perfume is delightful.

–14– The storm began about 11 last night, and has continued without intermission till nearly noon today. I cannot describe the thunder; it is unlike any I have ever heard; as to the rain upon our wagons covers I can only compare it to millions of shot, falling on sheets of copper; sleep is out of the question as well as conversation; for though Aunt and I were in the same wagon, it was with difficulty we could make each other hear. Of course there is no chance of proceeding, so I made up my mind to a days needlework; being on the top of the hill, we are not inconvenienced by the surrounding waters. We are 45 miles from human habitation, but we are as merry as larks, and our now small company, much happier than when there was so many of us. Our long anxiety is, whether we shall be to late to go to the valley this year.

–15– Heard from a stranger, that there are no wagons within 70 miles of us; so it is not likely that Hawkins will overtake us now. Started at 3 P.M. and by throwing a deal of brushwood into the creek, we were able to cross it, and made about 8 miles.

–16– Fine weather. Came to a dense forest, except where it has been partially cleared for the road. Found a deserted log house. A creek runs along the hollow, which from the accumulated waters has overflowed its banks. The Captains sounded it and found

its depth 40 feet, so we must remain here, until another
bridge is made.

–17– An equestrian traveller came up, who is on
his road to Kanesville, but he too is obliged to wait
till the bridge is completed. here are gooseberries in
abundance, giving us a nice variety in our fare.

–18– Saw a traveller on foot, and without a coat
approaching on the opposite side of the creek; as
he came toward us, he told us he was on his way to
St. Louis. He left Kanesville 2 days since, and had
walked the distance. He tells us there are 200 waggons
waiting there, so we think we shall not be too late
at last. He had passed six wagons yesterday 40 miles
off, we suppose them to be those of Margetts &. Finished the bridge by twelve. had dinner and started;
crossed the bridge safely, and went over some mile
of prairie; came to another creek found it too wide
and deep to cross, and no timber to make a bridge,
so tried to head it by going 2 miles round; had to
go over a dreadful piece of bottom land, entirely under
the water, had to put 7 yoke of Oxen to each waggon,
at first going off, the Captain's waggon tongue broke;
they lashed it together with ropes, and set off again;
found on getting to the opposite hill, that there was
another bottom to cross, worse than the last; and a long
steep hill to finish with; we had to increase our teams,
to 9 yoke to each waggon, and were even then obliged
to stop every few minutes for the cattle to recover
breath. Eliza's wagon and mine, went over first so
that by the time all had got over, (3 hours) we had
our kettles boiling, tea made, and supper ready, as
soon as the sun went down, the lightning began to
flash, which was a good thing for our men, as they

were thus enabled to see and avoid, a deep serpentine
ravine, which crossed the bottom, they came in completely exhausted.

–19– It has been a very stormy night; started at 10,
came to a high hill, where we have waited all day,
for the river to fall, so that we can make another
bridge; Mended the Captains waggon, plenty of wild
fruit.

–20– Still waiting for the river to fall; the stranger
who overtook us on the 17th, still remains with us;
he tells us he has been possessed of considerable property, as a stock-raiser, but has lost everything through
the villainy of his partner; his object in going to Kanesville, is to endeavour to get into some way of business,
he cares not what. He is from the state of Virginia,
where he has left his family.

–22– Sunday– Still waiting– we had a prayer meeting this afternoon; the first we had in 8 weeks; it
seems to have put new life into the men. The weather
is very fine, and the river falling fast. I call this Spot
Greenwich Park, as it has some resemblance to it,
only on a very large scale   we hope to be able to make
the bridge and cross the river tomorrow.

–23– Got the bridge finished, got the wagons across
and over a swamp, by 6 P.M. and encamped on a hillside; no fruit here, but plenty of mosquitoes.

–24– Started at 9, arrived at Nitchany-Boatany
[Nishnabotna] river   met a lad returning from the
Bluffs, to [Mt.] Pisgah, who gave us the startling
information, that the Indians had refused to allow
the Morman camp to pass through their territories.
Crossed the river in safety, and came upon a swamp

one and one half miles long, had to put 12 yoke of oxen to each waggon; the mud in some places being over the axles. got over safely, and encamped on a hill.

–25– Started at 8, came to 7 mile creek, called at a farmhouse   found the creek to deep to cross, and no timber to make a bridge, concluded to lay stringers across, and draw the wagons over by hand, the oxen could swim over; were joined by a traveller from Dubuke going on foot to Kanesville, he stayed with us, and shared our supper.

–26– Got over the stream in safety; halted to dine— then went on again untill we came to a deep ravine which they had to half fill with brush in order to cross, the stream at the bottom, was 3 feet wide, but we all got over on a plank, but Eliza, who managed to fall in, receiving no injury but a thorough wetting, and a slight graze on the side, travelled on till stopped by a thunderstorm near to a wood so turned out the cattle to feed and went to bed, thankful that we have a shelter in these awful storms. Surely this is a dreadful spring.

–27– Started at 5 o'clock, came to a farm; the first sign of cultivation we had seen in the last 100 miles, the farmer came up and spoke to us, and gave us some lettuces, and spring onions, which were quite a treat; we passed through some splendid groves of trees, and meadows, crossed a ravine, and encamped near a wood.

–28– We have had a deal of rain, during the night, and have been much bothered with some cattle, belonging to a farm close by, some of them got at our herrings, which were in a box under one of the wagons, and eat them all, tempted by the salt. got up; had our breakfast, paid a visit to the farmhouse; bought some butter, milk and eggs, also some cows, with their calves, for 30 dollars, found the river we had to cross, so much swollen as to be half a mile in width; crossed in a ferry boat in safety, got to a hill and encamped.

–29– Sunday, remained in camp at Macedonia, a Mormon town containing 5 houses; visited two of them, the inmates treated us very kindly. We got some mutton, (I bought a whole sheep for a dollar) and some green vegetables. In the evening Margetts came back to tell us the company was waiting for us at Kanesville; we started out, and travelled two miles, when rain came on, and we halted for the night.

–30– Started at 4 A.M. travelled on the Silver creek near which is a settlement; we forded the creek in safety, except breaking the Captains tongue-pin, and hounds; mended up with chains, and proceeded on, we arrived at Keg creek, (another small settlement) smashed up Jones's hind wheel against a stump, Jones made up his mind to stay behind at a Brother Dunn, whom he seemed to have been previously acquainted with, and we went on to a hill, and encamped.

July 1– Got to Centreville, where we stayed all day.

–2– Arrive at Kanesville, quite a pretty town, and the surrounding scenery very beautiful. walking with Mrs. Burkton this evening, in the outskirts. I heard the Whip-poor-will for the second time, the note somewhat resembles that of our Nightingale but not I think as sweet, it is more like a Wail.

–5– We stayed two days in Kanesville, where I purchased some more provisions, met with some pleasant people, and this morning recommenced our journey, crossed over the Missouri bottom, 4 miles wide, the whole distance under water, caused by the late heavy rains, most of the distance the water was running over the axles of the wagons, however we came out on high ground, in the midst of a wood; were ferried over in safety, and came up to the main camp, at 12 P.M.

–6– Found several of our shipmates in the camp and are organized. Mr. John Brown, being appointed captain of the whole, we mustered 42 wagons, with four other of the Bretheren, to take charge of 10 wagons each, subject to the orders of Mr. Brown.

–7– Started on this last division of our long journey crossing, from the steepness of the banks, came to the Elk-Horn, and encamped, 32 of us, Robin's ten having had some breakages's stopped behind to repair, we are now in the country of the Omaha's.

–8– Ferried over the Elk-Horn in safety, except one of Chatterley's company, who caught his hand in a chain, bursting one of his fingers, making a rent of one and one half inches long. Mrs. Joseph Pierce and I sewed it up between us, and dressed it as well as we could under the circumstances. Forded the next creek, Willis's dry goods wagon upset in the water, wetting most of the freight. Encamped on the bottom, which I am told was under water two weeks ago, making the river four miles in width, found many fine fish in the hollows, left by the receding waters, and millions of mosquitoes.

–9– Crossed Elk-Horn bottom, very hard days travel, plenty of chains broken, encamped by the side of the Platte river, where we found an Indian grave.

–10– Halted all day to repair damages, took the opportunity of wash up our dirty linen.

–11– Very sandy roads, but got on very well.

–12– Exceeding hot, passed another Indian grave, stopped at night by the side of a small lake, plenty of red root growing, of which we gathered enough to cook for our supper, it made a nice variety for our meal, nine wagons have overtaken us, and the travellers have requested to be allowed to join our company, we now number 54 (three others having joined us, since we left the Missouri river)   these new comers had started for Oregon, but had been attacked by Indians who had stolen some of their oxen and driven away the rest, they had recovered some few, and were returning to the frontiers, when they saw our company and then turned back.

–13– Proceeded onwards, found 10 of the strangers missing cattle which was quite a God send to them.

–14– One of our company shot a very fine garfish, in a stream by our roadside, and presented it to Eliza, that, stewed in the same manner as we used to stew Eles at home, made us a delicious supper, the fish weighed ten pounds, I had also gathered a quanity of red-root greens, which when boiled are quite as good as spinach, we are now on the Plains, in the Pawnee country.

–15– Came to the spot where the Oregon company lost their cattle, yokes and bows were lying in all directions, the boys found a nice yoke, just fit for my own cows, encamped at Plumb Creek.

–16-17– Very hard travelling, deep ravines to cross and a very hard and bad swamp, then a wide creek, with a very steep hill to finish with, encamped on the high ground, violent thunder storm, with rain during nearly the whole night.

–18– The men returned to the creek, to build a bridge, in order that Thomas's ten might get up to us, as they were unable to cross last night, having to mend a wheel, and this morning the waters had risen, so as to render the creek dangerous to ford. All got over in safety.

–19-20– We remained in camp repairing damages, this day at half past two o'clock, Sister Kempton died, she came with us from London, and was in her usual health till two days ago, Aunt Bateman and I laid her out, and sewed her body up in a sheet, she was buried by the Brethern at sunset, on the summit of a small hill, where there are 5 more graves. Mr. Pierce was baptized this evening.

–21– Crossed the Loup-fork, all safe, and came up on the Bluff, 5 miles   very heavy road.

–22– Bad, sandy road, we saw numbers of frogs, hares, doves, and the skull of an Elk, with a message written on it, with a pencil, informing us that the Indians were on the lookout for opportunities to steal cattle, from the passing Emigrants.

–23– Crossed 3 deep ravines, 2 of them with water in them, upset one of Robins's waggons, going down to Wood river, which scared me, so I preffered wading to riding, as the water at the fording place was only a few inches deep, the rest got over in safety   travelled one mile, when Robin's smashed one of his wheels on a stump, so encamped by the river.

–24– The hottest day, we have had, crossed 14 miles of prairie, then came to the side of a wood, when we were met by a hot wind, one of my finest Oxen fell down, and died in a few minutes, several of the teams were suffering in like manner, though mine was the only one that died.

–25– Not quite so hot to-day, but we travelled quite slowly on account of the weakness of the cattle, arising from the hot wind of yesterday.

–26– Came near to fort Kearney, where I bought an Ox to take the place of the one who died, he cost me $30.

–27– Sunday– remained in camp, prayer meeting in the afternoon.

–28– Came in sight of Buffalo, our company shot a young one, and we enjoyed a meal of fresh meat, our Captain of fifty who has crossed the Plains five times and is consequently well acquainted with the country tells us, that sometimes the Buffalo numbers 10,000 in a single herd.

–29– Met 3 waggons, 1 of them from Salt Lake which had overtaken the other two on the road, they report that 3 companies of fifties are 8 days ahead of us, and that we are still ahead of Elder Pratts company, which left Kanesville 2 weeks before we did, and in consequences of the high water, went around the Elk-Horn instead of fording it, making the journey 150 miles longer, from other reports too, we fear that his company has been attacked by Indians, Orson Hyde, who went on alone, they tell us has overtaken those ahead of us, but had been previously stopped by some Indians and robbed of nearly everything he had.

–30– Much bothered with Buffalo, which are very numerous; stragglers are apt to run in among our cattle, terrifying them very much, and it has been all the housemen to do, to prevent their doing mischief on encamping for the night, we saw another company of 115 waggons, about a mile before us they had endeavored to head the Horn, but found it impacticable, so aroused higher up, than we did; they have come 460 miles, have had a very trying journey, have had their cattle stampeded by Indians, and lost 18 head of them, Sister Kingeby who was among them was run over and killed, they are under Elder Phelps.

—31— Saw no Buffalo today, thunderstorm at night.

August 1— We are travelling in sight of the company ahead of us, and this evening two of our old shipmates who are with them, Sister Whitaker and Boss, came over to see us.

—2— Passed Elder Phelp's company, and came to a small creek in safety, making 100 miles since Monday morning, saw a few Buffaloes this evening, two of our people went out to shoot one, which they did but it being too dark to cut it up, left it intending to fetch it to-morrow morning.

—3— Sunday— The men went out early this morning to fetch in the meat, but found the wolves had been before them, and left them only the bones, however they shot two more, so that we have another weeks supply of fresh meat. One of the strangers in our company spoke at our meeting this afternoon and pleased us very much, by his testimony in our favor.

—4— A very heavy days travelling, we had to cross a great many sand hills, saw thousands of Lizards, snakes, and grasshoppers. Kay got his waggon tongue broke.

–5– A continuation of yesterdays difficulties, the country wild and romantic.

–6– Met a company of returning Californians, they had passed through Salt Lake City, where the people were just finishing their harvesting, which had been abundant, had not seen an Indian since Lomarie, but tell us that there is a Mormon company 15 miles ahead of us, with whom they encamped last night, this afternoon, the man who cooks for Robin's ten, was accidently run over, also one of the children, they were much bruised, but no bones broken.

–7– A terrible sand hill, and pass among mountains, Chatterly's hind wheel turned inside out, Mr. Conlett gave Elizabeth a puppy much to her delight, passed two graves, one that of a member of the old Independent church who died in August 1849, but the name too indistinct to be decyphered   the other: that of Hannah Hawks, aged 46, who died the same week.

–8– Very pleasant travelling all day, saw a returning Merchant train from Salt Lake, they had one of their waggons take fire, and on two of their men trying to extinguish it, their gunpowder exploded, and killed them both, shot 2 fine Antelopes to-day, this evening as one of Robin's men was milking he was nearly killed by the cows kicking, he was carried to his wagon quite insensible.

–9– Phelps company overtook us, all well, we afterwards passed them, saw Chimney Rock, I clambered to the top of a bluff in order to get a view of the country, the scenery grand, we encamped early.

–10– Sunday– Meeting as usual.

–11-12–13– Good traveling.

–14– Very heavy rain during the last, which has made the road very heavy, passed a very smart Indian one of the Sioux tribe, in the evening we found that quite a number of them, were encamped near us.

–15– Indians with us all day, very fine looking fellows, and very gaily attired, the dresses of the women some of them, nearly covered with beadwork, they came to camp with us, and stayed till dusk.

–16– Some cattle strayed during the night, and were not found till noon, I purchased 4 fine hams, at the trading post, also a yoke of Oxen for which I paid 65 dollars.

–17– Sunday– Compelled to travel part of the day in order to find grass, crossed the Platte river, and encamped, surrounded by mountains, covered with ceder, and pine.

–18– A very hard road all day, crossed some mountains but the view from the top, no pen can describe, we managed to get 20 miles, but it was hard work, did not get to camp till 11 o'clock. saw 4 Oxen dead on the road, and many wheels, axles, and tires, the results of former accidents, we had 2 wheels broken, Chatterly's and Robins's; loads of cherries and currents.

–19– Remained in camp all day, repairing damages, Sister Sharkey gave birth to a daughter, doing well.

–20– Very beautiful country, but very dusty.

–21– Horrible roads, crossed the Platte twice, encamped along with the Phelps company, by the river side.

–22–23– Very hard and bad travelling, deep ravines, and many sand hills.

–24– Sunday– At our meeting to-day, Bro. Thomas preached, of the first principals of the Gospel of Christ.

–25– Travelled 10 miles and encamped by the river, I was sent for to Sister Henderson, who had been sick for two days. In one hour, I was enabled to assist her in giving birth to a daughter, but the Mother is so much exhausted that I fear she will not rally again.

–26– Remained in camp all day, setting tires, Sister Henderson very low, the infant quite well. A hunting party, which set out yesterday, returned with plenty of fresh meat.

–27– Sister Henderson died to-day at noon, we buried her at 9 P.M., she left seven children.

–28– Crossed the Platte, Captain Brown passed the word, for all the waggons to keep as close as possible as there were Indians in the vicinity, on looking forward I saw a little army of them, about a mile distance, coming down the side of the mountain. our men at once loaded their guns, so as to be in readiness in case of an attack, but on our approaching the Indians, they opened their ranks, and we passed along, without any trouble, the Government agent was with them, in a buggy, and sitting between his knees, was the daughter of the chief, a pretty little creature of about 3 years old, who seemed to be quite pleased at our appearance, the agent told us that these were some of the Shoshones, that 3000 more encamped on the banks of the Sweetwater, 20 miles from us, that those present, were 90 of the principal warriors, with their families, going to a great counsel of various tribes, to endeavour to settle their differences, and bury the Tomohawk. They made a grand appearance, all on horseback, and very gaily dressed, some with lances, others with guns or Bows and Arrows, also a number of ponies, carrying their tents and the men passed on one side of us, the women and children on the other but all of them well mounted, their clothing was beautiful trimmed with small beads, altogether it was quite an imposing procession, after leaving them, our road was among mountains till we came to camp.

–29– We are among the Rocky Mountains, the country is a desert, except here and there a patch of grass, by the side of the small streams, the scenery grand and terrible; I have walked under overhanging rocks, which seemed only to need the presure of a finger, to send them down headlong, many of them resemble the ruins of old castles, and it needs but a little stretch of the imagination, to fancy yourself in the deserted hall, of a palace or temple, there seems to be much metal among the rocks. I picked up some specimens, which I am told are silver, and Iron ore, also some lumps of coal, which burn brightly, our road is so steep, as to seem almost like going down a staircase; killed a sheep to-day, which makes a nice change in our food.

–30– Very sandy roads, saw multitude of hares and rabbits, but had no time to shoot any, saw a few Buffalo; encamped by the Sweetwater.

–31– Sunday– Sermon from Elder G. D. Watt, on the new birth. Mrs. Richards an English woman who with her husband and 5 children are in our ten, gave me a fine fat hare this evening, which made us a delicious supper.

Sept. 4– Saw the snow capped mountains, for the

first time, our cattle began to show signs of fatigue, Richard Margetts had an ox die yesterday, and two of mine gave out.

–5– Remained in camp all day, to give the sick oxen a rest, killed 3 antelopes, and caught lots of fish.

–6– Comfortable travelling all day, crossed the Sweetwater river 4 times, encamped in a pretty spot by the river side, killed 2 antelopes.

–7– Started at noon, crossed a rocky ridge, called the Devils backbone. very barren country.

–8– Met the Mail from Salt Lake, with it was Dr. Bernhill [Bernhisel] the Utah delegate, all the news he brought was of a cheering kind, travelled on till noon, and halted for the rest of the day, on some very good grass, very pretty scenery.

–9– Several of the cattle had strayed, which delayed us an hour after our usual starting time, travelled 2 miles, when one of my oxen fell down and died, we think he had been poisoned, by picking up some Indian paint, as we were near one of their villages. One of Robin's waggons broke down, another a wheel, so leaving their ten to patch up, we came 19 miles, without stopping, (from the scarcity of grass) till we came to one of the Pacific Springs on the side of which we encamped. Robin's came in at night all but one waggon, which was too much shattered to bring on.

–10– Remained in camp all day. Fetched Robins's missing waggon, and mended the broken ones, one of Brother Norton's daughters had her leg broken by a kick from a cow, while milking; her father set the bone, and she seems to be doing well, no inflamation having appeared, 2 men came up with us; one from Alred's, the other from Cordon's company; they left on account of provisions growing short, and teams giving out; they tell us that the companies were throwing away all that they possibly could spare, in order to lighten the loads, that 19 waggons, had left Pratt's company, and overtook Cordon's; they had been visited by an Indian Party, who had robbed 6 of them, bidding the owners defiance, and telling them they had 500 Warriors on the other side of the hill. It seems our people were frightened and suffered them to do as they pleased, except one Englishman, who gave the Indians a sound thrashing with his whip-stock, there 2 men have started without any provision, taking their chance of meeting with other companies, they supped with us, and started on, as they travel in the night only, in order to avoid the high winds, which we constantly have in the daytime, though the nights are quite calm and pleasant. They hope to arrive in the Valley, in time to send out provisions to the various companies, who are behind, who we fear will be much distressed, two other men overtook us to-day having 6 mules, they are from Laramie, and tell us that there are a thousand Lodges, round the Fort, and many more expected; they seem to be apprehensive that there is trouble brewing; also that 2 Shoshones had been killed by a party of Cheyenes, that the Shoshones had in return slaughtered 27 out of 30 Cheyenes, they had fallen in with, on their way to the great Counsel of the Tribes; poor prospect this of peace among them, as those 30 were actually delegates from their own people. The atmosphere is much warmer, since we crossed the mountain ridge.

–11– Pretty good travelling all day, except the scarcity of grass, encamped on Pacific Creek, the wolves very troublesome all night, with their howling, which was accompanied by the barking of all the dogs in camp.

–12– Very heavy sandy roads all day.

–13– This morning the general strike took place, among Robins's teamsters, there has been dissatisfaction for some weeks, owing to the scantiness, and inferior quality of their rations, and Mr. Robins, refusing to make any improvement, the men shouldered their blankets, and set off intending to take their chance for provision, on the road, as they go along. An hour afterwards, the camp started, by noon the captain had overtaken the men, and expressed his wish that they would return, in order that there might be an investigation of the matter; they agreed to do so, and we went on till sun-down, and encamped on Big Sandy river, to the great joy of ourselves and cattle, who had not seen grass or water, for 18 miles, one Captain then supplied the mutineers with a tent, and plenty of Buffalo-robes, and we all retired for the night.

–14– Sunday– Lovely morning, after breakfast, Walter, William, and Derrick, went out with their guns, in hope of finding some game, but were disappointed, turning out our last ham, for dinner, during the morning Robins held a confab with his men; when on his promising to supply their wants in the eating way, 6 out of the 9 agreed to remain with him, the other 3 would have nothing to do with him, on any terms. 3 waggons from Salt Lake came up to us; they had brought out provisions, but to my chagrin had sold all they had to the companies ahead of us, and were then going to meet those in the rear, in order to see if they needed any assistance; they also told us, that there were some waggons laden with flour to meet us, so we hope to see them in a day or two. Meeting in the afternoon. Sermon from Cap. Brown, on the Kingdom of Heaven, Elder Margetts spoke after him. John Tout, who has been baptised during the week was then publicly received into the church, and the meeting closed.

—15— Came among timber to-day near Green River, passed through some very beautiful country, and we were just the ones to appreciate it, having seen nothing but sand and wild sage, for 300 miles, with now and then a mountain stream to break the monotony of the scene, we forded the river, a wide rushing stream, and clear as Crystal, along the sides the cottonwood trees were numerous, we traveled through this beautiful scenery, for several miles, on looking down the banks, which are very steep, except at the fording place, I observed a white sandy appearance among the pebbles, so being blest with a tolerable share of the failing, of which our first parents left so plentiful a supply to their posterity, I managed to scramble down to the water edge, and on taking up some, first looking at it, and then tasting, I found it to be pure salt, how it got there I cannot imagine, as the water is quite fresh, and we are at an altitude of 6500 feet above the level of the sea. We encamped in a grove of timber, on the banks of this beautiful stream, which seemed like a paradise, after the long stretch of desert country, through which we have been travelling for the last 4 weeks. While we were sitting at supper, a stranger visited us, he told us he was a servant at a trading post 2 miles off, and came to inquire if we wanted any cattle, or provisions, what have you got? (said I) Bacon, and Whisky madam, any butter? No butter. Any groceries or fresh meat? No madam, but there is plenty at Fort Bridger 50 miles further; after some more palaver, 9 of our young men, (Walter among them) went back with him to the post, and purchased us some bacon, which we found of very good quality, the Trader told them, that he had lived among the Indians for 15 years, and has not visited the states, for 10 years, his habitation was surrounded by the Indian huts, belonging to the Snakes, who had among them four of the Utah Squaws who had been taken prisoners when children, and adopted into the tribe, each of the white men, (4 in number) had an Indian wife, and each their own habitation, several hundred head of cattle and 150 horses, and seemed to be very happy in their wilderness way of life.

–16– This morning, 3 of the Indian women paid us a visit, remaining with us, until we started; we came almost at once on sandy, barren road, which extended for 15 miles, all the streams were dry, and we travelled along the bed of one for some distance, the banks of which were very high and steep, indeed in some places perpendicular, it was dusk before we arrived at a camping ground and both men and cattle were much fatigued.

–17–18– Still heavy, sandy road, but good camping grounds, Elder Robins taken suddenly ill yesterday, we were afraid he was going to have a fever, but became better this morning. 3 oxen died yesterday.

–19– Arrived at Fort Bridger, and to my great joy, I was able to purchase 40 pounds of very fine fresh beef, I never saw finer in the London Markets, and that is saying a good deal, also as a great favor got 3 pounds of potatoes, for which I paid 50 cents, the beef was only 10 cents the pound; travelled on till we came to Muddy Fork, & encamped.

–20–21– very romantic scenery all day, mostly ascending untill we arrived at the rim of the great Basin, where we encamped, the feed being very good. Sister Derrick was delivered a fine little girl this morning at one o'clock we have had gentle but incessant rain all night, to our very great comfort, as the dust has been almost choking us, for the last 3 weeks, with a continued west wind, which just blows in our faces. Obliged to travel to-day for want of water; the scenery is sublime, our road being between and round high mountains; we crossed over one, so long and steep as to make it very hard on the Oxen, we had 10 yoke to each waggon; on descending we came to Bear River, a swift stream, abounding with trout, and thickly bordered with trees of various kinds; we encamped on its banks; Eliza has been very ill all day, I am very uneasy, as I fear it will cause a premature birth, Mrs. Derricks doing pretty well.

–22– As I feared, my dear girls labor came on during the night, and at daybreak a little grandson was born to my very great joy. I have some fears for its life, but I do hope our Heavenly Father will spare it to us, and make it a blessing to us all, and an honorable member of His Kingdom; the children are all overjoyed. I lost another Ox today by poison.

–25– The country for the last 3 days, has been beyond description for wilderness and beauty; we are indeed among the everlasting Hills.

–26– We had this day a view of Salt Lake Valley, from the summit of a mountain, 7245 feet above the level of the Sea; here we were met by several men with teams, ready to assist those who needed help. Among others man of the name of Cadbury, from Camden-Town, who had been in the Valley 2 years; the descent of the mountain was awfully steep and dangerous, for about four miles. I took our little stranger into my arms, and walked the distance, for it was as much as Eliza could to hold herself firm in bed, Mrs. Derrick's daughter did the same by their babe, so the two ladies, "in the straw" were the only ones who remained in the waggons. When I arrived at the base of the mountain, I turned to look at the coming waggons, and was actually terrified to see them rushing down, though both wheels were locked, but no accident occured, and we are now at the entrance of a narrow defile between rocks measuring 800 feet perpendicular height, with a serpentine stream running through it, which we shall have to cross 19 times.

–27– In about an hour after starting, we came to a deep ravine, over which was thrown an apology for a bridge, we got over without accident, but how it was that there were no waggons overturned or Oxen killed seems almost miraculous. Our road afterwards was through a forest of small timber, which made it very unpleasant travelling, till we arrived at Brown's Creek, so named after our Captain, who was one of the Pioneers to the Valley, 4 years ago, one and three

fourths miles from this we came to a clear spring of
water, and encamped for the night. Mrs. Derrick
doing well, Eliza has suffered much from the rough-
ness of the road, which has been worse to-day, than
any part of the journey since leaving Kanesville and
our Captain gives the comfortable assurance to us,
that it will be still worse tomorrow.

-28- Of all the splendid scenery, and awful roads,
that have ever been seen since creation I think this
days journey has beaten them all, we had encamped
last night at the foot of a mountain, which we had to
ascend this morning. This was hard enough on our
poor worn out animals, but the road after was completely covered with stones, as large as bushel boxes,
stumps of trees, with here and there mud holes, in
which our poor oxen, sunk to the knees, added to all
this there was the Kanyon Creek, a stream of water
running at the bottom of a deep ravine, which inter-
sected our road in such a zigzag fashion, that we had to
ford it 16 times at a descent of 15 to 20 feet and of
course an equal ascent, and that in some places nearly
perpendicular. One of my own teams were forced down
a decline, with such rapidity, that one of the oxen
fell into the stream, and was drowned before it could
be extricated, this makes 6 oxen I have lost on the
journey, the mountains on each side of us seem to be
solid rock, but in the crevices on their sides trees are
growing in abundance, and the tops covered with
groves of splendid fir-trees; in some places large pieces
of rock have been detached, and have rolled down
the mountain side, many of them as large as a small
house, in some instances, the rocks lie directly across
the road, which occasion much difficulty in travelling,

in one spot, the rocks had the appearance of a ruinous gateway, through which we had to pass, the opening was very narrow, only one waggon could go along at a time, and that along the bed of Kanyon Creek, which seems to have forced its way through the opening I have described, it then turns off to the side of the road, which is immediately under overhanging rocks for some distance the grandeur of the scenery to my mind takes away all fear, and while standing in admiration at the view Milton's expressions in his Paradise Lost came forcibly to my recollections— "These are thy glorious works, Parent of good, in wisdom hast thou made them all." – and I seemed to forget all the hardships of our long journey, suddenly I heard a sound as of rushing water, on my left hand, and looking in that direction, I observed that the mountain stream buried itself among some bushes, and sure enough there was the prettiest waterfall I had seen yet. I cannot describe it as it deserves, and alas! I am no artist or I would make a drawing of it; however the cataract in itself, was comprised of 15 separate falls, over as many pieces of rock, the whole perpendicular height, being about 35 or 40 feet, it struck me with both awe and delight, and I felt as though I would like to have lingered a long time watching it, I dare say many would laugh at me, and they are welcome, if doing so affords them any pleasure; however the shouting of the teamsters, warned me to keep moving, if I did not wish to be left behind. On going about a quarter of a mile from this lovely spot, we came upon 7 waggons all in a row, every one of them with a broken wheel or axle; the sight made our company very careful for fear of being in the same

hobble passing there; as well as we could in the narrow road, we came to some others, and soon after
some more in the like fix, making in all 17, we picked
our way, as well as we could, and at about sunset, we
emerged from the Kanyon, and caught a faint view of
our destined home; we encamped in a hollow, just
at the entrance of the valley, and night came on, befor we could obtain a good look about us, I then began
to find that I was very tired, so went into the waggon
and found Eliza had suffered much, from the jolting
of the days travel; thank God however it is over now,
and they tell us that 5 miles tomorrow, will bring us
into the said Salt Lake City, and that after crossing
the hill, at whose base we are now resting, we shall
have a road, as smooth as a bowling stream.

–29– [September]   Rose this morning, with a thankful heart that our travels were nearly finished, at least
we hope so; after breakfast, and looking after my two
patients, who are doing even much better under the
circumstances than might have been expected, and the
babies first rate, I ascended the hill before us, and had
my first view of the city, which is laid out in squares,
or blocks as they call them here, each containing 10
acres, and divided into 8 lots, each lot having one
house; I stood and looked, I can hardly anylise my
feelings, but I think my prevailing ones, were joy, and
gratitude for the protecting care had over me and mine,
during our long and perilous journey; well we started
at 11 o'clock and came to Mrs. Wallace's house, having
a letter of introduction to her from her husband, whom
I left in England fulfilling his mission. She received
me most kindly and desired me to have my waggons
brought inside her inclosure, at the same time offering

me, any convenience her house afforded. In the course of the afternoon I received calls from several of the neighbors, who bade me welcome, and gave us invitations to their homes, but I hope in a day or two, to be able to meet with a home, so that a roof may once more cover us, as we have been living in our waggons 24 weeks his day, and I shall be glad to get into a habitation, where I can sit down, and think over all that has passed, on this lengthened journey.

Oct. 6– During the last week, I have purchased a small house; with an acre of garden attached to it, there are only 4 rooms, but we can manage for the winter, the garden is in good cultivation, and has growing a patch of Indian corn, also potatoes, cabbages, carrots, parsnips, beets, tomatoes – watered by a little stream, which runs through the center, the house is 40 feet from the road, and fronts the public square, I have also bought a three-year old Heifer, which supplies us with milk, so that we are now comfortably fixed for the present at least, all in good health, with the exception of Eliza, who still remains very weak, our dear little Babe too, begins to grow a little, and I hope will be given to our many prayers, but he is very small and very delicate.

–13– Delightful weather, the sun shining gloriously, Eliza much stronger the babe improving, and the rest of us in first-rate health. I had a wish to visit a Sulphur Lake, about four miles distant; so after dinner we yoked up, and went in the waggon; Walter, William, Eliza, and I leaving Aunt to keep home, and have the kettle boiling against our return, we found the ride very pleasant by the side of the mountains, passing a small lake, of warm water, supplied by a spring, at the foot of the mountain. A narrow stream from the spring had been conveyed to a Bathing house, very near, which contains 8 commodious baths, into which the warm water is continually flowing, there is also a large room used for dancing and some smaller used as refreshment rooms, after taking a good look here, we reentered the wagon, and one hours ride brought us to the Sulphur Lake, which we smelt long before we reached it. This is much larger than the warm-spring lake, and the water is only tepid, although supplied from a spring of boiling water 100 yards distance. We alighted, and walked to its source, which is at the bottom of a solid rock, where is a small arch, about large enough to creep into, on hands, and knees. We managed with some difficulty, to get close to the opening, and there sure enough was the water boiling, furiously and of a bright green colour; the strong sulphurous stench here, was almost intolerable, whenever a slight breeze sent the stream into our faces, still I doubted its being so hot as represented, so in order to be convinced, I very cautiously stepped on some pieces of rock, until I stood alone quite close to the bubbling water; by this time I began to believe what I had been told, as my feet began to feel much warmer than pleasant, however determined to make sure, I plunged in my hand, but was glad to draw it out again much to the amusement of my companions. The stream from the source is (as I have said) 100 yards, which accounts for the lessened heats at the edge of the stream, the grass is covered by a yellowish white deposit, which I am told, is pure sulphur; we tasted some of the water, and found it so strongly impugnated as to be very disagreeable. We clambered on to the top of the rock,

which overhangs the spring, and looking forward we
had a view of the lake, and to my astonishment, its
surface was covered with wild Ducks, I may say without exaggeration ten thousands of them; they are
excellent eating, I am told, not having the fishy taste,
common to our wild fowl, beyond this we could distinctly see the great salt lake, 22 miles distant. And
here I would mention one singular fact, (at least to
us English folk) and that is the extreme clearness of
the air, enabling us to see objects at a very great distance; this property of the atmosphere, I have noticed
ever since we left the Missouri River; standing where
I did, I should not have supposed the Lake to be more
than 3 miles off. While crossing the Plains, I have
frequently noticed different objects, which I imagined
I should have little trouble in reaching on foot, and
on enquiring the distance, have been told they were
perhaps 20 or 30 miles distance; in particular one
morning while at breakfast, I observed a rather singularly shaped hill, directly in our road, and as usual
felt an instant desire to mount to the summit, our
Captain of fifty coming past at the time, I called his
attention to it, saying that I would start a little before
the camp, in order to have a view of the surrounding
country from the top; "why" said he, "are you aware
of the distance that hill is from here." I replied I
supposed it to be two or three miles, he smiled. "Well"
said he, "if we are able to reach that hill tomorrow
night, I shall be very satisfied with our teams, as it
at least 26 miles before us", but I am running away
from my story; after enjoying the prospect for some
time we returned home without inconvenience.

Nov 4– I have just returned from a little journey

of 40 miles, to a place called Ogden, where I have purchased 20 acres of land. I spent a week in the neighborhood, and am pleased with the locality. I am to have a small house built during the winter, and in the spring, the younger boys with myself will go there and commence farming. Walter's family, with Uncle and Aunt, will remain in a house in Salt-Lake-City. While staying at Ogden, I was shown several specimens of the produce of the country. I brought home with me, a pumpkin weighing 53 pounds, but I saw some weighing 90, also potatoes weighing 3 lbs. and perfectly sound throughout. Well I arrived at home, and found all well, and our dear Babe much improved.

Dec. 25– A delightful day ushered in not by the ringing of bells, for our city does not possess any, but by the firing of cannon. At daybreak, the Nauvoo Brass Band had assembled, and, serenaded the city for two hours; At 10 A.M., the carpenters shop was thrown open for an entertainment to the men employed on the public works, who with their families, numbered between 6 and 700; the building was comfortably fitted up with seats, tables and convenience for making tea, the Governor with several members of the Legislature were present with their ladies, and when the floor was cleared for dancing, a good band having been engaged, took partners, and wives and daughters of the workmen, as the workmen in their turn took the wives and daughters of their employers; the company seperated at 10 P.M.

March 22nd– Removed to Ogden, accompanied by my son William, and the younger children, and now I suppose I have finished my ramblings for my whole life.

An Enterprising Woman in California

INTRODUCTION

As in our first volume we are including at the very end a letter published in an eastern journal quoting from a woman who had gone west with the covered wagons. This anonymous quote tells of the rich opportunities women had because they were so rare in the mining regions. Her first sentence reads, "I have made about $18,000 worth of pies — about one-third of this has been clear profit." Well, as they say, "That ain't bad." As a matter of fact, she did much better than most men who went seeking the golden treasure.

Our other items in this volume have involved a process of making known to the reading public women who had been heretofore anonymous. This last item — unsigned — must remain anonymous.[1]

We have before us, says the *Boston Traveler,* a private letter from a lady, though a hard-working woman, in California. It would interest our readers, we have no doubt, as it has us, were we at liberty to publish it entire. The writer appears to keep a restaurant or eating-house, in a mining village. Among her visitors she accidentally discovers the son of an old Connecticut acquaintance, and finding he was endeavoring to induce his father and mother to visit California, she writes this letter to encourage them forward. After an introductory explanation of who she was, and where they became acquainted with each other, she goes on to say:-

I have made about $18,000 worth of pies — about

---

[1] From *Hunt's Merchants' Magazine and Commercial Review,* New York, Vol. 26, no. 6, June 1852, p. 777.

one-third of this has been clear profit. One year I dragged my own wood of the mountains and chopped it, and I have never had so much as a child to take a step for me in this country. $11,000 I baked in one little iron skillet, a considerable portion by a camp fire, without the shelter of a tree from the broiling sun. But now I have a good cooking stove, in which I bake four pies at a time, a comfortable cabin, carpeted, and a good many "Robinson Crusoe" comforts about me, which, though they have cost nothing, yet they make my place look habitable. I also hire my wood hauled and chopped. I bake on an average about 1,200 pies per month, and clear $200. This, in California, is not thought much, and yet, in reality, few in comparison are doing as well. I have been informed there are some women in our town clearing $50 per week at washing, and I cannot doubt it. There is no labor so well paid as women's labor in California. It is hard to work to apply one's self incessantly to toil, but a few years will place you above want with a handsome independency. I intend to leave off work the coming spring, and give my business into the hands of my sister-in-law. Not that I am rich, but I need little, and have none to toil for but myself. I expect to go home some time during the present year, for a short visit, but I could not be long content away from the sunny clime of this yellow land. A lovelier or more healthy climate could not be, and when I get a few friends about me, I think I shall be nearly happy again.

Index